THE GLOBAL BUSINESS ENVIRONMENT

THE GLOBAL BUSINESS ENVIRONMENT

AN INTRODUCTION

MONIR H. TAYEB

SAGE Publications
London • Newbury Park • New Delhi

© Monir H. Tayeb 1992

First published 1992

SAGE Publications Ltd
6 Bonhill Street
London EC2A 4PU

SAGE Publications Inc
2455 Teller Road
Newbury Park, California 91320

SAGE Publications India Pvt Ltd
32, M-Block Market
Greater Kailash – I
New Delhi 110 048

British Library Cataloguing in Publication Data

Tayeb, Monir H.
  Global Business Environment: Introduction
  I. Title
  338.8

  ISBN 0–8039–8444–8
  ISBN 0–8039–8445–6 Pbk

Library of Congress catalog card number 92–50635

Typeset by Mayhew Typesetting, Rhayader, Powys
Printed in Great Britain by Biddles Ltd, Guildford, Surrey

Contents

PART V THE INTERNATIONAL MANAGER'S WORLD

Acknowledgements

I would like to express my deep gratitude to Professor David J. Hickson of the University of Bradford Management Centre (UK), Dr Alan Cheney of Air Products (USA), and to Dr John Nichols of the University of Bath, for their generous and constructive comments on an earlier draft which have greatly helped to improve the book.

My special thanks and indebtedness go to Sue Jones of Sage Publications for her unfailing encouragement and professional advice throughout the period of preparing and writing this book.

It goes without saying that I am responsible for any remaining defects in the work.

I am also grateful to *The Economist, Financial Times, Industry Week* and *Time* for granting me permission to reproduce some of the articles in boxes throughout the book.

Abbreviations and Acronyms

AC	advanced country
ACP	America–Caribbean–Pacific
ASEAN	Association of South East Asian Nations
BKPM	Investment Coordinating Board [of Indonesia]
BNL	Banca Nazionale del Lavoro
CACM	Central American Common Market
CIM	computer integrated manufacture
CIS	Commonwealth of Independent States
Comecon	Council for Mutual Economic Association
EC	European Community (see also EEC)
ECU	European Currency Unit
EEA	European Economic Area
EEC	European Economic Community (see also EC)
EES	European Economic Space
EFTA	European Free Trade Association
FDI	foreign direct investment
G7	Group of 7 (the seven richest industrialized countries: United States, Germany, France, Japan, United Kingdom, Canada, Italy)
GATS	General Agreement on Trade in Services
GATT	General Agreement on Tariffs and Trade
GDP	gross domestic product
GM	General Motors [Corporation]
GNP	gross national product
GSP	Generalized System of Preferences
IBM	International Business Machines [Corporation]
IBRD	International Bank for Reconstruction and Development, generally referred to as the World Bank
IDA	International Development Association
IFC	International Finance Corporation
IMF	International Monetary Fund
ITO	International Trade Organization
LAFTA	Latin American Free Trade Association
LAIA	Latin American Integration Association
LDC	less developed country

MFA	Multi-Fibre Arrangement
MFN	most favoured nation
MIT	Massachusetts Institute of Technology
MITI	Ministry of International Trade and Industry [of Japan]
MPV	multi-purpose vehicle
NATO	North Atlantic Treaty Organization
NIC	newly industrialized country
NUM	National Union of Miners
NUT	National Union of Teachers
OAU	Organization of African Unity
OECD	Organization for Economic Cooperation and Development
OEEC	Organization for European Economic Cooperation
OPEC	Organization of Petroleum Exporting Countries
PLC	public limited company
PSE	producer subsidy equivalent
R & D	research and development
SDR	special drawing right
SPEC	South Pacific Bureau for Economic Cooperation
SPF	South Pacific Forum
T & GWU	Transport and General Workers Union
UAE	United Arab Emirates
UK	United Kingdom
UN	United Nations
UNCTAD	United Nations Conference on Trade and Development
USA	United States of America
USSR	Union of Socialist Soviet Republics (see also CIS)
USTR	United States Trade Representative
VAT	value added tax
VER	voluntary export restraint

Introduction

The historical and economic background

The first chapter introduces international business at national and company levels. The first section discusses briefly the reasons for and the nature of trade between nations. The discussion is then brought to the company level and the forms in which business organizations engage in international business. Various forms of internationalization, ranging from business activities without foreign management (for example, export and import) to those which involve foreign direct investment and managerial control, are outlined. Barter and countertrade are also dealt with in the section. The final section examines major reasons behind a firm's decision to engage in international business.

Chapter 2 gives a brief account of the historical evolution and the present state of the political and economic world within which international business operates. Events such as the Industrial Revolution in the eighteenth century, the two World Wars, the 1929 depression and the acquisition of their independence by former Western colonies, which changed the global scene considerably, are discussed.

The chapter is then brought up to the present time, via a discussion of the emergence of the USA and later Japan as economic superpowers, the North–South division, East–West blocs, and outlines the most significant challenges that firms engaged in international operations are likely to face. These are then dealt with in detail in the remainder of the book.

Major challenges to free international trade

In an ideal world, free international trade, based on the principle of comparative advantage, should benefit all. But in reality, restrictions of all kinds hinder the free flow of goods and services, even though the eventual outcome of these restrictions is an overall loss to the ultimate consumer.

Part II outlines some of these restrictions and Part III deals with efforts made by various countries at both regional and global levels to remove them in such a way as to bring about a fairer trade system.

Chapter 3 discusses the risks involved in international business which emanate from governments' intervention for both political and economic reasons. It defines political risk and suggests its likely sources, such as conflict of interests, threat to national sovereignty, perceived exploitation of national resources, and economic and socio-cultural factors. The chapter then outlines various forms of action that governments take in order to exert control and restrictions over the activities of multinationals and the ways in which the latter could deal with them.

Chapter 4 outlines some of the protectionist measures that governments take in order to improve their terms of trade with the outside world and to protect their domestic economy. It starts by discussing the political and economic rationale for protectionism, such as avoiding dependence on foreign products, protecting certain industries, full employment at home, restrictions on exports to hostile countries, and restrictions on imports from some countries as a form of punishment. The chapter points out the drawbacks that protectionism may entail, such as poor quality products and services, and retaliation by other countries.

One of the major problems faced by international companies is the differences between accounting, taxation and legal systems practised in different countries. Chapter 5 outlines these differences, and discusses their implications for multinational companies.

Western banks are currently facing a major crisis because of, among other things, the inability of some developing countries to repay their loans. Chapter 6 focuses on the extent of this problem and the proposed solutions for it. The chapter starts by describing briefly the global financial system and international banking. It is pointed out that because of the growing interdependence among various financial institutions and capital centres, these are becoming increasingly vulnerable to international crises such as the debt crisis. The discussion is then concentrated on the historical reasons behind the debt crisis, from both conservative and radical viewpoints. The last section of the chapter examines the solutions put forward by various international bodies so far.

Efforts to enhance free international trade

Chapter 7 focuses on major global institutions and agreements, namely, the IMF, World Bank and GATT, to highlight the steps taken by nations to bring down barriers to free trade. The performance of these international bodies is assessed critically.

Chapter 8 concentrates on regional agreements in various parts of the world, such as the OECD, EFTA and EC (in Western Europe), OPEC and ASEAN (in Asia), OAU (in Africa), CACM and LAIA (in Latin America), and SPEC in the Pacific Basin. The effectiveness of these organizations to protect their member states and to enhance international trade is examined.

Doing business with others

The chapters in this part include comparisons between, on the one hand, the European and American 'way of life', and on the other, the different ways in which some other nations conduct their social, cultural and business life.

Chapter 9 explores the possibilities of cultural influences on organizations and on their members' relationships with each other and with the outside world. The chapter consists of five sections. The first defines culture and outlines its scope. The second examines the likely origins of culture in primary and secondary social institutions.

The third section concerns the ways in which culture influences organizations from 'without', through institutions such as trade unions, political and economic structure, and consumers and other interest groups. The cultural origins of employees' work-related attitudes and behaviours, and the implications of these for organizations' management style and structure are also examined in this section. The fourth section of the chapter discusses the management of culture, which includes strategies ranging from cultural synergy to building organizations' own cultural identities which aim at suppressing cultural characteristics that may have been carried over from outside the organizations. The chapter concludes by discussing the transfer of management practices between cultures.

In the past three decades or so many researchers have sought to study the interaction between organizations and various levels of the environment, but only a very small number of studies have been carried out to examine the influence on organizations of the two major forms of the economic system of production, namely capitalism and socialism. Chapter 10 addresses this issue. Major differences between the two systems, especially in the areas of ideology and value systems, characteristics of class structure, ownership and control of the means of production, management of the economy, and the role of the state, are discussed.

The current political and economic events in East European countries, and the likely challenges they face in their attempts to move from a centrally-planned economic system to one based on capitalism and free enterprise are examined. The final section of the chapter speculates on the implications of the political reforms in ex-socialist countries for international business.

A major proportion of multinational companies' foreign direct investment is within industrialized countries, but the trend to move to less developed countries (LDCs) and newly industrialized countries (NICs) is on the increase. The reduction in the cost of production in an increasingly competitive world is more than ever becoming a significant determining factor in the choice of location of foreign manufacturing plants. LDCs and NICs are more likely to offer a competitive tender in this respect.

The first section of chapter 11 concentrates on less developed countries. Major characteristics which are common in almost all LDCs, such as the role of the state in the management of the economy, protectionism, inadequate infrastructure, poverty, and political instability, are discussed. The chapter then examines the position of the LDCs in the world of international trade, and discusses the way ahead for them. The final section of part one focuses on the opportunities and constraints facing the multinational companies which locate some of their foreign subsidiaries in LDCs.

The newly industrialized countries of South East Asia are becoming an increasingly competitive and formidable force to be reckoned with. They have made inroads in the markets which have hitherto been regarded as the domain of Japanese and Western companies. These NICs and some of the major reasons for their spectacular economic growth in the past three decades or so are discussed in the second part of chapter 11.

The success of Japanese managers in the past few decades has encouraged many researchers to study Japanese organizations in either single-culture frameworks or in comparative paradigms, in an attempt to establish whether or not Japan's distinctive culture accounts for the success of Japanese companies.

Chapter 12 identifies some of the salient characteristics of the Japanese culture in general and Japanese business culture in particular. In the light of these characteristics, some of the features attributed to Japanese organizations, such as the *ringi* method of decision making, employee-centred leadership style, non-class distinctions between management and workers, lifetime employment, employee commitment to company, team-work and quality circles, the practice of Just-in-time, and single-union agreements, will be discussed. The degree to which the Japanese organizations are uniquely Japanese phenomena is also examined. The chapter gives examples of Western firms which have in the past tried to apply one or more of Japanese management practices in their organizations, and evaluates their success.

The international manager's world

The concluding chapter draws on the previous parts of the book and examines the global opportunities and threats with which international business organizations have to deal. Strategic planning, interface activities, organization and the management style of multinational companies in the light of their global challenges, are discussed.

PART I

HISTORICAL AND ECONOMIC BACKGROUND

1

Firms and International Business

We are living in a complex world, where peoples and countries are more than ever interdependent. Mass communication media, fast and far-reaching transport systems, and satellite-based telecommunications are bringing together almost all parts of the world closer and closer. International business plays a significant part in this complex world. It not only moves goods and services from one country to another, it also transforms societies along the way. It is therefore important to know how international business operates and what challenges it has to face.

International business may be defined as commercial activities which span two or more countries. It can be studied at three levels: country, industry and company. This chapter concentrates mainly on international business at the company level.

Nations and international business

Countries engage in international trade mainly because they are not and cannot be self-sufficient. Various resources which exist in the world, such as raw materials (for example, oil, cotton), capital, labour (in terms of, for instance, education and skills), technology and technical know-how, are found in and are acquired by nations in varying degrees. For example, some countries might have vast reserves of oil (Saudi Arabia) or produce large quantities of coffee every year (Kenya), yet be deficient in technical know-how and engineering skills. Other countries, like Japan and Singapore, are very advanced in technological terms, but their natural resources are very limited or non-existent. Countries like the United States have both natural resources and human skills, but because of the advanced level of their economy, their supplies are not sufficient to meet the demand.

In all these and similar cases, the obvious course of action would be trade between nations. In principle, therefore, countries sell the commodities, products and technologies that they have in abundance and buy those of which they have less or none at all. In an ideal free-trading world, the comparative advantages of nations would guide the nature and direction of international trade and business. In practice, however, as we shall see in Part II, various factors hinder free trade and countries engage in international business for many other reasons as well as for their comparative advantage.

This is not to say that free or liberal international trade is always equally beneficial to all the countries concerned. Young modern economies, such as those of the less developed countries, have many vulnerable industries which cannot fend off competition in a 'free for all' market from the more powerful and experienced companies from advanced economies. These industries may have to be protected, through various trade policies, until they can stand on their own feet.

In fact, as we shall see in chapter 2, the United Kingdom was the only country to preach and practise the liberal trade doctrine almost to the letter. This was mainly because it was the first nation to industrialize, and because it dominated world trade until the second half of the nineteenth century.

Other nations, such as the United States, France, and Germany, which followed the UK on the road to industrialization, had more protectionist trade policies than did the UK. The same is true of Japan; it still is no advocate of free trade. The newly industrialized countries of Asia, especially South Korea, Taiwan, Thailand and Indonesia, started their rigorous industrialization process in the second half of the century with protectionist trade policies.

Nowadays, as the past forty years of GATT (the General Agreement on Tariffs and Trade) negotiations and various trade pacts show, many countries, economically advanced or otherwise, seek to maximize their national and regional interests through intervention in international trade. As has been pointed out, this does not necessarily coincide with their comparative advantage, and it is at variance with the views of economists and trade theorists.

Firms and the international market

The involvement of companies in international business is the level at which trade between nations is translated from principles and policies to actions and practices. In other words, the actual exchange of goods and services, and of money, usually takes place between companies, even if in some cases, such as the sale and purchase of arms, governments are directly involved.

The most prevalent and perhaps the oldest form of international business is the **import** and **export** of goods and services. Some firms may buy, or sell, or facilitate the import and export of commodities, products and services of other companies in international markets. Others may import raw materials and semi-processed goods for use in their own manufacturing operations, mainly because either these do not exist in their own country in sufficient quantity or they might be cheaper abroad. There are also companies which export their own products and services. Individual firms may, of course, engage in any combination of these forms of import and export activities.

Exporting firms could choose to have local partners or sales agents abroad to handle the sale of the goods once they arrive at their destination. Some will go further than this and operate their own transport and distribution network in the foreign country.

In most cases, imports and exports involve exchanges of money, usually in the form of hard currencies, such as the US dollar or the UK pound sterling. But sometimes the trading firms may import from or export to countries whose national currencies are not convertible, such as in the case of the former Soviet Union, China and some of the ex-socialist East European countries. In situations like these, products and services are usually exchanged for products and services under **barter** agreements.

In 1990, for example the former Soviet Union and an American firm, Pepsico, signed a $3 billion agreement according to which the Soviet Union would trade ships and spirits for expanded Pepsi production. Barter was used because the Soviet currency, the rouble, was not readily convertible to Western currencies.

Pepsico, which previously produced 40 million cases of soft drinks in the Soviet Union each year in exchange for the right to ship Stolichnaya vodka to the United States, would under the new agreement increase its numbers of bottling plants in the former Soviet Union from twenty-four to fifty. The expansion would be financed by larger vodka shipments over the next ten years and the sale or lease of at least ten Soviet freighters and tankers (*Time*, 23 April 1990).

Barter is in effect a form of **countertrade**. Sometimes a seller of goods or services undertakes to buy goods or services from its trade partner under the conditions of the contracts signed between their respective governments. This type of obligation based on contracts is called countertrade. Countertrade is a useful means of trading employed not only by the countries with non-convertible currencies, but also by many developing countries which wish to increase their exports and to attain better terms of trade with their international partners.

Another variation of countertrade is where the exporter of goods or services agrees to buy from the importer or from another source in the same country products and services for a specified value within a certain period of time.

Under yet another form of countertrade a firm which sets up a turnkey plant (see below) in a foreign country, or sells equipment or technology to it, undertakes to buy back the products of the turnkey manufacturing plant or those subsequently made by the companies which used the imported equipment and technology.

Some firms choose, for economic, technical and sometimes political reasons (see chapter 4 for details), not to export their products to some countries, but to **license** certain companies in those countries to use their production technology and components to produce similar products. An example of licensing is a car manufacturing company in Iran, Iran National, which used to import engine and other components of the Hillman Hunter from a plant in Britain. These components would subsequently be assembled, under the British company's licence, but under a different brand name, Paykan.

Franchising is very similar to licensing, with one or two differences. For instance, under licensing agreements, the products may in some cases be made under different names, but the franchised products are almost always made under the original company's brand name. The American company McDonald's, which has hamburger restaurant chains in many countries, is an example of this kind of international business.

A major difference between licensing and franchising is that whereas in the former case the parent company usually does not have much control over the operations and the quality of the finished goods in the host country, a parent company with franchises abroad has a greater degree of control over the quality of the final product, mainly in order to protect the reputation of its brand name.

This difference can be interpreted as an advantage of licensing over franchising. If, for instance, the products manufactured under licence with a local name do not live up to the original company's standards, the company's brand name will not suffer. But the products made under franchise using the original brand name can damage the reputation of the brand if they are not as good as the originals. If your Paykan car does not work properly you will blame Iran National, not the British plant which makes the Hillman Hunter, but if the hamburger that you eat in a McDonald's restaurant is not what you expect you hold the McDonald's company responsible.

One factor which all of the above forms of international business share in common is that the companies concerned do not have full managerial control over the foreign part of the operations. Another form of non-managerial foreign involvement is **portfolio investment**, whereby a company may decide to buy shares in one or more firms operating in other countries. These shares entitle the investing company to dividends but not to managerial control.

In other forms of foreign involvement the investing firm has control over the assets and the management of the companies concerned. Turnkey projects and foreign direct investment are examples of this kind.

In **turnkey** projects, a firm usually enters an agreement with a foreign government under which it sets up a plant in the host country; it brings in capital, technology, and managerial skills, and it operates the firm for a limited period of time, say ten years. At the end of this period the investor is expected to hand over the company to local interests and leave. During this initial period of operation the company is required to employ and train local people and to prepare them to run it later on their own. While the firm is operating within the specified period, the investor has the usual managerial power and control, which are relinquished at the termination of the period.

Turnkey projects are especially desirable in developing countries whose governments wish their people to learn to operate advanced technology; their companies get access to the latest skills and know-how, and thereby improve their economies without being dominated by powerful foreign companies.

Control of assets and management are the features which

distinguish **foreign direct investment** (FDI) from portfolio investment. But every country defines control, and by implication FDI, in its own way. In the United States, for instance, owning 10 percent or more of a company constitutes 'control' and thus counts as direct investment. In Germany the ratio is 25 percent, in Britain and France 20 percent (*The Economist*, 23 June 1990).

Foreign direct investment, however defined, has grown considerably in recent years. Every industrial country has more of its economy under the control of foreign firms than a decade ago. But the extent of foreign ownership varies tremendously across those economies. Only 1 percent of Japan's assets were owned by foreign-controlled firms in 1986, just 0.4 percent of its workers were employed by them. In the United States, by contrast, foreign-controlled firms owned 9 percent of the assets, employed 4 percent of the workers, and accounted for 10 percent of all sales. In Britain foreign-controlled firms owned 14 percent of the assets, employed one in seven workers and accounted for 20 percent of all sales. In Germany the foreign-controlled companies owned 17 percent of assets (Julius, 1990).

Foreign direct investment normally takes one of two forms. One is partnerships with firms, also known as joint ventures; the other is wholly-owned subsidiaries.

Joint ventures are companies with multinational ownership, usually involving two or three countries. Joint ventures can be established as such from the outset, or foreign investors can buy into a uninational company and change it to a joint venture.

There can be any number of reasons why some companies are established as or converted to a joint venture. Sometimes a company might face financial difficulties and, unless it is bailed out by another company, it will cease to exist. An electronics firm in the South East of Britain is an example of this kind. A few years ago this company was suffering from serious financial problems. The management decided to sell one-third of the company to a German firm and a further one-third to a Japanese multinational. The company was soon back on its feet and fully operational.

For companies which seek to expand their operations and markets but have limited capital and other resources, such as expertise and technology, a joint venture with a partner who possesses these can be an attractive course of action.

Joint ventures have their attraction for governments too. Some countries, notably developing and ex-socialist ones, need the technologies and skills of Western companies, but also want to be in control of their policies and operations. These countries normally allow foreign direct investment in their territories only in the form of joint ventures. The proportion of ownership by foreign investors and local interests vary from time to time and from country to country, but the host countries usually hold the overall controlling power.

These kinds of restrictions on foreign companies are not, of course, unique to the less technically advanced countries. Japan, a highly industrialized and advanced country with protectionist trade policies, has until recently been virtually closed to foreign firms, be it exporters of cars and electronics, or investors. It was only after many meetings, months of negotiations, and threats of retaliation, that Americans and Western Europeans were able to persuade Japan to open its market to imports and to allow foreign direct investment. Sweden, Finland and Norway also are among advanced industrialized countries with similar restrictions. In Sweden, for instance, foreign investors cannot own more than 40 percent of a company's equity and are limited to 20 percent of shareholders' votes.

Joint ventures have their drawbacks too. Partners have to share in the control and power over resources, policy and strategic decisions and over their business and technological 'secrets'. Risks of tension and disagreement between managers of the partner companies over these and other major aspects of the business can be very high.

Multinational companies may choose a **wholly owned subsidiary** as an option for foreign direct investment. They can set up a new plant or take over an existing one.

Setting up a new plant gives the managers the opportunity to 'build up' the organizational culture from scratch and to shape it in the way they want. Many Japanese multinationals operating abroad, particularly in the UK, prefer new plants. They recruit young high school graduates. These 'fresh' employees have no union membership experience and are not 'contaminated' by the 'them and us' culture of British industrial relations. The managers can then train the new recruits and implement Japanese management practices, which are based on cooperative management–employee relationships.

Companies have more freedom to choose the location of the plant. They can, for instance, set it up in 'development zones', where there are government tax and other financial concessions for investors. The usually high rates of unemployment in such regions also enable the foreign investors to dictate certain employment terms, such as no-strike agreements and single-union contracts.

Taking over an existing firm also has its attractions: an established market, customers, a distribution network, and the invaluable knowledge the management team has of local conditions and local 'ways of doing things'. But the companies that have been taken over also suffer from the drawbacks of joint ventures mentioned earlier. These require mutual understanding and sound managerial judgement on the part of the new team and the old one. The British subsidiary of a Japanese multinational manufacturing firm, Rainbow Corporation (pseudonym) illustrates this point.[1]

Rainbow first became involved in the existing British owned electronics firm as partners in a joint venture and later took over the ownership of the company as a whole. The new owners then decided to introduce technical, managerial and structural reforms in keeping with their own management philosophy.

The 'old' company managers and employees were worried about the uncertainties and confusion which could be caused by the change over, and therefore resisted the introduction of new ideas and a new management style. Also, as in some other British firms, a culture of 'them and us' was prevalent within the company which had created a division between the management and employees. This was regarded by the 'new' management team as a serious obstacle to the successful implementation of their proposed policies.

In order to remove these anxieties and obstacles, the management embarked on creating an atmosphere of cooperation and mutual trust. They tried to enhance the feeling of mutual belonging to the same 'family' by playing down the differences between various groups of employees, in terms of the company's attitudes towards them. The new climate thus created encouraged a high degree of commitment by the workforce to the company objectives, enabling the management to introduce the new policies and ideas with little or no resistance from the employees (see Tayeb, 1990b for details).

Why do some companies 'go international'?

The decision to go international is intertwined with the decision concerning where to go, and they are both guided by many considerations.

[1] Rainbow Corporation was first described in this form in a case study which appeared in Tayeb, 1990b.

The prime objectives of any business organization are to make profits, to grow and to increase its market power. Companies engage in international business when the possibility of achieving these objectives are either diminishing at home and/or there are great opportunities abroad.

Market saturation, fierce competition from domestic and foreign companies, high cost of production (wages, raw material, capital, land), and shortage of the required managerial and technical skills, are some of the reasons why firms might find further investment in home markets less attractive than in foreign markets. Also, there may be restrictive regulations at home which some firms might prefer to avoid. Regulations concerning reserve requirements, deposit insurance, or corporate taxes, for instance, have prompted many banks to move all or parts of their operations abroad and to set up subsidiaries in countries with less stringent rules.

There are many factors that may entice companies to invest abroad, ranging from lower production costs to tax incentives in host countries. The following are some of the factors.

The first group of factors are **market related**. Sometimes firms decide to enter a foreign market because their competitors are already there or are planning to do so, and they do not want to be left behind. The rush of many companies from the capitalist world to the ex-socialist countries in Eastern Europe is, in part, an example of this.

An established end-user market is another 'pull'. Dell Computer Corporation of the United States, for example, announced in 1990 its plans to set up a factory in Ireland to manufacture computers for the European market.

There may also be an untapped market or new opportunities such as the reconstruction of Kuwait after the Persian Gulf war of January–February 1991, which offer attractions to international firms.

Companies may want to 'get a foot in' a market, the entry to which might become harder at a later date. Investment in EC member countries by foreign firms is a move to ensure a firm footing in the Single Market planned for 1992. According to a study carried out for Sweden's Institute for Economic and Social Research, for instance, the country's forty largest firms all plan to boost their investment in the EC over the next few years, some choosing to set up joint ventures and others to buy whole companies (*The Economist*, 1 September 1990).

Secondly, there are **production related** factors. Closeness to raw materials, availability of resources, and advanced technology, can be powerful attractions to encourage firms to invest abroad.

Third are **personnel related** factors. High unemployment rates and weak trade unions in the target areas could be a good reason for foreign direct investment. Many of the Japanese plants recently set up in the United Kingdom, for instance, were attracted there because industrial relations legislation since the early 1980s have significantly reduced British unions' power. The Japanese managers could therefore push through their single-union and no-strike deals with the workers' representatives.

The type of workforce that companies need, that is, unskilled workers for humdrum jobs, highly skilled ones for technically advanced tasks, and generally hard working and committed employees, can also be a factor in deciding to go abroad. For example, Japanese manufacturers investing in South East Asia go to places like Indonesia and Malaysia, where the local workforce is receptive to Japanese ideas about management, can make 'zero defects' their guiding principle, and possess quality consciousness and discipline.

Fourthly, there are **risk related** factors. Investing in two or more countries can help reduce risks – this is the principle of 'not putting all one's eggs in one basket'. By doing so, companies can offset economic troughs in some countries against the peaks in others and benefit overall.

Cost related factors are a fifth group of considerations. Sometimes it is cheaper to manufacture goods in a foreign country than to export them to it. Major deciding factors, of course, would be the cost of labour (wages), raw materials, capital (interest rates) and transport.

Sixthly, there are **host government related** factors. Some governments offer various incentives such as tax concessions and grants, or impose import tariffs and quotas in order to persuade foreign direct investors to set up plants in their countries. Their main aims are usually to bring in capital, know-how and technology, to create jobs for their citizens locally, and to diversify their industrial bases.

Policies of this kind are not just confined to developing countries, as some might think. The British government under Margaret Thatcher's leadership, for example, enticed many multinational companies, especially Japanese, to the less economically prosperous regions of the country (for example, parts of Scotland, South Wales and North East England) by offering them various tax and capital concessions. Margaret Thatcher's

---

Box 1 *Where not to go – Japanese style*

Many Japanese manufacturers are planning to shift production to South East Asia in an effort to reduce costs and escape protectionist barriers in the United States and Europe.

Until recently Thailand, because of its free-market culture and relative political stability, was the favourite investment site in the region for many Japanese firms, which account for one-half of Thailand's recorded foreign investment. But many are hesitating and are becoming cautious for at least three reasons. One is creeping inflation. The second is Thailand's creaking infrastructure. The main problem is that Bangkok accounts for over half the country's economic activity. It has become a by-word for traffic jams, appalling telephones and more kinds of pollution than can be easily imagined. Its foundations are sinking at a rate of four inches a year into the estuary of the Chao Prays river. The third reason for Japanese restraint is that Thailand is facing an increasingly acute shortage of skilled labour. Toyota, which has recently opened its third plant in Thailand, is forced to send as many as 200 Thais a year to Japan for intensive training. Even though it has been established in Thailand since 1957, its most senior Thai manager is still only an associate director, four layers from the top.

These problems are forcing some Japanese companies to think again. Those that require a great deal of unskilled labour are now giving Thailand a miss and heading for Indonesia, where the average income is half that in Thailand. Those that need skilled labour and a functioning infrastructure are turning to Malaysia.

Source: *The Economist*, 2 June 1990

---

main objective was to bring badly needed investment and jobs to these depressed areas, though sceptics suggest that she wanted to crush the unions' power. Many of the prospective investors would only agree to set up their plants (for instance, Nissan in Washington, England) provided that only one union represented the workforce. Ford, the American multinational, had intended to set up a plant in Scotland in the late 1980s, but withdrew its offer precisely because it could not get the national and regional unions to agree to a similar deal.

Finally, there are **host country related** factors. The quality of the infrastructure in the target country, such as its distribution networks, telecommunications systems, roads and railways, is a crucial factor. Poor infrastructure is one of the factors which has made many multinational companies approach direct investment in East European countries with caution.

The present author's experience in India, in the course of the fieldwork for a comparative research project, brought home to me the importance of proper and adequate infrastructure in business negotiations. I was based in Bombay but had to conduct a series of interviews and meetings with a large number of managers in companies scattered around in the state of Maharashtra. It was almost always impossible to get through to the companies' switchboards without over an hour of continuous dialling; the telephone would not respond and would go dead after each trial. On one occasion I went to a company situated in Poona, an industrial city about four hours by train from Bombay, to meet the managing director at the pre-arranged time, only to be told that for the past week he had been trying to contact me by telephone in order to change the date of our meeting. The telephone system had let both of us down!

Factors such as political ideology, religious and other socio-cultural dispositions of people, commercial laws, and regulations regarding the environment, health and safety standards, are also usually considered carefully by firms before they decide to set up subsidiaries abroad.

For example, a firm which makes condoms may not find Eire (because of its anti-contraceptive laws) an appropriate country for its foreign direct investment location; nor would a food processing company producing pork products find Israel or Muslim countries receptive to its intentions to locate a subsidiary there.

Some countries, like Sweden, Germany and Norway, have very stringent environmental regulations which prohibit companies that produce toxic wastes, such as chemicals firms and nuclear processing plants, to operate on their soil unless they meet certain safety and environmental requirements and standards. But other countries are less particular in this respect. Britain, for instance, has welcomed (and still does to a large extent, despite protests by environmental pressure groups) nuclear and other highly toxic industrial wastes from other countries to be reprocessed in its waste-processing plants. The accident at the site of an American chemicals multinational, Union Carbide, in the Indian town of Bhopal in the early 1980s is another illustration of the lax environmental policies which can entice companies to take their operations to 'easy-going' countries. Later, the same company was not allowed to set up a new plant in the United States itself.

In many countries, especially the industrialized ones, a potential or actual captive market, rich and discriminating consumers, and a healthy economic atmosphere could be principal reasons for foreign direct investment. There is no reason, for instance, why a manufacturer of expensive compact disk players or other hi-fi systems would want to set up a plant in a low-income country like Bangladesh, where the market for its products is either non-existent or negligible. Unless, that is, the company can re-export all its products, and the Bangladeshi government also wants to get its share of the business, in the form of local employment, profit and export taxes, and the like.

2
The Global Scene and the Challenges Ahead

The environment within which international business operates consists of almost all nations, with all their social, cultural, political and economic diversities. These pose a unique challenge to multinational firms which has to be met if they are to flourish and indeed survive on the international scene. This chapter outlines some of the features of this global environment and the remainder of the book will discuss them in more detail.

It is useful at this stage to go back a little to examine the recent past which shaped the world of modern international business. The Industrial Revolution which originated in the mid-eighteenth century in Britain may be an appropriate point at which to start.

The Industrial Revolution and international business

The Industrial Revolution was one of the most significant landmarks in the history of modern societies. It was in a way the culmination of nearly three centuries of the intellectual explosion which followed the liberation of Europe from the grip of religious dogma, which had dominated all spheres of life through the Middle Ages – the emergence of the people from the age of ignorance, superstition, diseases, wars and destructions, and the dawn of the age of Enlightenment.

The Industrial Revolution, triggered off and pushed along by a burst of scientific ideas and engineering inventions, changed agriculture and the methods of production of goods. Mechanization replaced and/or complemented manual labour in the farms and on the shopfloors. Small scale, often family owned, cottage industries gave way to large scale mass production factories. This in turn encouraged a massive migration of people from rural areas to industrial centres. As a result, the close knit extended family structure was eventually transformed into a loosely coupled nuclear family system. The ownership of the means of production began to be separated from its control, and feudal societies based on a paternalistic master–serf structure changed to class-based societies in which the middle class was the dominant élite. They either owned the means of production or acted on behalf of the owning classes. The working classes possessed only their labour which they exchanged for wages.

This division of roles, that is, the ownership and control of the means of production on the one hand, and on the other the provision of primary commodity – in this case labour – in exchange for money, was to a large extent replicated on the international scene which was to come. Britain and other early-comers to the industrialized world, such as West European countries (and later the United States), dominated the world of business over the following two centuries.

By the middle of the nineteenth century, Western Europe and the United States had achieved an unprecedented technological level that was affecting the whole world.

Among the greatest technological changes of the period, which encouraged and indeed increased international trade was the application of steam to land and sea transport. Historically, the great cost of moving goods any considerable distance meant that only goods with a high market value in relation to their bulk – such as silk, spices and precious metals – were traded internationally. The extension of the railway network altered this position, not only by reducing the cost of land transport, but also by allowing relatively cheap transport over routes where it had been virtually impossible to offer any before. By 1869 the Union Pacific railway, climbing to 8,600 feet, had linked the east and west coasts of the United States. In many countries the length of railway track in operation increased tenfold in these years (Foreman-Peck, 1983).

The transport of goods by sea underwent similar changes. Shipping benefited from improvements in fuel consumption of marine engines throughout the second half of the nineteenth century. Steam could now provide lower transport costs than sail, especially on short routes.

The division of the world

The benefits derived from the inventions in manufacturing techniques and increased international trade were virtually confined to the industrialized and industrializing nations of the period. Various factors contributed to this situation, the major ones of which are discussed below.

Comparative advantage in technology was one such factor.

Western Europe and later the United States were bursting with technological inventions and scientific discoveries, while at the same time many countries, some of which were the cradles of civilization, were in the grip of hibernation and stagnation. In a way, these countries were experiencing their own equivalent of the Middle Ages at the time when European nations had emerged from theirs. While Europe was in the Dark Ages Asian countries, such as China, Iran, India and some Arab nations, were busy discovering, inventing and perfecting paper, printing techniques, gunpowder, algebra, alcohol, sophisticated irrigation networks, universities and other seats of learning, the then advanced laws and rules of administration, literature and the arts. But by the mid-eighteenth century the position of the two groups of nations had been completely reversed.

Even when these Asian nations, and later African ones, emerged into the modern ages and started their economic and industrial revolutions, they had further disadvantages in the technological sphere. Some of the modern technologies and techniques that they had imported from the more advanced nations were not appropriate to their climatic and socio-cultural conditions. Even today, some of the sophisticated machinery that is imported to the less advanced countries does not work there properly. There is, for instance, a shortage of skilled manpower to operate it or to maintain it when there is a breakdown. For example, an airline company in an Asian country had a series of accidents and crashes in its domestic route operations in the early 1990s. Technical observers blamed the inadequate training and knowledge of the pilots and other technical members of the crews of the planes for these accidents. Apparently the crews did not know how to operate properly the sophisticated foreign computers newly installed in the cockpits.

Technological disadvantages in the less advanced nations can further result in a lower per capita productivity, both in industrial and agricultural sectors, in comparison with their more advanced competitors. This weakens their position in the international markets.

Furthermore, low productivity in agriculture can be detrimental to the growth and expansion of the industrial sector. And this situation has been the case for quite a long time. Lewis (1978) argues that the problem of the late nineteenth century commodity producers was ultimately low productivity in their agricultural sectors, which engaged the great bulk of their labour forces. For these countries, and for others, as Foreman-

Peck (1983) points out, trade is worthwhile if the resources used to provide exports are less valuable than the imports obtained in exchange. The more productive the economy, the fewer are the resources needed to supply a given quantity of exports. Increased productivity in these countries' agriculture, as against increased output, would have allowed some of the agricultural labour force to move into manufacturing industry, but this did not happen to any significant extent.

The second factor contributing to unequal shares in the benefits of international trade among the nations, was the **colonization** of the majority of African, Latin American and Asian countries by the then imperial powers. As Foreman-Peck (1983) points out, a relationship between trade and colonization was by no means novel, especially towards the end of the nineteenth century, but the speed of the 'scramble for Africa' was remarkable.

Colonization had become necessary as a means of securing further sources of supply of cheap or even free raw materials and sources of demand for the industrialized countries' manufactured goods (Hobson, 1905). Lenin (1934) argues in this connection that the concentration of industry allowed the monopolists to divide the world between them, first into commercial empires and then into political empires, in order to safeguard their monopolies of markets and sources of raw materials.

The colonial powers, especially those which believed in liberal trade, imposed their ideologies on their colonies. Given that there were hardly any manufactured goods coming from the colonies, the barrier-free trade relations could only benefit the colonial powers. India, for instance, was a colony and unable to pursue an independent tariff policy. Under British political control during the first half of the nineteenth century, the trade regulations that were imposed on India would probably not have been allowed had the Indian government been independent. As a consequence of these regulations, the imports of cotton goods from Britain increased massively to become the largest category of imports, while cotton piece goods, formerly a major export, dwindled into insignificance (Chaudhuri, 1971; Maddison, 1971).

The third factor was the **slave trade**, which involved capturing young and physically strong men and women from African tribes and transporting them to the American continent to work on plantations owned by the white settlers. Although the international trade in slaves had been declared illegal by Britain and the United States by 1807, it continued until the late nineteenth century because its profitability was assured by the strength of Western demand for slave-produced goods, in particular cotton, sugar and coffee (Sheridan, 1976).

Trade in slaves, which provided a cheap and indeed free source of labour for these plantations, had harmful effects on African countries. The African economies suffered from a massive drain on their young people, in whom they had invested their resources from childhood to the productive age. Also, the economic development of these countries was hampered by the lack of security caused by slave raiding parties.

The harmful effects of the slave trade went beyond African countries to a number of other low income nations. The cotton produced by free labour in India and the Middle East, for instance, was less profitable and was therefore produced in smaller quantities, even after the American Civil War, than would have been the case if the slaves had never been trans-planted across the Atlantic. Indirectly, because of the slave trade India and the Middle East had their opportunities to gain from international trade reduced (Foreman-Peck, 1983).

The fourth factor was, and still is as we shall see in chapter 11, the **specialization** of the poorer and less developed countries in primary products and that of the advanced nations in manufac-tured and semi-processed goods. Primary products are subject to uncontrollable fluctuations in supply conditions, for example caused by drought or disease, and have a chronic tendency to decline relative to the prices of the manufactured goods in the international market. The primary products also have a much lower income elasticity compared with manufactured goods. Beyond a certain level of income, demand for primary products increases far less, or even ceases to increase, compared with the demand for manufactured goods. How many more cups of coffee can a millionaire drink in a day compared with a person with an annual income of, say, £25,000? Not very many. And how many more luxury items, expensive and sophisticated cars, gadgets and household appliances can the former buy in a year compared with the latter? Infinitely more. The nations that are specialized in making the second kind of products are bound to leave the producers of the first type behind by a very considerable margin. This role specialization, of course, has its roots in the factors just discussed above.

Moreover, developments in the last quarter of the nineteenth century brought increasing competition for primary product exports, which the less advanced countries were not able to fend off effectively. For instance, sugar prices were forced down by the expansion of subsidized beet sugar exports from continental Europe from the 1870s; new copper deposits were discovered and exploited in the United States and other countries, and the invention and commercialization of synthetic dyes greatly reduced exports of Indian indigo. The United States became the world's leading producer of cotton and tobacco, Japan became an important exporter of silk and tea, and the United States, continental Europe and Japan all developed advanced textile industries (Foreman-Peck, 1983).

The rise and fall of the dominant powers

The European and especially the British rise in dominance in the international economy went hand-in-hand with the extension of political control or influence. International economic relations allowed the rise of Western Europe to its powerful nineteenth-century position by despoiling and correspondingly reducing the income of the rest of the world. Physical violence, confiscation and theft in Asia, Africa and America by superior European military and political organizations caused divergent paths of economic development in the four centuries before 1850 (Foreman-Peck, 1983). Successful wars excluded other countries from lucrative markets, and allowed the accumulation of capital from profits (Barret Brown, 1974; Wallerstein, 1979). The employment of this capital in the world markets conferred a monopoly which was used to exploit foreign consumers by the charging of high prices, and to exploit foreign producers by buying at low prices. The economic development of Chile in the nineteenth century, for instance, was distorted by the industrial monopoly of Great Britain. This monopoly furthered Britain's development under free trade, but forced Chile to specialize in the production of primary products that were not conducive to economic development (Gunder Frank, 1967).

European political and economic power reached its peak in the last quarter of the nineteenth century and the years before the First World War. Within Europe, the rise of Germany to challenge Britain's former economic supremacy and to displace France from the political leadership of mainland Europe was the most fundamental change of the period.

Until then Britain had enjoyed a dominant position in the world, both politically and economically. It had presided over a massive empire which covered much of Asia, Africa and parts

of the Americas, and in which 'the sun never set'. By the beginning of the twentieth century, however, Britain had lost its lead
as the dominant industrial nation (Kemp, 1969; Mitchell and
Deane, 1962; Mulhall, 1899). Britain's share in exports to industrialized areas decreased while that of economically more
backward regions, including countries in which it wielded
political influence, increased (Sen, 1984). There were various
reasons for the decline of Britain's position, which continued
well into the twentieth century.

First, there was a shift in the comparative advantage in
manufactured products in the mid-nineteenth century as the
United States, Germany and other West European countries
industrialized. The British manufacturing sector, for instance,
suffered a decline in productivity and shifted its competitive
advantage towards natural resources, especially coal; but the
United States shifted from a position of competitive advantage
in natural resources to one in manufactured goods. By the end
of the 1920s, the United States was exporting more manufactured goods than Britain, largely because of its competitive
advantage in the rapidly growing sectors of chemicals, machinery and transport equipment, while the British industrial structure, heavily weighted towards textiles, suffered from the
import substitutions and international competition of the then
newly industrialized countries.

Secondly, after the Second World War, Britain's position as
an imperial power had been eroded considerably. A vast
majority of its colonies, beginning with India in 1947, became
independent one after another, and thereby adopted independent trade policies which were no longer so one-sidedly in
favour of their colonial ruler. The independence of the colonies
put an end to the massive reservoir of cheap raw materials and
to the sources of demand for British manufactured goods.
Moreover, Britain now had to face competition from these
newly freed countries in international markets.

While Britain was experiencing decline in its position, the
United States was gaining importance on the international
scene. By the end of the Second World War the balance of
power among the capitalist powers had been altered decisively,
with the United States emerging as the leader.

Although much of the United States' trade was within the
various regions of the country itself, and therefore participated
in international trade proportionately less than other industrialized nations, the rapid growth and sheer size of the
economy nevertheless meant that the overall impact of the

United States on the the international economy was immense (Foreman-Peck, 1983).

The strength of the United States' economy was such that it was able, mainly because of its huge post-war surplus, to finance the reconstruction of Europe through the Marshall Plan (Hutton, 1988), even though many European countries specifically discriminated against US exports, partly because of their inability to generate enough dollar earnings with which to pay for them (Patterson, 1966). The United States chose rapid European reconstruction and political amity because of what it perceived to be the greater immediate threat of the Soviet Union (Sen, 1984). The United States was also able to support massive world-wide investments by US multinational companies which created new industries in Western Europe, Australia, the Far East, Africa and Latin America (Hutton, 1988).

By the 1950s a new and fierce competitor, namely Japan, began to make its presence felt in the world of international business. Allen (1972), an economic historian of Japan, traces the earlier signs of Japan's rise among the industrialized nations to the beginning of the twentieth century. According to him, 'in the early months of 1915 it became clear that the country was on the threshold of a period of unexampled prosperity' (Allen, 1972: 97). This situation was to a large extent caused by the inability of countries in Europe involved in war to supply customers and their own additional war-time requirements. But there were also cultural reasons for Japan's economic rise. The country had suffered humiliation and a spectacular defeat in the Second World War, which for a culture that attaches immense significance to loss of face (Briggs, 1988; Tayeb, 1990b) could be buried and forgotten only under an equally spectacular victory, this time on the economic front.

The inter-war period was characterized by instability, unemployment, and the decline of trade, which culminated in the Depression of the years 1929–30. But in many countries the real per capita income increased and compared favourably with the pre-war period. Although Japan had suffered as much as most countries from the effects on trade of the Depression, it increased its exports faster than national income which in turn grew faster than those of other countries.

The Depression also brought about changes in economic thinking. Until 1929 the major economies were organized more or less on a *laissez-faire* basis. The Depression prompted eminent economists like Keynes to call for more government intervention in economic affairs. Governments, even in a country like

Britain, which was the birthplace of *laissez-faire* capitalism (Weber, 1930) began to play a more prominent and active role in their countries' economic and industrial policies, and even nationalized some industries such as coal, steel, railway networks and air transport.

Between 1945 and 1950 the strength of the Japanese economy and its shares in international trade relative to major industrialized countries, not surprisingly, slumped. But in the twenty years after 1950, the two major countries which suffered a decline in world markets especially for strategic industry exports were Britain and the United States. At the same time Japan and Germany improved their shares (Sen, 1984).

Britain's losses were incurred in part because of German competition in non-industrial markets during the 1950s. Britain had also become more dependent on semi-industrial markets since the outset of the twentieth century because of industrialization in Europe, and import substitution policies in semi-industrial markets subsequently had a significant impact on British exports (Maizels, 1970). Britain also suffered losses because of the United States and, increasingly, because of Japan (Batchelor et al., 1980).

A significant proportion of the decline in the United States' manufactured exports and the penetration of its domestic market was due to Japan. Severe competition was experienced by the United States in iron and steel and electrical machinery in the initial period, extending to a whole range of products in the 1970s (Roemer, 1976).

The growth of Japan's exports in manufactured products inflicted losses on other countries as well.

By the late 1970s, the United States' economy had lost its dominant position in the world export markets and also faced a challenge in its home market because of the appearance of competitive rival economies.

The rise and fall of the communist bloc

A major phenomenon which dominated much of the international political and economic scene after the Second World War was the division of the nations into Eastern (communist/ socialist) and Western (capitalist) blocs and their allies, with a small group of non-aligned countries, initiated by Yugoslavia's late Marshal Tito, outside these two camps.

The capitalist bloc consisted of the United States, the West European countries, Canada, Japan and their smaller and less powerful allies.

The communist system first came into being with the 1917 revolution, led by Lenin, in Russia in the 'ten days which shook the world'. But it was only after the Second World War that communism swept through a large number of countries, either through revolution and a *coup d'état* from within (such as China and Cuba) or through invasion by the Soviet Union (for example, in Eastern and Central European countries).

For over forty years the two superpowers – the United States and the Soviet Union – presided over a state of 'cold war' which dominated and determined the direction of many international political and economic decisions.

During this period, there was a minimal amount of trade and economic cooperation between the two blocs. The Eastern bloc countries conducted much of their trade among themselves, through Comecon (Council for Mutual Economic Association), and to a limited extent with other countries through barter, because of the inconvertibility of their currencies.

The Soviet Union treated its satellite countries as its own property, plundered their natural resources, and polluted their air, water and land with the toxic fumes and wastes of its steel, chemicals and armament industries. Furthermore, the Soviet Union crushed, indirectly through puppet regimes, or directly through military actions, any democratic and human rights movements which rose up in these countries.

The Eastern bloc countries were not members of international financial and trade institutions such as the International Monetary Fund (IMF) and the World Bank, and only Czechoslovakia and Poland participated in the General Agreement on Tariffs and Trade (GATT). Foreign direct investment by companies from the capitalist bloc in the communist bloc was either non-existent or very limited.

With the coming to power of Mikhail Gorbachev in the Soviet Union in the mid-1980s, first as Secretary General and then as President, a new political and economic era dawned in the Eastern bloc as well as the Soviet Union itself. Internally, Gorbachev initiated a series of political and economic reforms – *glasnost* (political freedom) and *perestroika* (restructuring). These aimed at installing democracy eventually throughout the country and transforming the centrally-planned economy into a decentralized capitalist social market which would be based on private enterprise.

Internationally, the Soviet Union entered into negotiations with the Western bloc to end the cold war; in 1991 it was formally declared as ended by the United States and the Soviet

Union. In fact, economic and especially political cooperation between the two superpowers had already manifested itself during Iraq's invasion of Kuwait and the Persian Gulf war in late 1990 and early 1991.

In 1989, the Soviet Union withdrew its support for the Communist regimes of East European countries and elsewhere. In November that year, in the wake of dramatic political events in Poland, a wave of popular revolutions swept through the communist countries of Eastern Europe, which ended the monopoly of the communist party and replaced it with political pluralism and democratically elected governments. These countries subsequently embarked on reforms and reconstruction of their economies on a social capitalist model.

The death of the Eastern bloc also brought an end to Comecon and the Warsaw Pact (the Eastern bloc's equivalent of NATO). It also exposed the serious problems and weaknesses of the Soviet Union's economy; the country could no longer be considered a superpower, at least in economic terms. The final seal to the fate of the Soviet Union's communism was achieved, inadvertently, by an unsuccessful *coup d'état* staged in August 1991, during the 'three days that shook the world', by the so-called hardliners who saw in the demise of Soviet Union communism their own fall from power and privilege.

The implications of the failed *coup d'état* went further than this. The Baltic states of Latvia, Lithuania and Estonia, which had been annexed to the Soviet Union by force since the Second World War, seized the opportunity and declared themselves independent. The remaining parts of the Soviet Union disintegrated into their twelve constituent republics, and the Soviet Union ceased to exist as of 31 December 1991. Eleven republics (the exception was Georgia) formed themselves into a loosely-connected group known as the Commonwealth of Independent States (CIS), with Russia by far the largest of all in terms of land mass, population, and economic and military power (see also chapter 10).

The world of international business today

Currently, although the world is no longer as divided along political and ideological lines, it is still divided into 'haves' and 'have nots'. In historical terms we are still close to a time when the world was dominated by no more than a dozen powers from what we now term the North (Arnold, 1989). Much of the rest of the world belongs to the South.

The 'haves' are the rich industrialized countries which are mainly situated in the northern hemisphere. They are characterized by high per capita income, high GNP, the manufacture of semi-processed and finished goods, the use of computers, capital intensive technology, high per capita consumption of electricity and other sources of energy, low level of natural resources relative to less-industrialized nations, mechanized agriculture, high rates of literacy, and long life expectancy (75 years in the United States).

The 'have nots' are the poor countries with predominantly agricultural economies, and mainly, but not invariably, situated in the southern hemisphere. They are characterized by dense population, low per capita income, a low rate of literacy, high rates of infant mortality, short life expectancy (just under 50 years in India), non-mechanized agriculture, and the export of usually one and sometimes two commodities.

The rich industrialized world plays the preponderant role in the international political systems; the less industrialized countries of the world are effectively almost excluded from participation in the decisions which affect the functioning and direction of these systems. International organizations such as the United Nations, the World Bank, the IMF and the GATT rounds of negotiations are dominated by the industrialized countries. Whenever the G7 countries (the United States, Germany, Japan, France, the United Kingdom, Canada and Italy) meet for their annual summit meetings, they discuss the economic conditions of the whole world and decide upon matters which affect all other countries, without any of these either being present or being able to influence the outcomes of the summits.

The contemporary world, although it has not indulged in great all-encompassing conflicts such as the First and Second World Wars since 1945, is still characterized by devastating regional and civil wars, as in the former Yugoslavia, the Middle East, Vietnam, Cambodia, Sri Lanka, Kashmir, Afghanistan, Iraq, Ethiopia, Sudan, South Africa. The list can go on and on.

Some of the less developed countries are in the grip of a debt crisis which has also crippled many multinational banks and other financial institutions. In the 1970s inflationary pressures both stimulated and later resulted from OPEC oil price rises. Investment capital, abundant from the OPEC oil surpluses of the 1970s, led to overborrowing by many East European and developing countries, and brought major debt servicing difficulties which were intensified by the 1980–2 recession in the industrial countries.

Box 2   *Japanese and American managers – do it my way*

Misunderstandings between Japanese and American managers are possible at nearly every encounter. They can begin at the first recruiting interview.

A large American company typically hires people to fill particular slots. Its managers know that Americans are mobile people, who have a limited commitment to any particular employer or part of the country. As a result, jobs are clearly defined and so are the skills needed to fill them. American firms hire and fire almost at will. In steel, cars, aerospace and other heavy-engineering firms, employees are routinely laid off in a slump and rehired when business picks up.

The assumptions, and so the expectations, of the Japanese managers of Japanese subsidiaries in the United States could hardly be more different. They hire people more for the skills they will acquire after joining the company than for their existing skills. Job descriptions merely identify the minimum which the firm expects from its employees. The Japanese company wants the managers it hires to make a long-term commitment and to search constantly for new ways to serve the company better. The firm assumes that its ability to retain and rotate workers will provide it with the necessary flexibility on labour costs.

Such an approach, however, is more feasible back home in Japan, where subcontractors can be squeezed more easily to cut costs or absorb workers. Such employment practices are more difficult to sustain in the United States, where even Japanese subsidiaries have to be more self-sufficient.

These different approaches explain much of the hostility between American and Japanese middle managers which plagues so many American subsidiaries of Japanese companies. The Americans feel impotent because of their inability to fire people. They are unsettled by the lack of such definable goals as operating-profit margins or calculations of discounted cash-flow in capital budgeting.

In the face of a conflict, the Americans believe that their Japanese bosses are indecisive or incompetent. Japanese managers do not share the American belief that conflict is inevitable, and sometimes healthy. They want to believe that employees form one big happy family.

In the United States such attitudes will not 'fly'. Most Americans prize their individual freedom far too much to make a Japanese-style commitment to any company. Shiseido, a large Japanese cosmetics firm, learned this lesson after it acquired Zotos International, an American hair-products company, in 1988 for $345 million. Two years later Shiseido replaced the Japanese manager in charge of Zotos with Mr Philip Voss, an American ex-army officer. Out went management by consensus. In came the hierarchy Americans understood. On top of the heap is Mr Voss, the kind of strong-willed boss Americans admire – or fear.

Source: *The Economist*, 24 November 1990

The international trade scene is characterized by both protectionism and liberalism at the same time. On the one hand, there are international agreements and regional pacts to enhance the free trade of goods and services across borders. On the other hand, there are increasing protectionist tendencies and government interventions, both in the industrially inferior countries, which feel vulnerable to domination by the richer and more powerful ones, and in the advanced countries where strong interest groups dictate or influence the trade policies of their governments.

In social and cultural terms, the world is, as ever, a patchwork. Various nations have different value systems, social norms, religious beliefs and political ideologies. Most countries have their own distinctive laws, administrations, policies, political allegiances and power struggles, and national priorities. There are also issues such as human rights abuse, racism, and ecological considerations with which people all over the world are involved.

Companies that engage in international business face a tremendous challenge in order to succeed and indeed to survive within this complex web of peoples and events. They always have to look over their shoulder for a political upheaval here, a new trade barrier there, a cultural misunderstanding in a third place (see Box 2). There is a constant stream of vigorous newcomers to the marketplace in addition to the 'old hands'. But the world also offers a large number of opportunities, potential or real, to international companies. The remainder of this book deals with some of these challenges, opportunities and threats.

PART II

MAJOR CHALLENGES TO FREE INTERNATIONAL TRADE

3

Political Risk

Political risk can be defined as the probability of domestic or foreign firms' activities being adversely affected by the actions taken by the state. This chapter deals with political risk involving foreign firms and international trade.

Governmental actions against foreign firms

Governments sometimes take various actions against foreign firms for political or economic reasons. These actions range from interfering in the foreign firm's managerial policies, to harassment and making the carrying out of its operations difficult, to outright nationalization and confiscation of the firm's assets.

Foreign firms may be required to include local people in their top management teams, and to use a certain proportion of local content in the assembly of imported components. They may be asked to build or contribute to the construction of local amenities such as roads, houses for employees, hospitals, schools and similar facilities in the areas where the firms are situated.

Governments might also take actions which are primarily aimed at driving the foreign company out of their country. These actions include encouraging the firm's employees to go on strike, and asking consumers to boycott its products.

Some governments require foreign firms to pay excessive licence fees and high taxes. Such charges can be increased to the point where making profits is not possible and the company is forced to leave.

In what is known as 'creeping expropriation', firms are not allowed to take their profits out of the country and/or are forced to invest them in specific governmental projects. Expropriation is the official seizure of foreign property by a host country whose intention is to use the seized property in the public interest. The ultimate harassment is, of course, nationalization or expropriation. Nationalization usually means with compensation, and expropriation usually means without.

There can be many reasons behind a government's actions against foreign firms operating in their territories, of which the most significant ones are the following.

The first is a change of, or a shift in, emphasis in foreign trade policies. An example of this is the decision of the Indian government, in the late 1970s to change, on protectionist grounds, the conditions under which foreign firms could invest and operate in India. This made it very difficult if not impossible for multinationals like Coca Cola to continue their presence in the country.

The second reason is a change of the government itself. This may occur through democratic channels such as elections, or through *coups d'état*, or through revolutions.

Democratic elections, although a less dramatic method of changing a government, can nevertheless have serious consequences for foreign firms. Take the government of the United Kingdom, for example. Since 1979 the Conservative Party has been in power and its economic policies have been based largely on the principles of non-intervention and free markets. In pursuit of these policies the government has embarked on a large-scale privatization of state-owned companies in various sectors, such as the telecommunications, water, electricity, gas, aerospace, petroleum, and car industries. The shares of these companies were sold not only to British individuals and institutions but also to foreigners, notably the French (the water industry), the Kuwaitis (petroleum), and many more. The opposition Labour Party has always threatened to re-nationalize some of these industries, especially water and electricity, should it be elected to power. The risks involved for the foreign (and the domestic) shareholders are obvious.

France is another example of a democratic country in which general elections could be a source of political risk. When the socialist President Mitterand was elected to his first term of office, he, following his election manifesto promises, nationalized banks and other financial institutions. Although he later returned to the private sector the vast majority of them, the fact remained that the nationalization of those organizations posed a serious threat and risk to the firms involved.

Political uncertainty and weak transitional governments can

also cause political risk. In the early 1990s international bankers who had lent money to India faced such a risk. The government had scarcely enough foreign exchange reserves to meet one month's loan and import payments (*Time*, 8 April 1991). The crisis was compounded by the lack of a proper government. Four weeks earlier the prime minister had resigned. Fresh elections were scheduled for a few months later, but until then a weak caretaker administration was in charge. Senior government officials were trying to avoid defaulting but had no mandate to rewrite economic policy or make a deal with the institutions that specialize in financial rescues, namely the International Monetary Fund and the World Bank.

Coups d'état are always viewed by foreign firms as a source of great risk, though this is probably not always so. In less democratic countries, such as some of the Latin American and Asian nations, a *coup d'état* was, and still is to a large extent, the only means by which people could change their governments. The coups are usually a way of settling domestic power struggles and scoring points among rivals. The new governments are likely to follow similar foreign trade policies to their predecessors.

Take Thailand for example. The generals who led the bloodless military coup in spring 1991 cited some familiar charges to explain the coup: government corruption, abuse of power and what they called 'national calamities'. There was also the issue of power. As *Time* (4 March 1991) points out, the military, which had traditionally played a leading role in Thai politics and economics, had felt for some time that its power and prestige were being eroded by democratic development and an economic boom that pushed technocrats and businessmen into the forefront of national life, while edging soldiers to the sidelines. At the same time, there was growing public discontent with widespread poverty and an infrastructure that failed to keep pace with economic development. The army saw itself as intruding into politics for a short time to solve a problem and then withdraw.

Attracting foreign investment and honouring contracts already signed remained a priority, in theory at least. The generals appointed a number of respected economic advisers in an effort to reassure international investors that business would carry on as usual and to ensure continuity in economic policy (*The Independent on Sunday*, 3 March 1991, Business Supplement).

However, the risk, real or imagined, may still to some extent linger on. For instance, foreign companies involved in projects to upgrade Thailand's infrastructure could face further difficulty in securing long-term financing from overseas, where the impact of the coup was much greater than in Thailand itself. The Japanese government, for instance, announced that it would suspend talks on new yen loans for Thailand for the time being, and most foreign bankers in Bangkok said it was unlikely that any substantial loan decisions would be made at least until a civilian government was installed by the junta.

Revolutions, like those which occurred in Iran and Nicaragua in the late 1970s, had even more serious consequences for foreign firms located in these countries and for the trade between these and the Western world. In both countries, the new governments took a hard anti-American line in their foreign policies. As a result, and especially in Iran, the assets of many American and other Western firms were confiscated without compensation. This in turn provoked the United States and its allies to impose on Iran and Nicaragua an embargo on trade and investment and a freezing of Iran's funds held in American banks. With the change of government in Nicaragua in 1990 and a shift away from anti-Western attitudes in the foreign policies of Iran in 1991, these countries might one day become again risk-free for foreign firms.

A third reason behind a government's actions against foreign firms is a change of relationships between governments caused by war (as the Persian Gulf War), or by political reforms (as in Eastern Europe) which could change the political climate within which foreign firms and international trade operate.

The invasion of Kuwait by Iraq in August 1990 affected mostly oil-related firms. But other firms suffered too. A British textile and fashion company, for instance, had an exclusive made-to-order range for Kuwaiti customers; they were rendered worthless after the invasion.

Beyond causing direct losses in trade and commerce, the Gulf crisis sparked a general reluctance to invest in a region that had been an important trading partner for industrialized economies. Even the neighbouring countries cancelled or delayed their capital projects. Saudi Arabia, for instance, had planned to construct 400 new industrial plants at a total cost of $40 billion in the following 5 years. The plan had to be shelved so long as the crisis was unresolved.

Another consequence of the invasion was the imposition of trade sanctions against Iraq by the international community. As a result, not only the Iraqi firms (and people) but also their foreign trading partners were affected considerably (see Box 3).

Box 3   *Sanctions against Iraq and international business*

At NEI Parsons, a subsidiary of Northern Engineering Industries in Newcastle-upon-Tyne, Britain, employees have abandoned work on what should have been one of their most lucrative projects in recent years, a $150 million contract to build four turbine generators for a power station at Al Shemal, 400 km north of Baghdad. Playing its small part in the world-wide sanctions against Iraq, the firm has announced layoffs of 650 workers.

Near Beasley, Texas, Jack Wendt, who farms 607 hectares of rice and grain, calculates that he will earn $72,000 less than in 1989 because of the sudden disappearance of the US rice industry's best customer, Iraq. In Paris, Airbus Industrie has put on hold a recently signed deal to sell five A310 wide-body jets to Iraqi Airways at about $70 million a plane.

The freeze on trade with Iraq and Kuwait is hurting many people, from US manufacturers of oil-field equipment to Irish meat producers to Italian shipbuilders. If UN sanctions produced a cutoff in trade with Iraq, they also led Iraq to suspend payment on outstanding debts. The result is dislocation and even hardship among Iraq's erstwhile commercial partners. . . .

As longtime suppliers of arms and ammunition to Iraq, several East European countries agreed earlier in 1990 to accept oil as payment for Iraq's debts. When the sanctions went into effect, Iraq owed Czechoslovakia $800 million and Poland $500 million. . . .

In even more dire straits are the crumbling economies of Bulgaria, which holds $1.2 billion in Iraqi debt, and Romania, which is owed $1.7 billion. Moscow also faces losses. Professor Alexander Arbatov of the USSR Academy of Sciences estimates that the Soviet Union might be forfeiting a potential gain of as much as $1 billion by cutting off sales of arms and agricultural products to Iraq.

As lenders in the most far-flung corners of the world, Japanese trading firms and German banks and investment companies are saddled with more than their share of Iraqi debt. Japanese trading firms hold about $5 billion in unpaid Iraqi bills, German banks about $2 billion. The embargo also leaves 40 German companies stuck with $2 billion in debt on business deals that have been partially completed but not paid for. . . . Large diversified conglomerates such as Daimler-Benz, Mannesmann and Ferrostaal can absorb such short-falls, but smaller firms with proportionately larger exposure are talking about hardship and calling for a government bailout. . . .

France is forfeiting about $600 million in export trade with Baghdad. Just weeks before the 2 August invasion, the telecommunications giant Alcatel CIT was hoping to clinch a $75 million deal for a central phone network for the Basra area. The contract 'no longer exists', says a company spokesman.

Turkey find itself in a particularly painful position. Exporters had expected to sell Baghdad $600 million worth of goods, mainly iron, steel and food products. Since the US and most European countries impose strict quotas on some of these imports and the markets for others are saturated, Ankara estimates that 75 percent of the products destined for Iraq will be effectively rendered worthless; no other foreign importer will be able to buy them. In addition, the 10 large Turkish firms that keep some of their assets in Iraq, including the construction companies Enka Insaat, Fuat Soylu and Guris Makina, could suffer combined losses of about $570 million if Iraq, as expected, seizes their property.

Italy's commercial connection to Iraq is a source of embarrassment. Baghdad owes Italian banks about $2.2 billion, mostly because of unauthorized loans made by the Banca Nazionale del Lavoro (BNL) branch in Atlanta, Georgia. That scandal, which is still under investigation in the US, led to the resignation of BNL directors and the dismissal of nearly everyone connected to the Atlanta branch. In addition, Iraq owes Italy more than $1 billion for warships that were built but never delivered. . . .

Source: *Time*, 5 December 1990

The defeat of Iraq in the war also caused casualties among foreign firms. Brazil's arms industry, which was the world's seventh largest arms exporter by the mid-1980s, was one such casualty. It was, according to *Time* (15 April 1991), an enterprise built largely on supplying Iraq's war machine, particularly during the long Iran–Iraq confrontation. With the end of that war and with Iraq's defeat in the recent Gulf conflict, Brazilian arms merchants seemed to have lost their lucrative market in the Middle East. Middle Eastern customers, impressed by the success of sophisticated US and European weaponry during Desert Storm, seemed unlikely to shop in Brazil when the time came to restock inventories or buy new hardware.

Sources of political risk

Political risk may occur at three levels: national, industry and firm.

At the national level, some countries seem to be more risk prone than others. Although it is difficult to generalize, nations that experience a greater degree of political instability are more likely to cause problems for foreign firms. Major factors which contribute to political instability in a country and are potentially risky for foreign firms include those which are related to the government, and those which are related to the country in general.

A change in government through revolution or elections or

just a change of leadership can lead to changes in the policies affecting foreign firms. These policies can be related to such areas as foreign exchange controls, foreign investment inside the country, taxation, price controls and profit remittances regulations, and a shift of emphasis in foreign policy towards certain countries.

The legitimacy of a government may sometimes be in doubt, in which case there is a potential for its overthrow and subsequent uncertainties as to future events.

The administrative machinery might be bedevilled with corruption and incompetence. This can force foreign firms, in their efforts to obtain a licence to operate in or deal with a country, to be caught in a complicated web of bureaucratic procedures and paperwork. They may also have to deal with corrupt officials who would manipulate the situation in order to extract commissions from the firms before granting them permission to trade. Once the permission is granted the firms have to co-exist with these people and procedures for as long as it intends to continue its operation in that country. Not knowing the rules of the game is likely to jeopardize the foreign firm's successful operation and therefore be a source of risk and threat.

Factors related to the country in general include terrorism (Lebanon), civil disorder, domestic tension (Northern Ireland), labour unrest, regional instability (the former Yugoslavia, the former Soviet Union), nationalism and resentment towards foreigners, and religious extremism (India). The country itself may engage in war or serious conflicts with other countries (the Iran–Iraq war from 1980 to 1988, Iraq's invasion of Kuwait in 1990).

At the industry level, the potential for political risk is greater for strategic industries, such as oil, steel, power stations, arms and weaponry, and high technology, than for non-strategic ones. For instance, a company making shoes is less likely to face hostility from the host government than a firm engaging in oil extraction or running nuclear power stations.

Developing countries are sometimes considered to be more risky than the more advanced ones. This, however, may not necessarily have anything to do with their level of industrialization. Rather, it may be because of political considerations. The reason could be, for instance, that they need technological know-how and capital from advanced countries in order to build their infrastructure and strategic industries. Ideally they would want to reduce and/or terminate this dependence as soon as they can. By implication, the foreign firms which are engaged in such industries are more likely to be nationalized – hence the higher risk propensity of developing countries.

At the firm level, political risk is potentially great if, for instance, the company produces a large amount of the host country's GNP; or if it is a subsidiary of a powerful multinational which can or does exert political and economic pressure on the host country. The company may be engaged in handling the host country's major natural resources, such as oil and valuable minerals. It may have access to and control over export markets. There could also be a conflict between the company's goals and the national interests of the host country. In cases such as these the host government might feel vulnerable and would want to take control of the foreign firm as soon as it could.

Forecasting political risk

There are many methods by which, it is claimed, political risk can be forecast, and which are dealt with by many other writers in any typical textbook on international business. The present book, therefore, makes only a brief reference to these methods.

Firms which intend to set up operations in a foreign country can choose simple procedures such as 'grand tours', 'old hands' and 'check lists'.

'Grand tours' involve sending senior managers to a potential host country on a fact-finding mission, to collect information on various relevant socio-political factors and make an estimate of its political stability. The obvious shortcoming of this method is the superficiality of the information collected. One cannot learn much about a country unless one lives there and mingles with people for a long time.

'Old hands' procedures involve seeking advice from other foreign firms which are presently dealing, or have in the past dealt, with the targeted country. Here again there is some doubt about the usefulness or relevance of the collected information. The effect of political risk on individual firms, as was discussed earlier, can be qualitatively different one from another, depending on what each firm does and what kind of political, economic and social impact it might or might not have on the host country.

'Check lists' involve ranking a given country on a list of potential political hazards, such as governmental stability, administrative competence, domestic tension, official attitudes towards foreign investment, prospects for nationalization, and so on. Here again the success of the method depends on the accuracy and reliability of the information on which the ranking is based.

There are also more sophisticated mathematical models, such as Delphic techniques, the Haendel–West–Meadow political stability index and the Knudsen ecological approach (see for instance Globerman, 1986), which, again, might or might not be successful in forecasting political risk.

It is important to bear in mind that political risk should be evaluated at the country, industry and firm levels. Also, because of the complexities of modern politics, it is not often easy or possible to forecast political risk. The revolution in Iran in 1979, which led to the overthrow of the pro-American regime of the Shah, was not detected as a probability by many foreign companies which were operating in the country at the time, and which were subsequently confiscated by the new regime. This was in spite of all the signs of people's dissatisfaction with the outgoing regime. Neither was the Iraqi invasion of Kuwait on 2 August 1990 considered likely by, among others, many eminent politicians the world over until it actually took place. In connection with the aforementioned *coup d'état* in Thailand, *Time* (4 March 1991: 50) points out:

> for weeks there had been confident predictions in Bangkok that a military coup was unlikely, despite obviously escalating tensions between the army and the elected government of [the] Prime Minister. The men in uniform, political analysts contended, would be unwilling to do anything that [might] disrupt a three-year economic boom. That seemed a reasonable judgement – until the tanks began to roll.

How can foreign firms reduce political risk?

Companies can employ a local workforce, borrow money from local banks and other sources of capital, and involve local interests in their business as much as possible. In this way, the company's sufferings, so to speak, will result in suffering for the local interests. For instance, if the firm recruits a large number of local people and owes a great deal of money to local banks, its financial losses or bankruptcy will directly affect those people and those banks. Also, if it is forced to fold or give up operations and leave the country, it will lose the assets and capitals which are largely owned by the local people anyway. Policies such as these would at the same time act as a deterrent and would prevent the local government from taking actions which might ultimately hurt its own people and institutions.

The foreign firm can control the internal market, and retain its legal rights over its brand name and trademark. In the event that the company is forced to close down no other firm can fill the gap. And if it is nationalized the new company or any other firm will not be allowed to use its brand name.

Sometimes the foreign firm can enter into negotiations with the government of the host country to sort out their respective requirements before setting up its plants there. Together they can work out arrangements such as the proportion of the profits the company can take out of the country, the extent to which it can use local raw materials and other natural resources, the extent to which local capital and people should participate in the ownership and management of the company, and how the transfer prices can be determined. These arrangements will eliminate future ambiguity as to where the company and the country stand *vis-à-vis* each other and the element of surprise and risk is therefore greatly reduced. It does not, however, mean that if there is a drastic change of government, the new regime will automatically or necessarily honour its predecessor's commitments.

Some firms might simply prefer joint ventures, licensing, franchising, or management contracts as better forms of foreign investment than wholly owned subsidiaries in countries with good market prospects but a high risk probability.

4
Protectionism

In chapter 1 it was argued that, in theory at least, trade between nations is conducted largely on the basis of competitive advantages. You produce and export the goods and services that you can make more efficiently than others, and import those that you cannot. In reality, however, governments often intervene in the free flow of trade. The extent of this intervention varies from a total control of foreign trade (China), to strict import–export and foreign investment regulations (India), to the protection of certain industries or sectors of the economy (France).

Governments step into the processes of international trade mainly to protect their domestic economy against foreign competition. But there are also political reasons for their actions. The following sections discuss some of these, and examine their consequences for the consumers, the ultimate end-users of international trade.

Rationale for governments' intervention in international trade

National defence needs and independence

The economic strength of a nation, as mentioned in chapter 2, goes hand-in-hand with political power and its real autonomy and independence. A strong economic base is in turn underpinned by a competent and strong military and defence system. The state, as the guardian of national sovereignty, will participate in and even control the economic and industrial activities of the country in order to ensure its development and strength. As Sen (1984: 79) points out,

> the necessity of state intervention in the economy because of the perception of national defence needs and the goal of economic autonomy, instead of allowing private enterprise to proceed independently, is highlighted by the timing of state intervention to ensure industrialization. The industrialization of Britain progressed relatively slowly compared to the pace of industrialization elsewhere later. Since Britain was the first country to industrialize it did not

perceive any serious military threat from the existence of other more advanced countries and the state in Britain intervened relatively little, allowing industrialization to proceed at a 'natural' pace.

If the state in France, Germany, Italy, Russia, and Japan had allowed industrialization to proceed at the same pace, intervening on the same limited scale as Britain, industrialization would not have occurred in the relatively short span of time that it did in these countries . . . . The perception of external threat from the prior presence of already industrialized countries prompted considerably enhanced state involvement with industrialization, and explains the rapidity of progress. Thus, while the process of industrialization and economic growth is influenced by endogenous factors specific to the internal dynamics of society, the timing and its character are primarily determined by the impact of international political rivalry and perception of national defence needs.

Barriers to entry raised by foreign firms

This is especially the case for less developed and industrializing nations. The presence of powerful and fully industrialized competitors raises barriers to entry in markets for the late arrivals to the scene. These countries have to import most of the basic investment and infrastructure inputs, mainly because of their less advanced technology, a lack or shortage of local skills, and the benefits of economies of scale already achieved by the advanced countries. This process inevitably makes the goods manufactured in the less advanced nations more expensive and therefore less competitive than those of their more advanced competitors. The governments of developing countries therefore impose import controls in order to protect their domestic firms.

Young and inexperienced local industries

The local industry may not be able to compete with foreign companies because it is not old enough to utilize well-developed managerial and technological know-how; it is not large enough to benefit from economies of scale; its products lack the quality of those of the foreign competitors; and its production process is not efficient enough to make the price of its products competitive.

Why would governments want to protect such 'hopeless' cases? There is a complex web of economic, social and political justifications for such protectionism. If you want to encourage new industries, say, in order to reduce your imports, you need to protect them in their early and most vulnerable stages till they can 'stand on their own feet' – this is known as the 'infant industry' argument.

The idea of infant-industry protection goes back to Adam Smith. It is often argued that new industries need to be sheltered when young. Without such help, enterprises that might be profitable in due course will fail to establish themselves. The infant-industry argument rests on the view that the market fails in some way; otherwise a new business would be willing to incur initial losses in the expectation of making larger profits later.

Short-sighted financial markets might be one such market failure. In many industries, the time needed for the initial investment to pay off is very long, and new businesses might find it difficult, if not impossible, to finance their initial investment. The British capital market, for instance, is one which is characterized by short-term interest, in contrast with that of Japan which is keen to finance long-term investments.

Being first-to-market is often advantageous, but there may be drawbacks as well. Sometimes a new company invests a great deal of money to start up, or to adapt foreign technology for local use, only to see that its efforts benefit others following it into the market. The first company into a new business is not fully rewarded because it cannot keep the benefits all to itself.

Because of market failures such as these new industries need protection and support. The problem, however, is that it is difficult to stop giving support. There is always the danger that protection for infant industries would be captured by vested interests and extended through the life of the product.

Industry protection, of course, is not confined to infants. Well-established industries might also seek protection. For instance, many US electronics companies have been lobbying for more trade protection against (in particular) Japanese electronics firms. This action is in response to new figures which suggest that the United States' share of world production of electronics hardware has fallen from 50 percent to 37 percent over the past 5 years (*The Economist*, 28 April 1990).

Employment policies

If governments want to maintain a high level of employment, they might encourage their domestic producers to engage more employees than they otherwise need and run overmanned organizations. As a consequence, they incur high production costs. The government then assists them in retaining their domestic market by erecting trade barriers and keeping efficient low-cost foreign competitors out.

Restructuring the economy

Some governments, especially those in developing countries, introduce protectionist measures in order to encourage a shift from agriculture to industry. Here, again, young industries need protection in their initial stages. Import controls can be employed in order to encourage foreign investors to help expedite the industrialization process.

The control of foreign trade can also be channelled to encourage diversification of domestic industries, to promote exports, to replace imported goods (import substitution) by those manufactured domestically, to shift the emphasis of the economy from producing primary commodities (with ever decreasing prices) to producing industrial goods (with ever increasing prices), and to achieve or maintain the equilibrium of the balance of payments.

Political objectives

Sometimes there are more overtly political reasons, both domestic and international, for trade controls.

Concerning domestic politics, major industrialized countries, even those which advocate liberal trade in the manufacturing sectors, protect their agricultural sectors against outside competitors. The Japanese market, for instance, is heavily protected in some foods, notably rice and beef, against imports. The European Community (EC) subsidizes prices within Europe and thereby grossly inflates its own output. As a result, huge surpluses of butter (the so-called 'butter mountain'), wheat and other crops are created that are dumped on world markets at give-away prices. Also farmers in other parts of the world are denied access to European markets because they cannot compete with heavily subsidized prices.

The reason for farm support in these countries is not, unlike in the developing countries, the restructuring of the economy. Rather, the support is largely in response to pressures from powerful farm lobbies. In France, Germany, and to a lesser extent Britain, for example, farmers constitute a major voting bloc in general and local elections.

Concerning international politics, governments may restrict exports to hostile countries. For example, Western countries used to ban exports of high-technology industrial and consumer goods to the Soviet bloc before the end of the cold war. The main objective here was to stop the communists from using Western technology to military advantage.

The US embargo on exports of grain to the Soviet Union after its invasion of Afghanistan in 1979 is another manifestation of political objective expressed through the manipulation of trade.

Governments may also restrict or boycott imports from certain countries as a form of punishment, for example the US boycott of imports of coffee from Nicaragua under the Sandanistas, and trade sanctions against South Africa by most nations as a means of bringing about the reform and indeed abolition of the apartheid regime in that country.

Some powerful industrialized countries export to less developed countries at a much lower price than world prices in order to influence them politically and otherwise.

Forms of trade control

For reasons such as those mentioned above, states intervene in and control international trade by creating barriers to the free flow of goods and services. These barriers can take various forms.

Direct control

This is direct control over prices, such as the practice of 'dumping' in order to create a market abroad; and over production and export to maintain market monopoly and power, for example, OPEC's control of the oil production and export quotas of member states.

Tariffs

Tariffs are taxes that governments levy on goods bought and sold internationally. They are not only a means of trade control and protection but also a source of revenue for governments. The level and amount of tariffs are usually a percentage of the value of the goods or their quantity. In either case the aim is to make the traded goods dearer for the end customers and hence discourage their trade. Whether or not tariffs are effective in achieving this aim depends on a few factors.

It depends on whether or not the tariff raised is greater than the price difference between the imported and the domestically produced goods. Suppose the retail price of a television set imported from Japan to Britain is £200, and its British equivalent is sold in High Street shops for £250. For the import tariff to be effective it has to be at least £51, to make the Japanese set dearer than the British one.

Further, the effectiveness of a tariff depends on whether or not the exporters of the foreign goods can absorb it in their profit margin. Suppose each television set in the previous example costs our Japanese manufacturer £120, leaving a net profit of £80. A tariff of £51 levied by the British government can easily be absorbed in the profit margin, leaving a profit of £29. In this case the Japanese manufacturer can sell the television set for £200, still £50 cheaper than its British rival, and make a profit.

In assessing the success of tariffs from the customers' side, the elasticity of demand for the imported goods is an important factor. This elasticity can be next to zero in at least two cases. First, when the imported goods do not have any domestic substitute, such as personal computers, or compact disc players exported to a country which does not have the technology to produce them. Second, when the imported goods meet quality standards that the domestically manufactured ones do not. In either of these cases, the amount of tariff may not affect the customers' demand for the foreign goods in question.

Tariffs would be less than successful if they could not be enforced properly or loopholes could make it easy for some to avoid paying them (see Box 4).

Finally, tariffs, and indeed other forms of barrier, are effective only to the extent that they do not provoke retaliation by exporter countries. We will come back to this point later in the chapter.

Non-tariff barriers

Subsidizing domestic goods to help them sell abroad is an example of a non-tariff barrier. Farm support subsidies, as mentioned earlier, are the most widely used policies, especially by the United States, Canada and the European Community member states.

Manufactured goods are also subsidized in many countries. The French government's support for Renault, the car manufacturer, in the form of a guarantee against the company going bankrupt and writing off its debts, is an example of subsidization in the manufacturing sector.

Refunds policy, used widely by the member states of the European Community, is a direct result of the agricultural produce price subsidy. They compensate exporters of processed foods and textiles for the fact that they have to pay high EC prices rather than low world prices for their ingredients. EC wheat costs more than twice world prices – £128 a tonne,

Box 4   *What's in a name?*

Protectionist ploys can make it just as profitable for importing firms to spend money on accountants, lawyers and lobbyists as on improving their products. Britain's Land Rover, a maker of four-wheel-drive vehicles, has shown consummate skill in steering around obstacles placed in the way of imports to protect domestic producers.

In 1987 Land Rover launched the Range Rover, a plush version of its stripped-down, cross-country model, in the United States market, but immediately ran into a problem. Vehicles like the Range Rover are classed as multi-purpose vehicles (MPVs) in the US. And with sales of such vehicles taking off in a big way, the US decided to tax the imported ones. The American customs service ruled that MPVs were not cars but light trucks, and so subject to the 25 percent tariff on trucks, and not the 1.5 percent which had previously been levied on MPVs when they were imported cars.

Land Rover was not pleased. How could anyone call a $40,000 Range Rover a truck? Complaining loudly paid off. The United States Treasury officials overruled their colleagues in the customs service by declaring that, provided an MPV had four doors (as the Range Rover does), it could be counted as a car but if it had two doors (like most of the smaller Japanese MPVs which were the real targets of the tariff), it was a truck.

In 1991 the United States introduced a tax on luxury cars, 10 percent of the part of a car's price that exceeds $30,000. The main effect of the tax is to increase the price of imported luxury European cars, such as BMWs, Jaguars and Mercedes. 'Conveniently' for American producers, few of their luxury cars sell for more than $30,000.

Again, Land Rover has found a loophole for its Range Rover. The United States Internal Revenue Service, the tax-collecting arm of the Treasury, says 'four-wheel-drive utility vehicles' are trucks. Suddenly Land Rover is happy for its Range Rover to be sold as a truck, though it still ships them to the United States as cars to avoid the 25 percent truck tariff. The reason is that the luxury car tax will not be applied to trucks with a gross vehicle weight of more than 6,000 lb – a measurement that includes the maximum load a truck is allowed to carry.

The company ran into one snag. Before the introduction of the luxury tax, the maximum weight of a Range Rover was 5,997 lb. The company decided to re-check its figures, supposedly after some changes on models sold in the United States. Guess what? This time the maximum weight of its cars – er, trucks – was 6,019 lb.

Source: The Economist, 2 February 1991

against £40 a tonne. Sugar prices at £450 a tonne compare with world prices of £170 a tonne (1990 prices). But EC-based manufacturers are compelled to pay EC agricultural prices. As this would make their non-EC exports completely uncompetitive, the EC 'refunds' them the difference. For instance, a 40 pence packet of crackers includes ingredients which cost around 16 pence. Of that the producers get about 8 pence back when they export them outside the EC, cutting the export price to around 32 pence a packet (*The Independent*, 6 December 1990).

Undervaluing currency makes the domestic goods cheaper, even though the cost of production may be equal or higher than that of the foreign competitors. For instance, suppose the value of the pound sterling in the foreign exchange market is equivalent to $1.75. At this rate, a £6,000 British car will cost customers in the United States $10,500. A devaluation of the pound by 20 percent (£1 = $1.40) will make the British export to the United States $2,100 cheaper overnight. At the same time, American goods will become 20 percent dearer for the British customers. If the price of a US-made personal computer before the devaluation was $1,750, the British customer would have to pay £1,000 for it. After the devaluation, the same $1,750 computer will cost the British importer £1,250.

Voluntary export restraint (VER) is where sometimes a government is worried about the harm that imports are doing to its country's products. It might require, perhaps with a threat of retaliation, another government to restrict its country's exports of the goods in question.

In the late 1970s and the 1980s the use of VERs spread from textiles and clothing to steel, cars, shoes, machinery, consumer electronics and more. The GATT's secretariat counted nearly 300 VERs and similar arrangements. Most protect the United States and European markets; 50 affect exports from Japan and another 35 exports from South Korea (*The Economist*, 22 September 1990).

Governments put **anti-dumping duties** on imports that are being sold in their market at prices that are too low in relation either to the costs of production or to the prices in the exporter's home market. Similarly, **countervailing duties** can be imposed on imports from suppliers that are subsidized by their governments.

Governments may introduce **regulations and procedures** governing the contents of imported goods, ostensibly for reasons such as health and safety, the environment, and technical standards, and this would effectively reduce imports.

The EC, for example, used to block pork and beef imports from the United States because it claimed that the slaughterhouses in the United States were unsanitary. In 1990 the United States blocked the imports of one brand of wine because it had not tested a drug used in its production. Germany's regulations specify the ingredients of lager in such a way as to make it more difficult to import lager produced by any other country. This last case is being changed as a result of the implementation of the Single Market directives (see chapter 8 for details).

Standard procedures can also be used to discourage foreign exporters. For instance French customs officials used to inspect every single box containing imported goods from Japan in detail, thereby lengthening the waiting and queuing time for trucks and lorries carrying these goods to French customs from ports. The usual procedure for the goods imported from other countries was random checking.

Sometimes governments arbitrarily increase the prices of the imported goods at the port of entry in addition to the tariff that they impose on them. The customs officials, for instance, calculate the tariff on the basis of their own (usually) higher evaluation of the goods, rather than the exporters' prices specified in the respective documents.

In some countries rules and regulations require the governments, when purchasing goods and services, to give preference to domestic suppliers over those from abroad, even though the latter might be able to offer better and cheaper deals.

In Japan, there is a 'large-scale retail store' law which gives small local shopkeepers the power to block the expansion plans of large retailers. These large retailers are Japan's biggest distributors of imported goods. The effect of the law on imports is obvious. Under pressure from other industrialized countries this law is expected to be reviewed in the near future.

Import and export **quotas** targeted at various countries for both political and economic reasons are other forms of non-tariff barriers employed by most nations. The EC for instance has currently a fixed quota for the cars imported from Japan, and it is intended to remain in force until nearly the end of the century.

Many multinationals nowadays include a certain amount of locally-made components in the production of goods in their subsidiaries. Some governments take this element of **local content** into consideration when defining the origins of the products. On the basis of this definition, they then decide whether or not to subject the products to tariffs or other import barriers.

The French government's attitude to Japanese manufactured goods, especially cars, is a good example in this connection. The government has currently an import quota imposed on Japanese cars, and extends the coverage of this quota to cars made by the Japanese in other countries. The French government defines such cars as Japanese unless at least 80 percent of their components are made in the host countries.

Consequences of protectionism

Winners and losers

The major costs of protectionism are borne by tax-payers (in the form of subsidies), by consumers (in the form of an increase in the price of goods and services), and by the economy as a whole (in the form of reductions in efficiency by driving resources away from more productive uses). Free trade promotes efficiency, both because it fosters competition and because it provides an opportunity to specialize and gain economies of scale. Competition also enhances the quality of goods and services.

Take, for example, the British and Indian car industries. The British government, especially under the Conservatives, has a virtually hands-off trade policy in the manufacturing sector. The local manufacturers face fierce competition from foreign makers, especially the Japanese, the Germans, and the French. As a consequence of this open-market policy, British consumers have a wide choice of models, different price ranges, high quality and reliable cars, with more and more safety and leisure features, and with an ever increasing life expectancy.

The Indian government has a heavily protectionist trade policy with strict import controls. Tariffs on imported cars are very high, making it virtually impossible for people, barring a small but extremely rich élite, to buy a foreign car. In the domestic market, the customers' choice of car is limited to two or three makes, the design of which goes back about forty years. The prices of the cars are very high for what they are, they lack quality, and are generally unreliable. The protectionist policy provides the Indian government with a rich source of revenue, and Indian car makers with a guaranteed market and a high level of profit. Indian customers are the ones who lose the most. (The current Indian government is, however, adopting a more open-door trade policy and intends to liberalize imports and exports gradually.)

Farm support policies are another example of protectionism which cause many losses though a few gains. A recent research study by the OECD (1990a) illustrates the cost of these policies.

The OECD developed a multi-sector and multi-country model to examine the full cost of farm policies – that is, the extent to which losses in efficiency and consumer welfare exceed the benefit to farmers – in the EC, Japan, the United States, Canada, Australia and New Zealand. To compare the degree of protection in different countries, the model used producer subsidy equivalents (PSEs), which measure the different types of support (subsidies, tariffs and price support) in a single indicator. The average effective level of subsidy in the OECD's model (expressed as a percentage of the value of the domestic production) rose from about 30 percent to 50 percent during the 1980s. Japan had the highest PSE in 1986–8, at 76 percent. Australia had the lowest PSE, at 12 percent.

The model was asked what would happen if agricultural support, based on the 1986–8 average, was to be eliminated. Farmers would obviously lose, but their losses would be more than offset by gains in the rest of the economy.

The world trade and prices in farm produce would rise, with huge gains for the large agricultural exporters. Australia's meat exports would rise by 215 percent. New Zealand's dairy exports would rise by 190 percent. Elsewhere farming would shrink – by 24 percent in Japan, 19 percent in the EC, 17 percent in Canada and 7 percent in the United States. At the same time, as resources were released, industry and services could expand. The model suggested that the elimination of farm support would send real household income higher everywhere by an average of 1 percent, varying from a rise of 0.3 percent in the United States to 2.7 percent in New Zealand.

This means that agricultural protection currently costs these countries an annual $72 billion (in 1988 prices) in lost income, equivalent to twice New Zealand's GDP. If losses in other industrial and developing countries were included, the full cost would be higher still.

Some argue that these costs are a fair price to pay for achieving certain non-economic objectives, such as security of food supplies, alleviation of rural poverty and so on. The OECD report examines this claim. It concludes that farm policies rarely achieve their objectives and that there are more efficient ways to do this, such as income supplement for the rural poor. Indeed, agricultural support policies may sometimes be detrimental to farmers' long-term interests. Where subsidies encourage more intensive farming, they can cause soil exhaustion and nitrate pollution.

Retaliation

One of the risks, and indeed dangers, of protectionist policies, is that they provoke other nations to retaliate. Sections 301 and Super 301 of the United States trade law, for instance, give the president broad authority to retaliate against foreign trade practices that 'unfairly' discourage American exports.

Section 301 deals with disputes about specific goods, and Super 301 is used to accuse countries of a broad range of unfair trade practices. Countries 'named' under Super 301 must reach agreement with the United States Trade Representative (USTR) within 12 to 18 months or face retaliation.

The threat and implementation of retaliation by North American and Western European countries against Japan is another case in point. Japan's is a protectionist trade policy. The officials are very reluctant to allow foreign exports and investors entry to their domestic markets. At the same time, they pursue a very aggressive policy of exports to, and investment in, other countries. Under a heavy pressure, such as the United States' threat of imposing 'Super 301' sanctions on the Japanese market, Japan is now slowly trying to correct this imbalance in trade.

Reduction in import dependence

Sometimes countries are able to respond to the others' protectionist measures by developing alternatives to the protected goods or finding ways of reducing their dependence on them. When in the early 1970s the OPEC countries raised the price of crude oil, the industrialized countries responded by funding and encouraging research into the feasibility of alternative sources of energy, such as wind, wave and solar power. Car manufacturers responded by making smaller cars, with fuel-efficient engines, and aerodynamic body designs, all of which reduced petrol consumption. Some countries like Germany and Holland developed ways to convert household waste into a source of energy. In Britain some innovative building engineers have for a long time been engaged in designing solar-panelled heat-saving houses.

5
Accounting, Taxation and Legal Practices

One of the major problems faced by international companies is the difference between accounting, taxation and legal systems practised in different countries. This chapter discusses some of the issues involved and examines their implications for multi-national companies.

Accounting practices

Accounting can be defined as a process resulting in information about business enterprises that is useful for making decisions about resource allocations (Mueller et al., 1987).

A distinction may be made between financial accounting and cost or management accounting. Financial or equity accounting is concerned primarily with the provision of financial information to those parties external to the business enterprise who provide capital to it (such as shareholders, creditors, bankers, government, economic analysts). Management or operational accounting is defined as dealing with accounting information for managerial and other macroeconomic decision-making purposes. This, in other words, is the application of accounting knowledge in the production and interpretation of accounting and statistical information for assisting management tasks, including planning and budgeting (Enthoven, 1977).

Variations in accounting practices

Accounting practices vary considerably from country to country, depending on their specific political, economic and social climates. Some of the major aspects of accounting practices which distinguish various countries are purpose and end-users, legal requirements, price fluctuations (inflation), and the level of economic advancement (Mueller et al., 1987).

Purpose

In some countries, such as the United States and the United Kingdom, the business climate is characterized by, among other things, a highly developed capital market, widespread ownership, and hence existence of numerous shareholders. In such countries accounting information is an important source of data about how well a company is doing. Financial accounting is thus directed toward the information needs of investors and creditors.

In countries like Switzerland, Germany and Japan there are a few large banks that satisfy most of the capital needs of business, and the ownership of the companies is concentrated in the hands of a few individuals and/or institutions (see chapter 12). Since the business enterprises have to deal only with a few creditors, direct access to the companies, rather than indirect access via reports, is the most efficient and practical way to monitor their financial situation. Therefore, in these countries financial reports tend not to contain as much information as in those mentioned above.

Countries such as France and Sweden offer yet another orientation of financial accounting. Here, the national government plays an active part in the management of the country's resources, and business enterprises are expected to accomplish the government's policies and macroeconomic plans. Governments also ensure that companies have adequate capital and are prepared to lend or even invest in them if necessary (for example, Renault car manufacturers in France). Financial accounting in these countries is oriented towards decision making by government planners. Firms follow uniform accounting procedures and reporting practices, which are aimed at facilitating better government decisions.

Legal requirements

Countries may be grouped into two broad categories, depending on whether or not they have a legalistic approach to accounting. The legalistic approach is found in the so-called 'code' law countries, such as Argentina, France and Germany, where laws stipulate the minimum standard behaviour expected. In most of these countries accounting principles are national laws, and are codified. They tend to be highly prescriptive, detailed and procedural. Also, the primary role of financial accounting in these countries is to determine how much income tax a company owes the government,

The non-legalistic approach is usually found in 'common' law countries, where laws establish the limits beyond which it is illegal to venture. Accounting practices in common law countries are determined by accountants themselves, and not by national legislators, and thus tend to be more adaptive and innovative. The United Kingdom and the United States are among the common law countries.

In some countries which are structured on a two-tier federal–provincial government basis, and which have a dual legal system, the situation is rather more complicated than in those with a single-tier government. In Canada, for instance, there are two legal systems affecting businesses. Both levels of government pass commercial legislation and regulations which concern such areas as incorporation, stock rules, maintenance of accounting records, preparation and publication of accounting reports, and the audit of these records. The federal legislation functions on a national level, and each province legislates only in its own domain (Evans et al., 1985).

Inflation accounting

Accounting in many countries is based in part on the 'historical cost' principle. This principle is itself based on an assumption that the currency unit used to report financial results is reasonably stable over time, that is, there is little or no inflation in the economy concerned. Companies record their sales, purchases, and other business transactions at the prices prevalent at the time these transactions take place, and make no adjustments to these prices later. Inflation, therefore, is not taken into account.

For countries with a zero or low rate of inflation, such as Germany and Japan, keeping records on this principle seems reasonable. But there are others, such as many in Latin America, the war-torn nations of Asia, and the newly democratized countries of Eastern Europe, which have a very high rate of inflation. For these, inflation accounting is obviously a more appropriate system. But there are only a few countries, notably in Latin America, in which companies routinely write up the values of their assets based on the changes in the general levels of price.

Brazil is one such country which has excelled in inflation accounting. A prominent feature of the Brazilian economy is the widespread use of indexation. Indexation was conceived in the mid-1960s as a temporary measure to be used until inflation could be brought under control. But because of a persistently high rate of inflation since then, indexation has come to stay.

Today, indexation permeates Brazilian economic life, from public finance to long-term debts, wages and salaries, savings accounts, and to housing finance. As far as business organizations are concerned they pay taxes on inflation-adjusted profits, and indexation protects them from involuntary decapitalization.

Level of economic advancement
Most multinational companies have their headquarters in the wealthy, industrialized nations (namely, Japan, Germany, the United Kingdom and the United States). These companies can, therefore, use sophisticated accounting systems and employ highly qualified professional accountants. But, as is discussed below, in the vast majority of the less advanced countries the level of education and human skill is generally low, and businesses are small and unsophisticated. Accordingly, accounting in these countries as an appropriate tool to satisfy their own particular needs, is simple and therefore may not be very advanced by Western standards.

Accounting practices in less advanced countries

In many developing countries, the state plays an active role in the management and development of the economy. One of the tools that the governments employ in devising their economic plans is financial reports and statements by companies (Evans et al., 1985). For these statements and reports to be useful to the central government, a certain degree of uniformity, accuracy of information, and timeliness is required. Yet these are the very qualities which are lacking in the vast majority of company reports (Enthoven, 1977).

A common feature of many of the developing countries is that their enterprise accounting is financial accounting. In the majority of these countries the management or cost accounting is either non-existent or practised to a very limited degree. Furthermore, accounting reports are prepared primarily to determine the amount of tax the companies have to pay to the government, and they act as a means of preventing fraud and tax evasion. The reports are not a means, unlike in many advanced countries, by which to inform shareholders and other stakeholders about the financial state of the company.

A major reason for the virtual absence of useful information in the accounting reports from the shareholders' point of view is that there are not very many general public shareholders, certainly not to the extent we see in more advanced countries.

As Enthoven (1977) points out, business ownership in many of the less developed countries is concentrated among a few individuals. No capital market may exist or if it does its field of action may be quite limited. The climate of trust and confidence needed to make a capital market viable is frequently non-existent. With the lack of broadly based investment by numerous minority shareholders, the need for protection afforded by the regulation of enterprises of this kind has not been felt and this situation extends even to accounting aspects.

Moreover, as mentioned earlier, financial statements are geared towards the requirements of commercial and tax laws and the prevention of fraud. As a result, accountants tend to be legal experts, and their expertise in 'real' accounting is, therefore, limited. Consequently, the amount of economically useful information generated by the enterprise accounting system for decision making is often inadequate and unreliable.

Furthermore, financial statements are sometimes delayed as long as several years, and are in any case unable to give a clear picture of the status and performance of companies. Therefore, investors, bankers, national statistical institutes, government or even management tend not to trust these reports. When evaluating the credit-worthiness of the borrowing companies, financial institutions which lend money to business enterprises, instead of relying on the report take other factors into consideration. These include the reputation and personal knowledge of the owners or the borrowers and substantial security pledged in the form of personal property.

A shortage of trained accountants and skilled managers is another feature of most developing countries. As a result, the use of management accounting systems has been hampered, especially in small firms and in less sophisticated industries. This shortage also affects foreign companies which would otherwise have fairly good accounting systems.

Another aspect of accounting practices to note is the absence of inflation accounting. Most high-inflation countries, such as Iran, still follow the historical cost principle, and as a result many of the items in the balance sheets are quite unrealistic and misleading.

Finally, foreign influence has been a major factor in advancing accounting practices in some of the developing countries. Thailand and Taiwan have, for instance, benefited greatly from the expertise of British and American professional accountants. Also, ex-colonies of the United Kingdom (for example, Pakistan, India, Malaysia), France (for example, French-speaking countries in Africa) and the United States (for example, the Philippines) have far more advanced and sophisticated accounting systems than do others. For instance, financial accounting and cost accounting are relatively highly developed in India, and the country has a large number of qualified accountants.

International accounting standards

Various international and regional organizations (such as the International Accounting Standards Committee, the International Federation of Accountants, the Conference of Asian and Pacific Accountants, and the African Accounting Council) have in the past two decades or so been set up to harmonize accounting principles and auditing practices. However, the complete success of these bodies in achieving their objectives remains to be seen.

Taxation

Multinational companies, unlike a domestic firm which is based in one country, come under the jurisdiction of more than one tax authority. Since each country has its own taxation rules and regulations, a multinational firm is subjected to various taxation treatments concurrently.

Moreover, countries differ in their position towards foreign companies. Some would like to encourage incoming foreign direct investment, and use tax incentives to this end while others use high taxes in order to discourage the repatriation of foreign firms' profits.

Countries also differ in the way they tax their own multinational firms operating abroad. Under United States tax law, for instance, the income of a foreign branch of an American parent company is treated differently from the income of foreign subsidiaries. A foreign branch is regarded legally as an integral extension of the parent, and its profits are automatically included in those of the parent company and taxed by the United States government for the period in which they are earned. But a subsidiary is viewed as a separate legal entity, and its profits are not generally taxable by the United States until they are repatriated to the parent company as dividends (Weekly and Aggarwal, 1987).

International firms and variations in tax laws

Location of operations
The differences in taxation laws and rules between various nations have of course significant implications for international firms. For instance, as discussed in chapter 1, companies might find countries with a low rate of tax and favourable incentives more attractive as the site for their production plants than high tax nations.

Form of operations
Tax laws can influence the multinational companies' decisions as to the type of affiliates they want to set up abroad. As Weekly and Aggarwal (1987) point out, given the United States' tax laws referred to above, an American international firm might, for example, decide to set up a branch rather than a subsidiary abroad, and include the operational losses of the early years in the overall profit and loss account of the company as a whole. This would reduce the firm's taxable profits.

Transfer pricing
Transfer pricing is another practice which can be employed to make the most of tax differentiations between countries. Multinational companies sometimes buy from or sell to their own subsidiaries and other affiliates across national boundaries. The price at which these transactions take place, the transfer price, can sometimes be arbitrarily recorded at a high level if the subsidiary concerned is located in a high tax country. In this way the subsidiary shows a much reduced profit or even losses in its books. Transfer pricing may also be used to repatriate a vast amount of money from a high tax country, ostensibly as a price paid for goods and services bought from a subsidiary in another country.

    However, some commentators (for example, H. Schaffner quoted in Wallace, 1982) argue that even where a multinational firm has a clear tax incentive for contemplating artificial pricing, the practical opportunities for manipulation are very limited, since such practices are under intense and continuous scrutiny by a number of different local tax authorities who would be quick to discern any unjustifiable fluctuations or deviations from a proper transfer price. Moreover, identifiable 'arm's length' (open-market) prices exist against which the genuineness of the transfer prices can be measured.

Tax havens

Multinational firms might create non-operating subsidiaries or branches in the so-called 'tax haven' countries in order to reduce or defer tax payments. Tax havens are typically very small nations with limited resources of their own, which deliberately keep their taxes exceptionally low in order to entice multinational firms to set up affiliated offices there. Barbados, the Bahamas, and Liechtenstein are examples of tax havens.

This arrangement appears to be beneficial to both the international firms and the tax haven countries. On the one hand, the firms use various devices to channel income into their tax have-based subsidiaries, where it is insulated from the higher taxes of the firms' home countries or the host countries in which operating affiliates are located. On the other hand, tax haven countries benefit from the employment and tax revenues that are generated by those corporate offices, and by the banking and other financial facilities that accompany them.

Moreover, tax havens offer companies anonymity, which they are able to maintain because they do not have 'double taxation' treaties with major economies (see below for details) and so no exchange of information is possible between authorities in the tax havens and elsewhere.

It has to be noted, however, that the amount of information and knowledge about the precise role and the extent of the arrangements between the tax havens and international firms is very limited (Adams and Whalley, 1977).

Double taxation

A major issue concerning the taxation of multinational firms is international double taxation, whereby a profit is subjected to more than one charge to tax under the system of two or more countries. There can be at least three reasons for double taxation (Adams and Whalley, 1977).

Dual residence is one cause of such taxation. A company resident in two or more countries which levy tax on the basis of residence would be liable to a full charge for corporation tax in each country.

Double taxation also occurs when a company is resident in one country and carries on a trade in another country through a branch or subsidiary located there. This is because systems of taxation generally levy tax if either the tax payer or the source of the income is located in the country concerned.

Double taxation sometimes arises because the countries

involved may have different concepts of what constitutes profit for tax purposes, or even though they may have the same basic rules for computing the profit, they may interpret the facts of a given case differently.

Countries usually agree, through multilateral and bilateral treaties (such as the OECD's Convention for the Avoidance of Double Taxation), to prevent multinational companies from being double taxed.

There are three principal methods of relieving double taxation (known as 'double taxation relief'). The first is the exemption system, where the profit is taxed in only one of the countries concerned and is exempted from tax in others. The second is the credit system, where the tax paid in one country is allowed as a credit against tax liability in the other country. The third is the deduction system, where the foreign tax is allowed as deduction from the profit liable to tax in the country concerned (Adams and Whalley, 1977).

Differences between these systems are further complicated by the different ways in which countries compute double taxation relief. Take the United States and the United Kingdom for example. Both countries have a credit system of double taxation relief; they employ different methods of calculating the maximum credit for foreign tax. The UK system requires each source of foreign income to be dealt with separately, even in cases where there are two or more sources of foreign income situated in the same foreign country. Under the UK arrangements a credit will be allowed for tax levied in the country of origin on income from a source located there, but that credit can only be set against the UK tax chargeable on the income from that source. It will therefore be impossible to set a surplus double taxation credit in respect of income from one foreign source against UK tax liability on another foreign source where the two sources concerned are situated in different foreign countries. Those limitations do not exist under the US system which calculates the maximum credit either on a per country basis or on an overall basis, but, unlike the UK, not upon a per source basis (Adams and Whalley, 1977).

Legal practices

A multinational enterprise falls simultaneously under a host of different legal systems. Even though, regarded as a whole, it extends beyond the controlling capacity of individual national company law systems, once an international firm has established itself in the host country, it automatically becomes subject to all the relevant laws of that state. Even mere branch offices are entirely answerable to the law of the host country. As far as the state's legal capacity to control is concerned, its sovereignty within its own territory is indisputable and supreme. The territorial sovereignty of a government thus carries with it full judicial control over all persons (including companies) located within its territory. No multinational enterprise has the power or authority to overrule governments (Wallace, 1982).

Different governments have different regulations regarding the international firms which operate within their territories. Some regulate closely the day-to-day business operations of the firms; some only control those larger-scale movements and operations of the foreign enterprise which could have a direct effect upon its domestic economy.

The Canadian government, for instance, reserves the right to regulate certain aspects of the operations of international companies, such as when an existing foreign-controlled firm wishes to diversify into new and unrelated industries within Canada. The expansion of already-established firms into 'related' businesses, is, however, left unhindered (Wallace, 1982).

Developing countries, especially those which are suspicious of the activities of the Western multinationals, are liable to monitor every single movement of the firms within their country and subject them to various rules and regulations.

The governments of most industrialized countries generally tend to exert rather less control over the operational activities of multinational companies (for example, their initial capital in-flows, local borrowing, intercorporate debt, transfer pricing, capital transfers among affiliates and profit allocations). The reason may be because not only do these countries 'host' the majority of multinationals but they also are 'home' to a large number of them. Therefore, unreasonable actions and unnecessary interference with the legal business operations of their 'guest' companies might provoke retaliation by fellow industrialized countries which host theirs. As Wallace (1982: 85) points out:

> Not only would such controls pose problems of application, and tend to increase disagreements and tensions between the host and the [multinational firms], but they would most likely engender reprisals affecting the hosts' own [multinational companies] operating abroad, not to mention generating fears on the part of domestic companies that similar controls could well be extended to their own operations.

Box 5   *Figures that make sense, please!*

If Soviet economic reform is ever to work, companies must know whether they are making money and be able to respond to changes in demand. This calls for 'proper' prices, which give firms signals about what customers want. Soviet firms have no such signals, and cannot quickly respond to any they get. They do not reliably know how much their products cost to make, how long they take to manufacture, or if they are profitable. In short their company-accounting is a disaster.

Soviet accounting practices date from the days when all that was needed was enough data to allow central planners to plot their five-year plan. Since the five-year plan system has already been demoted to little more than a hazy guideline, an accounting system based on that is now hopeless for everything else.

The present Soviet accounting system impedes economic reform in three main ways. First, it does not distinguish between recurring costs of production and general administrative expenses. It lumps together the cost of raw materials, wages and overheads (like the cost of head-quarters) into one huge category: cost of production.

In the West, accountants distinguish between the various components of production costs, and thus allow companies to identify and keep track of their individual expenses. Wages and administrative expenses and many other costs are incurred in one year, and cannot be rolled forward to the next. But the value of, say, stocks of products can be rolled forward, because the company can still sell them. In the Soviet Union such a distinction does not exist. This helps inflate the value of inventories; it makes it impossible for companies to know how much raw material they have in stock; and it disguises the true cost of headquarters (which many Western companies are now struggling to control). Worst of all, it makes it impossible for firms to identify the recurring costs or production.

The second flaw in Soviet accountancy is that it does not match revenues with expenses. Expenses are recorded when money is paid out: revenues are not recognized until the cash paid for a firm's products actually arrives. This might seem acceptable until you realize that a product shipped on 31 December is counted as an expense in that year, but if it is paid for the next day, the revenue is counted in the following year. The cumulative muddles caused by years of such mismatches are incalculable. (In the West revenues are recognized at the point of shipment, not of sale.)

Both these difficulties reflect a structural characteristic of Soviet business: time is not considered to be money, or even a problem. Soviet accounting practices presuppose that business is risk-free. No provision is made for future bad debts. Current assets are revalued only when state prices change, not to reflect changes in the economic climate: the last revaluation was in 1972. Intangible assets – like trademarks and patents – cannot be valued at all.

The third Soviet accounting deviation shows up worst when firms buy new assets or write off old ones. In the West, if a company acquires new assets (say, new equipment), one side of its balance sheet shifts (to reflect the cost to the firm of the new assets) while the other moves by the same amount (to record that the firm now owns the new assets). The company's basic capital remains unchanged. Not so in the Soviet Union. Under the central-planning system, Soviet enterprises receive all new assets free of charge from the state – so each one boosts the enterprise's capital. If a company writes off assets as they wear out, the reverse happens: the basic capital of the enterprise is debited. But, because so much Soviet equipment is clapped out, companies distinguish between money for replacing fixed assets (in what is called the 'product development' fund) and money for repairing them (in what is called 'amortization' fund).

This system of accounting separately for repairs is unheard of in the West. It distorts the costs of maintaining assets, and makes all kinds of useless spending look productive. In June 1990 it was scrapped for joint ventures in the Soviet Union, but still exists for domestic firms. Eventually the reformed system for joint ventures will apply to domestic enterprises as well.

Source: The Economist, 27 October 1990

Under international law, multinational firms are subject to 'national treatment'. This means that host countries treat foreign-controlled enterprises under their own laws, regulations and administrative practices in a manner consistent with international law, and no less favourably than they treat domestic enterprises in comparable situations (OECD, 1976). Although a vast majority of nations subscribe to the 'national treatment' principle on paper, in practice they do not fully adhere to it (Vernon, 1970).

In the past two decades or so there have been major attempts by regional and international organizations, such as the OECD and the United Nations' agencies, to harmonize laws and regulations affecting (and controlling) international companies. But so far they have only succeeded in issuing non-legally binding 'codes', 'guidelines' and 'declarations'. They are still a long way from providing, or even seriously proposing, a legal enforcement machinery that would be effective internationally. However, as Wallace (1982) points out, these international efforts are of unquestionable importance for the light they shed upon the subject in general.

Centrally planned countries

The accounting, taxation and legal practices affecting international companies operating in socialist and ex-socialist countries are, like all other aspects of these societies, currently in a state of flux, and undergoing tremendous change, even in those countries which still adhere to a planned economy (see chapter 10 for more details). It would be futile at this stage to speculate as to what forms those systems and practices might take and how they might affect international firms. Box 5 provides a snapshot of the former Soviet Union and the challenges it faced as of June 1990 regarding this matter.

6
The International Debt Crisis

Western banks are currently facing a major crisis because of, among other things, the inability of some developing countries to repay their loans. The present chapter focuses on the extent of this problem and the proposed solutions for it.

International banking

Any discussion about international business today would be incomplete without reference to the rapidly changing circumstances and functioning of global financial dealings centred on New York, London, Tokyo, Singapore, Hong Kong and elsewhere (Hutton, 1988).

As we saw in chapter 2, since the end of the Second World War the economic reconstruction of Europe, the emergence of Japan as a world economic power, and the liberalization of international trade have contributed to the globalization of business on a massive scale.

Alongside the internationalization of manufacturing companies, financial institutions and markets have also intensified their international involvement. Offshore markets, such as Eurodollar and Eurocurrency markets, have come into being, lending unrepatriated dollars to multinational companies.

Companies (and individuals) which receive US dollars in exchange for the services and products they sell, may choose to deposit their earnings in US dollar-denominated bank accounts located outside the United States. These deposits are known as Eurodollars, even though the banks concerned may be situated outside Europe. The origin of the term appears to be the former Soviet Union's dollar earnings which were kept in European banks to be used later for the purchase of goods from the West. The Soviet government kept its dollars in Europe perhaps because it did not trust the United States with which it was in a state of cold war.

The Eurocurrency is a generalization of the Eurodollar and includes also other currencies kept outside the countries which issue them as their national currency units. The Euromark is a mark-denominated bank account held outside Germany; the Eurofranc, a French franc-denominated account held outside France, and so on.

In the 1970s a vast increase in OPEC oil surpluses also provided a new source of dollar-denominated funds (known also as petrodollars) for 'recycling' and redeployment by Western banks on a global basis.

The move of the United States away from a fixed relationship of the dollar with gold and the introduction of at first flexible, and then floating, exchange rates for the world's major trading currencies further transformed the hitherto structured basis for international finance and trade. In order to survive national banks had to seek international markets and look for a future on a global basis (Hutton, 1988).

Similar developments led to greater freedom in other financial markets, such as London, New York, Singapore, Hong Kong and Tokyo. The introduction of electronic means of communication for all types of financial and other transactions accelerated the changes (*The Economist*, 7 April 1990).

The freeing of both national and international markets and the competition which now clearly exists between the world's leading financial centres, linked as they are by electronic trading, indicates the extent to which globalization has gone. As Hutton argues, the global linkage of financial markets means that the ups and downs, the confidence and activities in one part of the world can in a flash be translated to other markets.

As part of the increasing globalization of the financial markets major banks in the United States, Europe and Japan move around the world, and operate in various countries through representative offices, agencies, branches, the acquisition of foreign banks and the establishment of subsidiaries.

The internationalization of the banks' operations helps them to acquire timely and accurate information about money and foreign exchange market development and about the quality of their borrowers. By moving abroad, banks can also avoid reserve requirements, deposit insurance, corporate taxes and the like. For example, many US banks opened London and tax-haven offices to avoid US regulations. Similarly, many Japanese banks have opened New York and London offices to avoid domestic restrictions and to exploit special opportunities (Levi, 1990).

However, while overseas offices may make banks more profitable by avoiding domestic regulations, at the same time they make banks and the banking industry more vulnerable and subject to crisis. As was mentioned earlier, the interdependence of the global operations of banks and other financial institutions and markets means that crises spread rapidly throughout these institutions. One such international crisis is the Third World countries' debt problem.

The debt crisis

The debt crisis first became apparent when in August 1982, on what has been called the 'Mexican weekend', Mexico announced it could not meet scheduled repayments on its almost $100 billion of external debt. Within one year of that announcement, forty-seven other debtor nations had declared their inability to repay their debts.

The economies which have suffered most from the debt crisis are low-income nations, including several in sub-Saharan Africa, which have the least ability to repay their debts, and the middle-income countries, such as Brazil, Argentina, Mexico, Venezuela, Egypt, Indonesia, Nigeria and the Philippines, which have large external debts and debt servicing problems.

The debt crisis concerns also a number of East European and other centrally planned countries, such as Poland, China and India. These could face servicing difficulties if future concessional flows of exports fall.

The background

There are at least two distinct explanations why we experience an international debt crisis. These two views are not incompatible; rather they emphasize different aspects of the crisis.

The **conservative view** considers the debt crisis as a short-term liquidity problem, and attributes its origins to the favourable conditions for international borrowing in the 1970s. These were low interest rates (about 5 percent), the availability of billions of petrodollars in Western banks, and a promising prospect of economic growth and increase in exports in a large number of the Third World countries, to which the loans were subsequently made.

In 1973, the Organization of Petroleum Exporting Countries (OPEC) suddenly cut oil production so that the price of oil rocketed (see chapter 8). The result was a huge inflow of US dollars to the Middle East oil producers. They placed large parts of these revenues as deposits in the United States and European banks. These banks now had enormous funds at their disposal, waiting to be invested. As a consequence, many of these banks actively promoted loans to Third World countries. They went on a 'wild' lending spree, assuming that a country could not go bankrupt and default. For example, for the largest US banks, developing-country loans at the start of 1982 amounted to 7.9 percent of their assets and 150 percent of their capital (Levi, 1990).

What was obviously overlooked by the bankers was that some countries, although they might not become bankrupt, especially in terms of their own currency units, could be in a situation where they would not have enough hard currency to repay their debts. In other words, these countries were bankrupt in terms of dollars and other hard currencies. And the Third World countries' debt was denominated in hard currencies especially US dollars (Levi, 1990).

A number of events, some of which had not been foreseen by either the lenders or the borrowers, occurred in the late 1970s and resulted in the debt crisis by early 1982. In 1979 there was another sharp increase in the oil prices initiated by OPEC. Many non-oil producing Third World countries had to face higher bills for their imported oil.

The oil price rise was exacerbated by a fall in commodity prices. The price of non-oil primary goods which are the main exports of LDCs fell by 31 percent between 1978 and 1982. According to the United Nations Conference on Trade and Development (UNCTAD), the fall in commodity prices from 1981 levels cost the developing countries $38,000 million between 1982 and 1984. They fell sharply again in 1985, leading to further loss of income.

In addition, at this time a recession had swept developing and developed countries alike, so the quantity of commodities sold also declined along with commodity prices. The result was that many of the Third World countries were unable to raise enough hard currency to repay their debts. The loans, as Levi (1990) points out, had been sought and granted because of an expectation of increasing commodity prices and export revenues, and yet the very opposite occurred.

Also, the United States had a balance of payments deficit, and, as an anti-inflationary monetary policy, it increased interest rates in October 1979. The US prime rate was now over 20 percent. This made the payment of interest difficult for many borrowers, and repayment of the loan itself just about impossible (Levi, 1990). Saddled with enormously high oil import and debt service bills certain developing economies began to look shaky. Borrowing was now being 'eaten up' by the payment of these two bills.

After 1981, some members of OPEC, such as Mexico and Nigeria, also began to suffer. This was largely because of a fall in the price of oil (a fall in hard currency earnings), which had in turn been caused by the reduction in demand for oil because of the recession and of the competition from new sources of supply.

All these developments led to increasing shortages of foreign exchange in developing countries. And while these countries tried to increase their exports, the industrialized countries were restricting access to their markets, through protectionist policies.

In August 1982, Mexico, Brazil, Argentina, Venezuela and the Philippines announced they were unable to meet payments due to commercial banks. Many of the economic conditions which affected Mexico so seriously also affected the rest of Latin America. The problem spread throughout the region and African debtor countries followed soon after.

The **radical view** takes the distant as well as more recent history of economic developments in the world into consideration and apportions the blame to the governments of the industrialized countries, multinational enterprises, international banks, the IMF and other similar international institutions, and the Third World nations themselves.

This alternative view is based on the structure of the world economic order. Almost all the Third World countries, with the exception of a few, were the colonies of, or under the political influence of the now defunct European empires and the United States. The colonial division of labour was based on the unequal exchange of manufactured goods from the industrialized countries for the agricultural products, minerals and raw materials from the colonies. The problem has been aggravated by rapid price fluctuations of and a steady decline in the relative prices of primary goods. In 1959, for instance, 24 tons of sugar could buy one tractor, in 1982 this had been increased to 115 tons. Moreover, the industrialized world continues to spend billions of dollars every year on agricultural subsidies, which makes it almost impossible for the Third World nations to compete in agriculture in international markets.

There were other factors which also helped the process along. Many multinational companies established subsidiaries in the developing countries in order to secure the supply of raw materials and so, perhaps inadvertently, prevented the local industry from taking full advantage of these resources. As a result of the deteriorating terms of trade most developing countries remained dependent on a relatively narrow range of exports. They suffered chronic trade and balance of payments deficits, and therefore required external borrowing.

The élite groups in a vast majority of the debtor countries were, and still are, also to blame. A large proportion of the borrowed funds were diverted away from investment in the development programmes for which the loans had been made in the first place, and which would have generated income to help service debts. Instead, much of the funds had been spent on arms, prestige show-case projects, foreign investment (capital flight), or even deposited in private Swiss bank accounts. According to a United States Federal Reserve report, the twenty largest debtor countries spent 20 percent of the increase in the loans between 1976 and 1980 on arms, and 50 percent of the loans in many countries left the country immediately, to foreign banks or investments. Between 1978 and 1982, 30 percent of the increase in aid to Argentina, Brazil, Mexico and Venezuela went into overseas assets or banks.

Some of the funds were also used to subsidize consumption. The politicians found it difficult to remove these subsidies, for fear of social and political unrest. As a result only a small proportion of the financial aid was put to use efficiently.

Proposed solutions

For obvious reasons, such as the hardship suffered by ordinary people in the debtor countries, and the threat of bankruptcy of many of the Western banks with all its consequences, solutions had to be found to the crisis. Since 1982, international institutions such as the IMF and the World Bank as well as relevant governments and private banks have proposed and helped implement various programmes to solve the crisis with varying degrees of success.

The 'Mexican weekend' in 1982 marked the transition of the debt crisis from a commercial crisis to an economic and political crisis. This incident exposed the fact that there was no international mechanism for collecting debts from sovereign debtors.

Initially, a series of two-year tied-over deals by the IMF and the World Bank was put in motion. The two institutions made $12 billion of stand-by credits available to the six largest Latin American debtor nations on condition that they adopt austere economic policies. These policies included the devaluation of the currency and the elimination of government price subsidies, and were designed to bring about the structural changes needed to deal with the problems in the long run. Another short-term measure, prompted by fear of the collapse of highly exposed US banks, was taken by the United States Treasury and Federal Reserve. A $1.7 billion credit was granted to Mexico to help it maintain its schedule payments. Brazil and Argentina also received grants from both the United States and other Western countries.

Later, long-term solutions were proposed by government officials, mainly in conjunction with the IMF and the World Bank, and commercial banks. Some of these are discussed below.

The Baker plan

In 1985, the US Secretary of the Treasury, James Baker, proposed $20 billion of additional private bank lending to the debtor nations, and offered to arrange $9 billion of new loans from the World Bank and the Inter-American Development Bank. The Baker plan aimed to provide additional commercial loans to fifteen heavily indebted countries in conjunction with loans from the World Bank. The plan showed recognition that the economic interdependence among nations required that debtors be able to continue buying crucial imports. However, it failed because the funds provided by the banks and official sources were less than expected, and the debtor countries failed to make full adjustments. Most of the new loans were used to pay accumulated interests.

The Brady plan

In 1989 Nicholas Brady, who was the US Secretary of the Treasury at the time, put forward a new plan which was approved by the IMF and the World Bank. According to this proposal, the resources of the IMF and the World Bank would be made available to support voluntarily agreed debt and debt service reduction deals between the debtors and private banks. This has made the debt reduction a central feature of the new financial packages negotiated between indebted nations and their commercial bank creditors. The plan, agreed to by a committee representing nearly 500 creditor banks, allows each creditor to choose one of three options. They can: forgive 35 percent of the principal of old loans; reduce interest rates to 6.25 percent; or provide new loans. Also, under the plan, the debtor countries must pursue strong and sustained programmes of adjustment, including measures to encourage the return of capital that has left the country.

The Brady plan represents a change of debt strategy, in that instead of encouraging new bank lending in return for 'good behaviour', the plan advocates a negotiated reduction of debt. Also, it places the onus of reduction on commercial banks rather than on the tax payers in creditor countries or on the debtor nations. The Brady plan explicitly acknowledges for the first time that indebted developing countries are unable to repay all their debts, and that a debtor's ability to pay should be a factor in deciding what it should repay. The plan encourages voluntary market-based reduction, but not wholesale forgiveness.

The plan, however, is vague and relies on the generosity of others, but it was always intended that its details would be worked out only through specific creditor–debtor negotiations, particularly in its first test case in Mexico.

The IMF and World Bank programmes

The IMF and the World Bank for their part, provide funds to promote debt reductions. They do this in two different ways. They reimburse the debtor countries for the cost of buying back their debt. Alternatively, when the debt is exchanged for new bonds carrying reduced principal or interest payments, the IMF and the World Bank provide resources to back guarantees that an agreed amount of these reduced payments will be made. Creditor governments are also encouraged to continue rescheduling and maintain export credits for their reform programmes.

The programmes which are initiated by the IMF and the World Bank or are proposed by others in conjunction with these two institutions, carry with them a prerequisite or what is called 'conditionality'. According to the conditionality rule, debtor countries individually accept a major rescheduling of their debt, and where necessary some new money, in return for major structural adjustments in their economies (see also chapter 7). The structural adjustments typically involve the reduction of import barriers and adoption of other open-door economic policies, raising interest rates to market levels, dampening down demand, the devaluation of currency, the withdrawal of subsidies on fuel and staple food, and deep cuts in government spending. For example, in July 1986 Mexico signed a $1.6 billion loan agreement with the IMF that included the following conditions: the budget deficit would fall by 3 percent over the following 18 months, monetary growth should be restricted to reduce capital flight, and national interest rates should exceed the inflation rates (Melvin, 1989).

The IMF has been criticized for imposing such conditions, which restrict economic growth and bring down living standards in the countries that seek loans from the IMF. The view of the IMF, however, is that adjustment programmes are unavoidable in the debtor countries which face repayment difficulties. The adjustments required are aimed at promoting growth in the long run. While there may be short-run costs of adjusting to a smaller role for government and fewer and smaller government subsidies, in the long run the required adjustments should stimulate growth to allow debt repayments (Melvin, 1989).

The track record of the austerity programmes has been mixed. There has been some encouraging progress. Some countries, notably Mexico, have succeeded in building their industry to compete with foreign firms, and so have earned the much needed hard currencies. But there also exists the threat of protectionism in industrialized countries, for example the imposition of tariffs or quotas, to restrict the inflow of imports. Also, the debtor countries which have agreed to implement the programmes could face other problems, such as flight of capital, high unemployment, falling standards of living, inflation, and political and social unrest. Moreover, as a result of the liberalization of trade and opening of their internal markets to foreign investment, it becomes easier for multinational enterprises to gain advantages, compared with the domestic firms.

The Toronto and Trinidad terms

An economic summit in Toronto in June 1988 decided on a package of rescheduling debts and lower interest rates than the market levels. To qualify under this scheme a country would have to be heavily indebted, with a high debt-service ratio, and be implementing appropriate economic reform policies.

The Trinidad terms were the outcome of a meeting of the Commonwealth Finance Ministers which took place in Trinidad in September 1990. Under these proposals, which were put forward by the then British Chancellor of the Exchequer, John Major, only the poorest countries (with an average per capita income of less than $600) which spend 25 percent of their export earnings in debt servicing, and have an IMF adjustment programme, would be eligible. The Trinidad terms would write off up to two-thirds of the $30 billion debt owed by these countries

Box 6   *Mexico's debt crisis*

Mexico is a middle-income developing country, with a per capita GNP of $1,820 in 1988. Manufacturing and commerce have become Mexico's major economic activities, although energy production (oil and natural gas) and agriculture remain important. Mexico's non-oil exports are nearly twice as large as its exports of petroleum products, with manufactured goods alone exceeding petroleum product exports since 1985, and growing more rapidly.

Mexico experienced rapid growth in the three decades through 1970. The growth of real GDP, largely based on expansion of the private sector, averaged over 6 percent, or double the rate of population growth. However, because of a policy of increased government intervention in economic affairs, high fiscal deficits and rigid exchange rate policies, Mexico began to experience severe balance of payments problems in 1976. The authorities subsequently embarked on an adjustment programme supported by the IMF through an extended arrangement.

Aided by rapidly increasing oil production and prices, as well as large foreign financing, economic activity rebounded during 1978–81, with public sector spending providing the main impetus to the expansion of domestic demand. The high growth in government expenditure, an economic slow-down in industrial countries, and higher international interest rates combined to produce a large deterioration in the fiscal and balance of payments accounts by 1981. The fiscal and external deficits that resulted were financed primarily through substantial foreign borrowing from commercial banks, with net external public debt rising by $20 billion, or 60 percent, in 1981 alone.

The situation deteriorated further in 1982. The resulting squeeze on foreign reserve, accentuated by capital flight, forced the Bank of Mexico to withdraw from the foreign exchange market twice during the year, leading to a sharp depreciation of the peso. In August 1982, the authorities announced their inability to service fully the country's external debt. Subsequently, the government imposed strict exchange and trade controls and nationalized the banking system, and Mexico began to develop external payment arrears on private sector debt service.

The combination of a large public sector deficit and the lack of foreign financing led to a rapid acceleration of inflation from an annual rate of under 30 percent in 1981 to almost 100 percent in 1982.

At this point, Mexico was a highly regulated economy with severe macroeconomic imbalances and limited access to external creditors.

In late 1982, a new administration adopted an adjustment programme. This was supported by the IMF with an extended arrangement covering 1983–5, while Mexico obtained additional financial resources and a re-scheduling of its external debt from official and commercial bank sources. The programme called for a major strengthening of financial policy and a liberalization of exchange and trade controls; it provided for a large initial devaluation, followed by frequent adjustments in the exchange rate based on projected inflation. This led to some improvements which did not last long. In mid-1986, the Mexican Government responded to the worsening economic situation by adopting a new economic programme, which the IMF supported with a stand-by arrangement. Financial support was sought from all of the creditors that had financed Mexico's development in the past, with a view to restructuring Mexico's external debt from official and commercial bank sources and offsetting the loss in export earnings. Fiscal and monetary policies were tightened, the exchange rate was depreciated sharply in real terms, and substantial efforts were made to liberalize trade and privatize public sector enterprises. These efforts, aided by a marked increase in oil prices, led to a sizable improvement in the balance of payments, allowing Mexico to enjoy a period of moderate economic growth in 1987.

Mexico has undertaken structural adjustment measures to open its external trade system, rationalize public sector enterprises, make the tax system more efficient, ease restrictions on foreign investment, and deregulate specific economic activities. These reforms are helping to increase economic efficiency and are paving the way for medium-term growth.

Source: IMF, *One World, One Economy*, 1990

to Western creditors. However, the United States rejected these proposals in the London summit meeting of the G7 in July 1991, even though the leaders of the seven richest countries had agreed on the need for extra debt relief for these countries.

For middle income debtors which do not stand to benefit from the Brady plan, because they owe the bulk of their debt to governments, but which are not poor enough to benefit from Toronto and Trinidad terms, the Paris Club agreed to offer longer repayments periods than usual when these countries rescheduled their debts, providing they are following strong adjustment programmes.

The Paris Club

One of the most important arenas for debt rescheduling in recent years has been the Paris Club, which, as Melvin points out contrary to what its name implies, is not an official organization with a continuous life. The term Paris Club refers to irregular meetings of creditor governments, usually the Western developed countries, with debtor nations. Sometimes a debtor country is unable to persuade its creditor countries to extend to it further loans, and it is therefore in danger of defaulting on existing debts. In such cases, the indebted country may contact the French government and request a meeting with the debtor's official creditors. There appears to be no special reason for holding such meetings in Paris, beyond the tradition of meeting there and the French government's willingness to host such activities. The debtor must apply for a stand-by credit arrangement with the IMF before the meeting is held. The Paris Club meetings involve negotiations between the debtor and creditor governments for rescheduling repayment in terms of both timing and costs (Melvin, 1989).

Other debt-servicing schemes

Some schemes, initiated by debtor countries, involve their buying back the debt at a discount, either by making once and for all partial repayment, or by having the bank exchange it for an equity holding in the debtor country or for a bond with a longer maturity. This scheme is generally known as the 'debt for equity swap'. As Melvin points out, the size of the debt equity swap market remains quite small, accounting for 1 or 2 percent of total developing country debt held by commercial banks, as of 1987.

Some Latin American countries have signed debt-for-nature swap agreements. This policy entails creditor banks selling debt, again at a discount, for hard currency given to conservation organizations. These organizations then trade the debt for currency bonds which are used to finance conservation activities in the debtor country. Ecuador, Bolivia and Cost Rica have agreed to exchanges of this kind. Although the proportion of the debt relieved through such schemes is very small, they nevertheless provide resources which would not otherwise be available for conservation projects.

There has also been at least one case where debts have been swapped for political cooperation. In 1991 the so-called Coalition countries wrote off around $6,000 million of Egypt's debt to their governments and national institutions to show their appreciation of Egypt's cooperation in the Persian Gulf war. The country's debt to the banks and private institutions stands (BBC Radio 4 news programmes, 25 May 1991).

Various solutions to the debt crisis, some of which were discussed above, attempt to tackle the problems within the

current international financial structure. The Western governments as well as many international banks regard the debt crisis
as one of liquidity problems rather than insolvency. They
generally tackle the problem on an *ad hoc*, one country at a time,
basis with different actions appropriate for different countries.
They propose to continue loans to these countries, although on
a much lower basis. It will still be possible to ensure growth,
they feel, as it is a question of going for better business policies,
and effectiveness and efficiency in spending the money. The
rate of recovery will depend on the recovery of the world
economy.

An alternative set of solutions, however, would recognize that
there can be no real recovery from the problem of Third World
debt unless these countries' position in the world economy is
improved fundamentally. Various steps, from increasing their
voting powers in international institutions such as the IMF and
the World Bank, to allowing them better terms of trade with the
industrialized world, should be taken to ensure the eradication
of their financial problems over a long period of years (see
chapters 7 and 11 for more details).

PART III

EFFORTS TO ENHANCE FREE INTERNATIONAL TRADE

7

Global Monetary Institutions and Trade Agreements

This chapter focuses on three major global institutions and agreements, namely the International Monetary Fund (IMF), the World Bank, and the General Agreement on Tariffs and Trade (GATT), to highlight the steps taken by nations to improve international trade and to bring down barriers to free trade. The success of these institutions is examined.

The International Monetary Fund

The origins of the IMF can be traced to the Great Depression during the 1930s. The effects of the Depression were devastating. Banks failed by the thousand, the price of agricultural products fell below the cost of production, land values plummeted, factories stood still, and tens of millions of workers lost their jobs.

The Depression spread also to international finance and monetary exchange. The amount of monetary transactions among nations contracted. Some governments severely restricted the exchange of domestic for foreign money and even searched for barter schemes that would eliminate the use of money completely. Other governments, desperate to find foreign buyers for domestic agricultural products, made these products appear cheaper by selling their national money below its real value in an attempt to undercut the trade of other nations selling the same products. This practice merely evoked similar devaluation by trading rivals. The relation between money and the value of goods became confused, as did the relation between the value of one national currency and another.

Between 1929 and 1932, prices of goods fell by 48 percent worldwide, and the value of international trade fell by 63 percent (IMF, 1990).

Several international conferences were called in the early 1930s to address world monetary problems, but they ended in failure. In the early 1940s simultaneous proposals to establish a new international monetary system were put forward by the United States and the United Kingdom. The British plan, the proposal for an International Clearing Union, was drawn up by John Maynard Keynes in collaboration with British Treasury experts. It provided for the founding of an international bank which would be able to grant credits (in the form of book money and not actual capital) to member countries to the extent of 75 percent of their average imports and exports during the period 1936–9.

The plan put forward by the United States government, the preliminary draft outline of a proposal for a United and Associated Nations Stabilization Fund, was prepared by a team headed by H.D. White, an Assistant to the then Secretary of the Treasury. It was based on the establishment of a fund of at least $5,000 million to which member states would transfer a part of their foreign exchange reserves. This fund would serve to grant credit, within certain limits, to the signatories.

After the publication of two further plans, one by the French and one by the Canadians, and consultation with several countries, including the Soviet Union, Britain and the United States arrived at a mutually agreed report, which was published on 21 April 1944. The proposed system would be supervised by a permanent cooperative organization, and would provide for the orderly conversion of one currency into another, the establishment of a clear and unequivocal value of each currency, and elimination of the restrictions and discriminatory practices that had brought investment and trade to a virtual standstill during the 1930s.

The final negotiations for the establishment of the International Monetary Fund took place among the delegates of forty-four nations gathered at Bretton Woods, New Hampshire, in July 1944. The IMF came into being on 27 December 1945 and began operation in Washington DC in May 1946. It then had thirty-nine members.

The IMF's membership now stands at over 150, and includes almost all independent countries. Until 1991 the involvement of the Soviet Union in the IMF was confined to sending delegates to the Bretton Woods Conference held in 1944. In July 1991, a meeting of the seven richest industrialized countries, the so-called G7, agreed to admit the Soviet Union as an associate member of the IMF. Later in the same month the Soviet Union applied for full membership.

The IMF aims to promote international monetary cooperation and to facilitate the expansion of trade. It furthers the achievement of its objectives by providing a permanent forum for consultation between members and also by giving advice through surveillance of economic policies. It makes available financing to members when they face balance of payments difficulties and provides technical assistance to enable them to improve their financial management.

The IMF's resources consist of the subscription that each country pays upon becoming a member, and annually thereafter. These are called 'quotas', and the sum of the quotas constitutes the capital base of the IMF – the primary source of the financing it provides to members. A country's quota is calculated to reflect its economic importance relative to other members. The IMF, through an analysis of each country's economic weight, determines the amount of quota each member will contribute. Quotas are reviewed every five years and can be raised or lowered according to the needs of the IMF and the economic conditions of the members.

A country's quota represents its share in the IMF's capital and determines many aspects of its relationship with the organization. First, the quotas form a pool of money that the IMF can draw upon to lend to members in financial difficulty. Second, they are the basis for determining how much the contributing member can borrow from the IMF or receives from the IMF in periodic allocations of an international money known as special drawings rights (SDRs). Third, and more importantly, the quotas determine the voting power of the members. Those who contribute most to the IMF are given the strongest voice in determining its policies. Thus, as of 1990 the United States has about 180,000 votes, or about one-fifth of the total; the Maldives has 270.

If a member borrows money from the IMF, it pays various charges to cover the IMF's operational expenses and to recompense the member whose currency it is borrowing. An IMF member earns interest on its quota only if other members borrow its currency from the pool.

The IMF is historically closely allied to the World Bank. When the IMF was established it was not seen as a development agency, but as a permanent means of establishing a world multilateral system of payments. It is a form of cooperative deposit bank. Members with balance of payments problems can draw, over a period of 4 years, up to four times their deposit quotas in exchange for their own currencies. Then, if a member wants help over and above its full drawing rights, it is obliged to submit to stringent IMF conditions. These **conditionalities**, as they have become known, go beyond normal banking requirements.

Throughout the debt crisis that began in 1982 (see chapter 6), the IMF has played an important role by providing policy advice and financial assistance. This assistance usually stimulates lending and debt reduction from other sources. The IMF's strategy in this respect has three main elements. These are to ensure that debtor countries pursue growth-oriented policies and reforms; multilateral, official, and private sources provide adequate finance; and all countries collaborate in maintaining a favourable global economic environment. The strategy also places emphasis on measures by debtor countries to promote investment and repatriation of flight capital.

How well is the IMF doing?

Of all the United Nations specialized agencies, the IMF is arguably the most controversial, at least in the eyes of the less developed countries (Arnold, 1989). The voting power is one such controversial case. As was mentioned earlier, votes in the IMF determine policy, and voting power is determined by a country's 'quota'. As Table 7.1 shows, the top ten quota holders have just over 58 percent of the vote and the rest of the membership (140 countries) has only 41.7 percent of the vote. It is interesting to note that there is only one Third World country in this group, Saudi Arabia, and this is a country which does not need loans from the IMF in any case. The five richest industrialized countries account for over 42 percent of the IMF quotas and dominate voting accordingly. This means that the projects and loans which are eventually approved by the IMF will have an inevitable bias towards political and economic preferences of this dominant block.

An examination of the list of ten largest users of the IMF's resources since its establishment is also revealing. African countries are missing from the list, and with the exception of the Philippines (with a total loan of less than one-fifth of that granted to the United Kingdom), Asian countries are also absent (see Table 7.2). Zambia, Pakistan and Sudan are among the

Table 7.1   *IMF top ten member states' quotas*

	Percent of total quotas
United States	19.62
Germany	6.10
Japan	6.10
France	5.48
United Kingdom	5.48
Saudi Arabia	3.79
Italy	3.40
Canada	3.20
Netherlands	2.55
China	2.50

Source: IMF (1990)

Table 7.2   *Ten largest users of the IMF's resources since 1945*

	Total loans from the IMF (US$ million)
United Kingdom	16,423.1
Mexico	9,627.2
India	7,912.0
United States	7,645.2
Argentina	7,519.9
Brazil	7,333.3
Yugoslavia	5,179.4
Italy	4,160.3
Philippines	3,787.9
Turkey	3,508.2

Figures at 31 May 1990.

Source: IMF (1990)

current users of the IMF's credits (as of 31 May 1990). These three countries between them have an outstanding credit of only $2,526 million.

The IMF's 'conditionality' has also become a major bone of political contention between the IMF and many would-be Third World borrowers, and as we saw in chapter 6, it has been criticized for imposing conditions and austerity measures that restrict economic growth and lower living standards in borrowing countries. The typical conditionality involves reducing government spending, raising taxes, and restricting money growth. Such policies, although they are intended for the borrowing government in order to permit the productive private sector to play a larger role in the economy, could also cause a lot of prolonged hardship to the poor majorities in these countries, as witnessed in the shanty-towns of Mexico and Brazil. Moreover, many of these measures are politically as well as economically damaging to the recipients.

The plight of African nations is a case in point (*Time*, 21 May 1990). Some of the poorest African countries, notably Zaïre, Benin, Gabon, Ivory Coast, Tanzania and Zambia, overspent badly in the 1970s, suffered plunging commodity prices in the 1980s, and today find themselves totally bankrupt. Desperate for hard currency, each country has been forced into structural readjustment programmes, which entail strict and painful austerity measures, in order to obtain IMF loans. The IMF also has pressed African regimes to liberalize their politics as well as their economies. However, lip service to reform notwithstanding, it remains unclear just how committed these well-entrenched regimes really are to giving up the total control they have enjoyed.

Also, there are cultural impediments to the adoption of Western-style democracy in these countries. Deep-seated ethnic animosities, for instance, pose a threat to stability as these inexperienced countries move towards competitive democracies. Many African leaders have long maintained that if multiple political parties were permitted, they would inevitably form along tribal lines, inviting bitter and perhaps bloody confrontations. The Ivory Coast is home to at least sixty different ethnic groups; Zaïre has 200. While this argument has often been overblown to justify repression, ethnic and tribal rivalries inevitably complicate the growth of democracy. Furthermore, these countries lack the critical mass of educated voters that is essential for the growth of democracy. Most debilitating of all is their sheer poverty, which makes it extremely difficult for a pluralist political system to thrive. The best assistance that the IMF and other similar institutions can offer, if they really want to see democracy take root, is first to give a helping hand to the continent's economy.

The IMF is not a source of aid but a source of short-term funds to tide countries over immediate problems when their economies are in crisis. But the problem for the Third World nations is that the IMF has come to be seen, with its seal of approval which Western bankers require if they are to lend, as a kind of police force for Western capitalism, prescribing the policies which developing countries should follow, and which are not necessarily what these countries want or need (Arnold, 1989).

The World Bank

The International Bank for Reconstruction and Development (IBRD), generally referred to as the World Bank, began operation in 1946 and, like the IMF, came from the Bretton Woods deliberations. Membership of the World Bank is open to all members of the IMF. In mid-1985 the membership stood at 148.

The original objectives of the World Bank were to assist the post-war reconstruction of West European countries, and to promote the expansion of international trade and the equilibrium of balance of payments. Its initial loans, totalling $497 million, were granted to France, Denmark and Luxembourg in 1947. Later, as the European Recovery Programme was implemented and completed, the Bank's activities and objectives shifted towards the less developed nations. It has now become the largest source of development finance for these countries.

Two affiliated institutions were later established to complement the activities of the IBRD, the main body of the World Bank. These are the International Finance Corporation (IFC), established in 1956 and the International Development Association (IDA), established in 1960.

The loans made by the IBRD are based on economic considerations, and carry variable market-based interest rates which are usually one half of one percent above the average cost of borrowing. The World Bank's loans have to be repaid over 20 years (plus a period of grace), with very little concessional element about them. The loans are either made to governments or have to be guaranteed by governments.

The IDA is the 'soft arm' of the Bank. It provides wholly concessional assistance, and grants soft loans on easy terms to the governments of the poorest countries. In 1981 the criterion for these was a per capita GNP of $371 or less. This was raised to $391 in 1983. The loans are for 50 years and without interest, although there are certain service charges. The IDA is dependent for its funds upon replenishments negotiated every 3 years from its principal donors. Its loans go only to the poorest countries.

The main objective of the IFC is to provide support for the private sector in developing countries. The IFC can make equity investments, and provides loans without government guarantees.

Almost all the World Bank loans are for specific projects. Initially, most of the loans were used on infrastructure programmes, such as roads and railways. The projects varied in size from the large-scale Kariba Dam in Central Africa to small thermal power stations in many countries, but they all consisted primarily of extensive civil works such as dams or harbours, or the supply of manufactured equipment such as electricity generators or locomotives and rolling stock. Since the early 1960s the Bank has widened the scope of its operations. Today, it lends for a variety of projects in agriculture, education, population planning, tourism, telecommunications and water supply, in addition to projects for electric power, transportation and industry.

Apart from granting or guaranteeing loans for development projects in less developed countries, the Bank also provides technical assistance to these countries, which in most cases have little or no expertise in the field of investment projects. To help less developed nations in the preparation of development programmes, the Bank is able to call upon a large number of experts who provide information on the profitability prospects of certain projects, their general repercussions on the economy of the country in question and the most appropriate financing methods. Before a member state makes a formal application for a loan, the project is analysed by the Bank's experts and, if need be, amendments are proposed.

How well is the World Bank doing?

By and large, the technical assistance with which the Bank has been associated has been effective. But whether or not the World Bank and its affiliate institutions are doing enough to help the developing countries is open to question. Like the IMF, the voting power of the member states is a relevant issue here. The World Bank is owned by its members, with each country subscribing to shares according to its GNP. In practice this means that the Western industrialized economies led by the United States, which has 19.91 percent of the voting powers, effectively control the Bank's policies. Table 7.3 shows the voting power of the top richest member countries.

With the addition of Italy and Canada, the Western countries have 50 percent of the votes. The planned quota reallocation, agreed to in 1990, allocates 15.1 percent of the votes to the United States, 8.7 percent to Japan, and 29.7 percent to the twelve member states of the European Community. This will

Table 7.3   *Voting powers in the IBRD and the IDA*

	IBRD (%)	IDA (%)
United States	19.91	19.13
Japan	6.63	8.03
United Kingdom	5.75	6.72
Germany	5.58	7.07
France	5.57	3.75

Source: Arnold (1989)

Table 7.4   *The top five borrowers of the World Bank, 1978–85*

	$ million	%
India	5,382.6	20.7
Brazil	3,391.1	13.0
Mexico	2,122.0	8.2
Romania	1,450.1	5.6
Indonesia	1,429.4	5.5

Source: Arnold (1989)

give 53.7 percent of the total voting power to the fourteen most industrialized countries. By contrast with the above figures, twenty-four African countries have a combined vote of only 2.03 percent, while another group of nineteen Africa countries plus Trinidad and Tobago have a combined vote of 2.67 percent. The fifteen nations in the Middle East between them have 5.36 percent of the voting power or slightly less than Britain.

Because of the overwhelming dominance of the Western countries' voting power the crucial issue for the less developed countries is the kind of developments the World Bank encourages and is willing to finance.

Then there is the question of who gets most out of the Bank. Table 7.4 shows the five leading borrowers of both the IBRD and the IDA over the period 1978–85. Over this same period, total lending of the IBRD and the IDA came to $26,013.9 million. As Arnold argues, it is debatable whether five countries out of a membership of 148 for the IBRD and 133 for the IDA should be allowed to borrow 53 percent of total lending. What criteria, for example, permit two of the most indebted nations in the world – Brazil and Mexico – to borrow on such a scale from the Bank while others find it hard to obtain the loans they require?

Another issue is the attitude of the Bank towards its poorer members. As the largest source of development aid, the World Bank is clearly of the greatest significance to less developed countries. The Bank's review of the state of development in these countries, however, as some commentators argue, is too often delivered as though from on high. Thus, for instance, in relation to Africa, generally regarded as the poorest and least developed region, the Bank is perceived to act as if it is owned by the rich countries of the North and is doing African countries a favour when it provides loans (Arnold, 1989).

One of the World Bank's most acclaimed documents on Africa (World Bank, 1981), according to Arnold, was badly received in Africa. Its analysis of the continent's problems was accepted, but the Bank was perceived to have descended upon the continent like a *deus ex machina*, analysed its ills and then prescribed solutions with far too little reference to what Africans wanted or were trying to achieve. It has been argued that such attitudes, as a rule, are the story of the aid relationship. Furthermore, most of the solutions offered are too much associated with market-force policies favoured by the West (Arnold, 1989).

There is also the question of the Bank's limited financial resources. One of the major holders of the world's surplus funds – the OPEC countries – will understandably not provide the World Bank with the assets which it so urgently needs, unless they are given decision-making power within this institution.

Any additional funds which the governments of the major oil-producing countries are prepared to lend to the World Bank would also increase its ability to raise money on the private capital markets. At present, this is limited by a statutory gearing ratio (that is the ratio of borrowing to capital) of 1:1. Such a gearing ratio is absurdly low (Mananyi, 1983).

Furthermore, there is a need for greater subsidization of lending to the developing countries which can no longer afford to borrow substantially from the commercial banks, but which are not so poor as to be able to take advantage of the concessional loans offered by the IDA. For many of the poorest countries, however, even generously subsidized loans will be beyond their reach. They will therefore need to remain an absolute priority for direct grants in national development policies (Mananyi, 1983).

The General Agreement on Tariffs and Trade

One of the features of, and indeed one might argue a cause of, the Great Depression in the early 1930s was the protectionist trade policies which had plunged nations into a vicious circle of tariffs and retaliations. This problem was high on the agenda of the Bretton Woods Conference in 1944.

The Conference had envisaged a new institution, to be called the International Trade Organization (ITO). It was to have been a full partner of the IMF and the World Bank, with departments covering employment policy, economic development, restrictive business policies and commodity agreements, as well as commercial policy, that is, tariffs and trade. But the charter creating the ITO was never ratified. As a 'stop-gap', the governments settled on a compromise agreement about international trade. The result was the General Agreement on Tariffs and Trade (GATT).

Four decades later, this interim arrangement is still in place. A small secretariat in Switzerland monitors the trade policies of the member countries (twenty-three of them at the beginning, now over a hundred), serves the various committees that they set up, and helps to settle trade disputes.

The immediate short-term objective of GATT was to provide an orderly framework for the conduct of trading relations, and to ensure that these trade relations did not revert to that prevalent in the 1930s. In the long-run, the aims were to provide a system of rules and codes of conduct, a framework for the progressive elimination of trade barriers which would make it more difficult for individual nations to take unilateral action and which would therefore minimize the risks of a repetition of the 1930s.

GATT's principles

There are three guiding principles which are embodied in the articles of GATT. These are non-discrimination, reciprocity and transparency.

Non-discrimination, sometimes also referred to as the principle of national treatment (equal treatment of foreign and domestic companies), is the most important principle of the GATT system. The principle is intended to ensure that any bilateral agreement on reduction of tariffs and quotas should be immediately extended to other member states in a non-discriminatory manner. Similarly, if quantitative restrictions were imposed to safeguard domestic industry the restriction had to apply to all importing countries, rather than any particular group. The principle is also known as the 'most favoured nation' (MFN) rule, which implies that every country is treated as favourably as the most favoured.

Although the MFN principle has been crucial to the process of tariff liberalization in the post-war period, there has been a number of departures from the principle. The Multi-Fibre Arrangement (MFA), which has controlled and regulated trade in textiles since 1961, is the most significant example of this kind. As the system has developed controls have become more restrictive and have been extended to an ever-widening product coverage.

The principle of **reciprocity** lays down that countries which accept tariff concessions should offer comparable concessions in return, and it is designed to encourage genuine multilateral trade liberalization and therefore to increase the global benefits from less restricted trade. This principle is exclusively concerned with agreements based on lower tariffs all round. It does not permit governments to threaten to raise their tariffs, even if such a threat might force other governments to lower theirs, thus levelling the playing field.

Also, embodied in the principle is a recognition that there are 'free rider' problems associated with trade liberalization. Specifically, certain countries may be content to benefit from lower tariffs in their export markets without offering concessions on imports to the home market. As well as ensuring that consumers on the home market do not share in the gains from trade liberalization, this may also frustrate the liberalization process itself. Furthermore, the presence of a reciprocity obligation serves to help defuse domestic political resistance to tariff liberalization (Greenaway, 1983).

Transparency forbids the use of direct controls on trade, such as import control and other non-tariff barriers, except under certain specified circumstances, such as a balance of payments crisis. Member countries are urged to replace non-tariff barriers with tariffs and then 'bind' the tariffs, that is, not to raise them again. For any given amount of protection offered to domestic producers, non-tariff barriers do more economic harm than tariffs. Tariffs, especially when bound, foster a climate of certainty. And because their impact is easier to judge (hence the term 'transparency'), they have the further advantage that they are much more amenable to negotiated reduction.

As *The Economist* (22 September 1990) puts it, reciprocity and non-discrimination, with a little help from transparency, are an exceptionally powerful 'double act'. Suppose a government is willing to lower its tariffs against imports from a certain country in order to gain access, thanks to reciprocity, to that country's market. If a deal can be struck, non-discrimination then requires that government to lower its tariffs on such imports regardless of which GATT member states they come from. This, in turn, sparks another round of tariff-cutting, as the third parties are themselves obliged to reciprocate. In this way, the benefits of agreements arrived at by large economies with clout at the negotiating table are automatically extended to smaller countries, which might otherwise be left out. At the same time, the system makes sure that 'any initial spark of liberal intentions is fanned into a healthy flame'.

There are certain exceptions to each of the above principles, recognizing the fact that there might be political, economic and other constraints that limit the freedom of individual governments to act according to the rules of the Agreement. For instance, under circumstances such as balance of payments difficulties, and the need temporarily to protect domestic industry from market disruption, member countries could employ direct controls. Also, under Article VI, discriminatory action against goods which are dumped by a particular country is permitted via the imposition of countervailing duties (an exception to the MFN rule).

The obligation to reciprocity is waived with respect to the LDCs which are 'contracting parties', as the signatories to GATT are called. The waiver has been questioned in recent years, with many industrial countries complaining that some of the newly industrialized countries have developed their industrial bases to a sufficient degree to honour the principle of reciprocity. In this respect, the United States, which has been more reluctant than most to see the abandonment of the MFN standard, now concentrates its arguments on the idea of 'graduation', whereby developing countries lose elements of their special treatment gradually as their economies advance (McGovern, 1986).

The most important exception to tariff liberalization according to the MFN criterion is contained in Article XXIV, which lays down rules for the establishment of free trade areas and customs unions (see chapter 8), within which preferential treatment may be accorded to co-partners.

Negotiations rounds

At the operational level, GATT fulfils its functions through a process of continuous consultation. There are also periodical **rounds** of negotiation on trade liberalization which are conducted under the auspices of GATT. These negotiations are aimed directly at the progressive elimination of trade barriers. The rounds, numbering eight so far, started in Geneva in 1947. (See Greenaway, 1983, for an excellent assessment of the first seven rounds.)

The latest one, the Uruguay Round, was launched in September 1986 at a ministerial gathering in Punta del Este, Uruguay. The round was to be completed in December 1990, but due to deadlocks on certain areas of negotiation (see below), its completion date was extended to 1992. Box 7 is a snapshot of a typical GATT round of negotiations, held in this case in Geneva in 1990. It illustrates the complexity of the issues, interests, power games and problems involved in the talks.

One of the main tasks of the negotiators in the Uruguay Round was to work out a general agreement on trade in services (GATS). Such an agreement could become as significant as the creation in 1944 of GATT, which covers manufactured goods. Negotiations on intellectual property, direct investment and new rules governing international competition were also included in the round.

Services now account for about one-fifth of world trade, and their importance is growing. But there are no international rules to govern the variety of businesses described as services, ranging from banking to tourism. Any agreement on services would be designed to extend internationally agreed rules to the fast-growing cross-border trade in services, worth more than $600 billion a year. It would also promote moves to dismantle trade barriers and to open markets to foreign competition.

The United States and other rich industrialized countries are the main drive behind a services deal. Their service sectors, such as banking, insurance, transport, telecommunications, tourism, construction, consultancy and public services, account for well over half of their national output and employment. In the United States, the world's biggest exporter of services, nearly 70 percent of GDP comes from services, which employ three-quarters of the country's workers, and represent 18 percent of its total exports. But even in developing countries services often account for nearly half of GDP and considerably more in some of the newly industrialized nations (*The Economist*, 5 May 1990).

Box 7   *GATT's Uruguay Round – old MacDonald in the way*

On 23 July 1990 top trade officials from over 100 countries will meet in Geneva in search of a way to save the three-year-old Uruguay Round of trade liberalization talks. Their biggest problems lie on the farm, the United States and the European Community are still deadlocked over the United States' demands for basic reforms in farm trade.

That leaves negotiators nerve-wrackingly short of time to reach agreement before trade ministers meet in Brussels in December to complete the round. Without a deal to cut down state support for agriculture – which now costs Western tax payers and consumers $245 billion a year – and to open up domestic markets to farm imports, efficient farm exporters like Brazil and Argentina say they will not sign other deals on services, intellectual property, direct investment and new rules governing international competition. The United States regards these as essential to the success of the negotiations.

Behind the scenes in Geneva some progress is being made, but not enough. On 2 July the Dutch chairman of the agricultural negotiating group will make suggestions on all four areas under discussion: domestic supports such as guaranteed farm prices (as in the EC) or top-up income payments to farmers (as in the United States); border measures such as tariffs and quotas that restrict imports; export subsidies; and the use of plant, animal and human health regulations as import barriers.

A concession is emerging on ways to cut farm protectionism at the border and to reduce internal supports. Most countries seem willing to agree a single formula to measure, and so reduce, the myriad kinds of domestic subsidies. State spending not designed to boost production directly, such as infrastructure and advisory services, will probably not be included in any such formula, but most other types of subsidy will.

On border measures the United States has persuaded the EC and most other countries to convert all non-tariff measures to tariffs as a prelude to reduction. Negotiators are trying to sort out the technical problems. Left for later are four awkward issues:

- Japan's desire to keep border restrictions on 'essential foodstuffs' (translation: rice!). The Japanese government seems to be hoping the stand-off between the United States and Europe means that its rice-import ban will escape attack. Equally unacceptable to many is the EC's proposal for a two-tier tariff, part fixed (and subject to negotiated reductions) and part variable to compensate for substantial shifts in prices of currencies. The United States and the 13-strong Cairns Group of agricultural free traders say two-tier tariffs are just a disguised form of the hated variable levy, already used by the EC to keep out imports. But the EC's concerns may be met by a safeguard mechanism against sudden import surges, which the United States has already suggested might prompt a temporary tariff 'snapback'.

- Much more difficult to resolve will be the conflict over the EC's controversial demand for 'rebalancing' – the freedom to raise tariffs on foodstuffs (such as oilseeds) now imported duty-free to compensate for overall tariff cuts. The United States and the Cairns Group say rebalancing is out of question. Europe, insisting it needs such flexibility, refuses to back down.

- On export subsidies there is an impasse. The EC argues that cuts in domestic price-supports will automatically lead to lower export subsidies (one is a mirror image of the other). But it says its dual-pricing system, which fixes domestic prices higher than world prices, is sacrosanct. The United States, among others, wants export subsidies scrapped. The EC says this penalizes its system of farm support, while the US's income top-ups will escape more lightly. The United States' income support is a less trade-distorting way of helping farmers than Europe's price guarantees.

- Clearly the US will not achieve its 'double-zero' goal of eliminating export subsidies within 5 years and most other protection within 10 years. It does not expect to. But the United States and its supporters do want specific cuts in subsidies and a genuine gesture towards reforming the system of farm supports. That will need big concessions from the EC and an overhaul of the European Community's common agricultural policy. This, in turn, will mean painful compromises between the EC's own members.

Source: The Economist, 30 June 1990

Free trade in services will mean adjustment costs as well as benefits. Governments may have to alter some regulations on services, including rules intended to protect consumers from unscrupulous finance companies or unqualified architects. The changes would be needed to conform to yet-to-be-decided international standards, if the existing rules inadvertently distort trade.

For services covered by the agreement, the same principles as those of GATT will apply, namely, non-discrimination, reciprocity and transparency. As in the case of GATT, there will also be 'graduation' (progressive lowering of remaining barriers) and safeguards and exceptions, such as appropriate flexibility for developing countries whose poverty might justify higher, but temporary, barriers. Other rules would cover state aids, regional trading blocks, and mechanisms for bargaining and dispute settlement. If established, the accord would probably have its own small secretariat in Geneva alongside GATT, and it would be open to all GATT members to become signatories.

Provisions for specified exceptions are to be made in the Articles of the Agreement. For instance, the framework deal will apply to all types of services trade, whether supplied across frontiers, at home to foreign customers, or by foreign companies in foreign markets. But countries will be able to put 'reservations' on specific services which they want to keep out of the liberalization arrangements first time round. With respect to the principle of national treatment, the signatories initially will be able to back out of this for named services. Poor countries would still be able legally to bar foreign banks from setting up subsidiaries; the rich ones would be able to forbid foreign accountants or architects from practising unless they qualified locally or had qualifications recognized as equivalent. These barriers would then be lowered by negotiations in subsequent bargaining sessions.

How well is GATT doing?

For most of its life, especially the first thirty years, GATT has worked remarkably well, despite its awkward start. In a series of trade rounds, governments cut the average tariff on manufactured goods from 40 percent in 1947 to less than 10 percent in the mid-1970s. Since then the average tariff has fallen even further, to roughly 5 percent. In addition, by the late 1950s, the governments of advanced industrialized countries had established a modern system of international exchange and payments, with fully convertible currencies. As a result, tariff liberalization spurred remarkably rapid growth in world trade. Between 1950 and 1975 the volume of trade expanded by as much as 500 percent, against an increase in global output of 220 percent (*The Economist*, 22 September 1991).

From the mid-1970s, however, the GATT system began to struggle. Several factors contributed to this.

Proliferation of protectionism

GATT was partly, as Bhagwati (1991) argues, a victim of its own success. As trade expanded, businesses everywhere were exposed to fiercer competition. Trade policies had a correspondingly greater effect on the well-being of firms and their workers. Governments resorted to all kinds of trade protection. As a result, the proliferation of protectionism put the unparalleled world growth enjoyed under the GATT regime during the post-war years in serious danger.

One of these protection devices is 'voluntary export restraint'

(VER). As was discussed in chapter 4, in the late 1970s and the 1980s the use of VERs spread from textiles and clothing to many more industries, such as steel, cars, shoes, machinery, and consumer electronics.

Some of the protectionist measures employed by various governments are in response to the pressures exerted by various interest groups and lobbies. For instance, the United States government, under pressure from the Treasury, and from the shipping and aviation lobbies, insisted on the exclusion of banking, shipping and aviation services from the Uruguay Round's agreement. The US would accept a comprehensive coverage only if, for certain services, countries can back out of the commitment to grant most favoured nation treatment (*The Economist*, 22 September 1990).

Agriculture (the farming lobby) is another area where some countries, especially Japan and those comprising the European Community, have protectionist measures firmly in place, in the forms of farm support and import barriers. The European Community attracted most of the blame for jeopardizing the Uruguay Round of trade talks by refusing to make significant cuts in farm support subsidies. Major agricultural exporting countries, including, the United States, Australia, Canada and several Latin American nations, pushed for 75 percent cuts in domestic farm supports. But the EC stood by its proposal for only a 30 percent reduction in domestic agricultural supports over 10 years starting in 1986. This concession would make the actual value of the reduction 15 percent (*The Economist*, 24 November 1990).

Bilateral trade agreements
Bilateral deals and free trade zones pose a further danger to the success of GATT. The United States, for instance, has already signed a bilateral agreement with Canada and is in the process of completion of a similar deal with Mexico. The United States is set to make such deals with every country in Latin America, and intends to make trade deals with other countries, such as Japan, Taiwan and those in the EC, on a one-to-one basis. In this connection, the President of the United States spoke proudly of 'an American free-trade zone running from the Arctic circle to Cape Horn' (*The Economist*, 8 December 1990).

In addition, the United States intends to open its markets on its own if it cannot do so in concert with other nations. But, at the same time, it has the so-called 'super 301' procedure, that threatens retaliation against any country that will not open its markets to the US companies.

The European Community might also find it profitable in the future to engage in bilateral negotiations with its external trade partners.

Such bilateral agreements break away from the even-handed principle of multilateral trade embodied in the Articles of GATT and could undermine the whole GATT system, and risk a repeat of the 1930s trade war. Moreover, the gradual division of the world into large trade groupings will leave many nations in Africa, the Middle East and Asia – most of the world's poorest – to fend for themselves, because, as we shall see in the next chapter, these countries have not as yet been able to form successful regional trade blocks.

The structure of power in GATT

The existing power structure in GATT is another factor which undermines its ability to fulfil its main objectives, namely fair and free trade.

There is an obvious imbalance of power in the structure of the GATT system. The principal industrial nations conduct all the negotiations, and agree on a package of tariff cuts which benefits them to the greatest extent. The smaller countries more often than not have little choice but to accept the package. The special treatment accorded to the less developed countries, is in itself no more than a *de facto* reflection of this power imbalance (Greenaway, 1983).

Some commentators (for example, McGovern, 1986) further argue that the special treatment of the less developed countries in GATT, and indeed in other international agreements, are merely notional rather than substantive and real. The wrangling among the powerful members of GATT over farm subsidies and the exclusions of certain services from the general rules of the Agreement underline the irony of the developing world's position. The states which have for so long emphasized free trade are determined not to allow the developing world fair access to the market for that trade to take place.

Special rules for developing countries have been unsuccessful in other respects as well, especially in the Uruguay Round. For instance, there have been ritual demands from developing countries such as India for the preferential treatment of their exports of services, while they continued to enjoy protection at home. Other Third World proposals would require foreign entrants to guarantee transfers of technology and to abide by special conditions including the use of local labour and material.

None of these demands is acceptable to industrialized countries (*The Independent*, 6 December 1990).

Another reflection of the negligible role of the Third World countries is the fact that a services agreement could survive without their support. Western negotiators think the draft under discussion could win support of all the OECD's twenty-four countries and the more advanced poor ones. Together these account for the bulk of world services (*The Economist*, 5 May 1990).

Proliferation of multinational companies
Finally, as *Time* (15 April 1991) argues, GATT seems to be losing ground in its central responsibility, namely trade in manufactured goods. Direct investment is changing the face of trade. Large multinational corporations rely increasingly on offshore manufacturers and operating subsidiaries. Sales by US-owned companies abroad, for instance, are already more than double the total of all US exports. British companies derive 39 percent of their profits from sales by overseas subsidiaries versus just 5 percent from exports.

8
Regional Trade Agreements and Pacts

A vast majority of regional agreements take the form of either a free trade area, or a customs union, or a common market. According to Lintner and Mazey (1991: 30–1):

1. A **free trade area** is one of the most basic forms of international economic integration. It consists of an arrangement whereby participating countries agree to practise free trade among themselves by dismantling all tariffs and other barriers to internal trade within the area, and to retain independence over their trade policies in relation with the rest of the world. That is, each country decides what tariff it should charge on imports from countries outside the free trade area, subject of course to other international agreements such as the General Agreement on Tariffs and Trade.

2. A **customs union** involves a greater surrender of economic sovereignty. It is an arrangement whereby countries agree to abolish all internal tariffs and other trade impediments, as in the case of the free trade area; but also agree to practise a common and coordinated trade policy towards the rest of the world. A customs union concerns solely trade in goods and services, and involves changes that represent both an enhancement of free trade and (potentially) a retreat from it. Customs unions infringe the 'most favoured nation' clause of GATT, which forbids discriminatory tariff changes. This clause had in fact to be amended to accommodate the creation of customs unions.

3. A **common market** implies still greater integration. It is a situation whereby members agree to take the customs union a step further by additionally promoting the free movement of labour and capital between the participating countries, that is, the right for people and money to move at will throughout the area concerned. A common market is an area of internal mobility for goods, services and factors of

production. Entry from the rest of the world is restricted: for goods and services by a common external tariff, and for factors of production by any prevailing exchange and immigration controls.

Beyond a common market, economic integration takes the form of monetary and economic union, which is likely to involve a single currency for the area as well as substantial joint determination of macroeconomic and microeconomic policies (Robertson, 1973).

Europe

The Organization for Economic Cooperation and Development

The OECD was created by a treaty signed by eighteen countries in Paris on 14 December 1960. The Organization was the successor to the earlier Organization for European Economic Cooperation (OEEC). The OEEC itself was formed to implement the Marshall Plan for the European Recovery Programme in the post-war years. The emphasis at the time was to encourage the governments concerned to cooperate in developing production, liberalizing trade, facilitating multilateral payment, and reducing tariffs.

After the achievement of its main objective of the administration of the economic recovery programme in Europe, attention was later concentrated on new areas of activities.

In January 1959 a Special Economic Conference was set up in Paris to review the functioning of the OEEC and its relationship with other European economic organizations, especially the then six-country European Economic Community (also known as the Common Market). Further discussions at governmental levels led to the establishment of the OECD which began operation in 1961.

The new organization included as its members also the United States and Canada and it ceased to be a purely European organization, and its new name reflected this. Other industrialized countries such as Japan, Finland, and Australia also joined later. The membership of the OECD currently stands at twenty-four countries.

The current aims of the OECD, as laid down in Article 1 of the Convention, are:

1. To achieve the highest sustainable economic growth and employment and to raise standards of living in member countries, while maintaining financial stability, and thus to contribute to the development of the world economy.
2. To contribute to sound economic expansion in member as well as non-member countries in the process of economic development.
3. To contribute to the expansion of world trade on a multilateral, non-discriminatory basis in accordance with international obligations.

To secure these objectives and to supervise their implementation, the OECD has set up a number of committees and review bodies. For instance, there is an Economic Policy Committee composed of senior officials with major responsibility in the framing of national policies, whose task is to keep under review the economic and financial policies of member countries, in order to adapt them to common objectives. The Development Assistance Committee compares and improves methods for providing capital to underdeveloped countries. There is a Technical Cooperation Committee which is mainly responsible for establishing and supervising technical assistance programmes for countries 'in process of developing'.

The OECD also looks at international trade as one aspect of global policies which affect developing countries. Measures to increase their earnings from exports are a necessary complement to financial and technical assistance. Together member states grant a substantial proportion of the total financial and technical aid to developing countries.

The OECD, like many other international organizations, has also carried out technical studies on environmental matters such as pollution, aircraft noise and traffic congestion for a number of years as part of its scientific research programme. It has also attempted to relate these matters to general policies for economic growth (Robertson, 1973).

The European Community

The first moves towards European integration were made as long ago as 1952 with the establishment of the European Coal and Steel Community. This was followed by the signing of the Treaty of Rome by six countries on 25 March 1957, which led to the establishment of the European Economic Community in 1958. The original members were France, Italy, the Netherlands, Luxembourg, Belgium and Germany. Over the years the United

Kingdom, Denmark, Ireland, Portugal, Greece and Spain have also been admitted to the Community. The idea behind the Treaty was to strengthen the economic power of the member states and to increase their influence in the world.

The main objectives of the European Economic Community (EEC), as set out in Article 3 of the Treaty of Rome, were:

1. The elimination of customs and restrictions on imports and exports between member states.
2. The establishment of a common customs tariff and a common commercial policy towards third countries.
3. The abolition of the obstacles to the free movement of persons, services and capital between member states.
4. The setting up of a common agricultural policy.

Provision was also made for four institutions of the Community – the Assembly (the European Parliament), the Council of Ministers, the Commission and the Court of Justice – to oversee the implementation of the objectives.

The single European market

The Community intended to be much more than a customs union and it was designed to bring about the adoption of common economic and social policies by the participating states. The subtle change of the name from European Economic Community (EEC) to European Community (EC) over time reflects the fact that the Community is about more than just an economic grouping. But it has not yet succeeded thoroughly in being so in practice.

The development of the EC since 1957 has been uneven and erratic. Nationalism, economic recession and enlargement of the Community have all served to delay and divert the process of European integration. Yet significant changes have occurred which have served to consolidate and strengthen the legal basis, institutional framework, and policy competence of the EC. The result has been a complex intermeshing of the Community's and its member states' economic, legal, and political systems (Lintner and Mazey, 1991).

In recent years there has been increasing pressure on the participating governments to take bold action to deal with Europe's economic decline. There has also been a greater realization that the economic problems of all the member states have much in common and would benefit from being tackled on a joint basis. Increasingly businesspeople, economists, national politicians and Members of the European Parliament have begun to realize that Europe's revival is dependent on the creation of a continental market. In fact, many have come to regard this as an essential pre-condition of the Community's future prosperity. Ordinary citizens too have increasingly questioned the value of the Community when so many obstacles to free movement remain (see various EC publications).

At the heart of this renewed impetus is the recognition that, unless it can make full use of the potentially vast single market that the twelve member states constitute, the Community will continue to lose ground and markets to its main competitors, namely the United States and Japan.

In the absence of a single European market, the member states remain largely separate markets, ranging in size from 366,000 people in Luxembourg to around 80 million in Germany. Even the German market, the largest European national market for industrial goods, is less than half the size of the Japanese market or a quarter of that of the United States. On its own each European country simply cannot compete effectively with the large resources of Japan and the United States. Only a single European market of 340 million people, which allows business to flourish on a large scale, both in terms of manufacturing and of research and innovation, can provide the base and the environment to meet the challenge (OOPC, 1988).

Development of new processes and products offers an example of the damaging effect of this fragmentation (OOPC, 1988). Taken as a whole the countries of the Community spend as much on research as Japan. But because this effort is fragmented it means that it cannot be used effectively. By spending on a national basis, a great deal of the research is unnecessarily duplicated and valuable resources are lost as the wheel is constantly re-invented. The splitting up of research budgets also means that many large projects simply cannot be undertaken by any single member state. Then, once a new product is to be launched, it has to be adapted to meet the requirements of a host of different national standards. This adds further to the cost that the consumer has to pay for the final product.

In the end all these obstacles mean that even in those sectors where individual national industries are efficient, the added costs make many of their products uncompetitive on the world market. This indirectly serves the interests of the Japanese manufacturers, who from the base of the large Japanese home market, can do the equivalent research and development work much more economically and produce for all markets in bulk.

The creation of a single European market is intended to make it possible and necessary for European companies to do the same and not produce simply to meet the needs of small separate markets.

Against this background, in 1985 a major step was taken to materialize some of the hitherto unaccomplished objectives of the Community. The Commission was instructed by the member countries to investigate and report on various ways in which this could be done. A White Paper containing legislative proposals was subsequently submitted by the Commission in order to remove barriers within the community. The report resulted in the Single European Market Act.

The main objectives of the Act are:

1. To complete the free market area within the EC.
2. To promote and stimulate economic growth within the EC.
3. To achieve full integration of the different member states' economies.
4. To stimulate restructuring and rationalization of major EC industries to enable the EC to compete effectively in global markets.

The Act called specifically for the removal of physical, technical, financial and legal barriers to trade between the member states, leading to the establishment of a single internal market within which people, goods, services and capital can move freely. This was then gradually translated into a series of about 280 regulatory measures, known as **directives**. These measures were proposed and negotiated and were intended to be adopted by the member states by the 1992 deadline.

Major guiding principles behind these directives are harmonization, mutual recognition and competition. The principle of **harmonization** is intended to diminish the existing differences between member states and to create a common approach to a vast number of policy and regulatory areas. Table 8.1 shows the extent to which the harmonization of standards and policies is proposed to be implemented. In some cases, such as indirect taxation (for example, value added tax, or VAT for short) the policy is that of approximation rather than complete harmonization. This means narrowing the scope of VAT and excise duty rates in Europe.

Sweeping away different national product standards and replacing them with a set of Euro-norms would be a Herculean task: Germany alone has some 20,000 standards, France, 8,000

Table 8.1   *Scope of harmonization within the EC*

Agriculture
Codes of practice and professional qualifications
Competition
Customs documentation and control
Customs levies and indirect taxation
Energy
External relations
Financial institutions and company law
Health, safety and consumer protection laws
Industrial relations and industrial affairs
Information technology and innovation
Regulatory processes and systems
Research and development
Science
Technical standards
Telecommunications
Test and conformance procedures and names
Transport

and Britain 12,000 (*The Economist*, 8 June 1991). This is where the principle of **mutual recognition** comes into the picture. According to this principle, a standard developed in one European country should be accepted in another providing it meets certain basic requirements in health and safety, as laid down in EC legislation. In other words, goods and services which meet the requirements of supervisory authorities in one member state can be freely sold in all member states with no further registration or certificating required.

The principle of **competition** is another aspect of the single market which the EC Commission has been working hard to promote. The establishment of one community market rather than twelve member states' markets requires a Community-wide competition policy within the single marketplace. The Treaty of Rome clearly states its opposition to restrictions on competition which affect trade between member states. However, in practice, especially in such areas as telecommunications, energy, and public procurement, many such restrictions exist. The EC Commission is determined to open up the national markets in these as well as other restricted areas to further competition.

The EC officials originally had hoped that the single market would be in place by 31 December 1992, but due to various technical and political difficulties this target has not been met fully (see below).

Many of the directives, which embody the majority of the original proposals, have been gradually turned into EC and national laws and put in place. But there are certain controversial issues, notably political and monetary union (involving a single currency, one monetary policy, and one central bank), industrial relations (the Social Chapter), frontier controls, and direct and indirect taxation and other fiscal policies which have remained unresolved. These issues have aroused nationalistic feelings among some member states, especially the United Kingdom, which considers them as infringements of its national sovereignty.

Finally, as a report prepared by a consultancy firm, Ernst & Young (1990) points out, while the barriers to exporting and importing will be reduced, the EC will remain an 'Uncommon Market':

- Consumption patterns will continue to vary due to differences in language, culture, climate, history, population structures and topography.
- National preferences will persist. While mutual recognition enables trade, customers may still specify national standards.
- Distribution systems vary between countries and will not be substantially affected. Access to distribution systems will remain a barrier to trade.
- While public purchases will be opened to international competition, differing concepts of value for money and purchasing systems will persist.
- Business practice, legal systems and many national regulations controlling business operations will continue to differ.
- While national currencies are maintained, selling to fellow EC member states' markets will remain exporting.

Implications of the single market for business
The single market provides domestic and foreign business firms with both opportunities and threats. The EC firms operating within the market will no longer be protected by their governments' economic and non-economic interventions, such as technical standards, tariffs, and quotas. Consequently, all but the smallest firms and those with the most specialized niche markets will face an enormous increase in competition, where only the most efficient and powerful can survive.

Also, the home market is no longer demarcated by national borders, it now consists of over 340 million Euro-citizens. This fusion of national markets will offer firms opportunities for economies of scale, thus strengthening their ability to compete with the United States and Japanese firms on equal terms. However, only large companies may be able to reap the benefits of economies of scale. Small firms will have to either find a small specialized niche for themselves or go bankrupt or be acquired by their larger rivals. For the same reason, companies will increasingly be inclined to merge and form larger entities. This is already happening. According to a recent set of statistics published by the European Commission, the number of mergers and acquisitions made by Europe's 1,000 leading firms leapt from 227 in 1986–7 to 492 in 1988–9.

The newly-merged companies will however face a less homogeneous market than do their Japanese and US counterparts within their respective home markets. National preferences and tastes in the EC countries are far more varied than those in Japan and the United States. Take, for example, washing machines. The French want their washing machines to load from the top; the British load theirs from the front. The Germans insist on high-powered machines that can spin most of the dampness out of their washing; the Italians prefer slow spin speeds, and let the southern sun do the drying. Combined with national differences in electrical standards, the complexity of creating so many different machines overwhelms economies of scale (*The Economist*, 22 October 1988).

For firms outside the EC, the single market conjures up the image of a 'Fortress Europe'. The Commission officials and other Community authorities have worked hard to dampen this fear. They have, for example, insisted that the total barriers erected around the Community will not be more than the sum of those already existing in the individual nations put together.

But outsiders are sceptical about this. Their scepticism is justified by the recent introduction of new or extension of certain old protectionist measures under pressure from various lobbies within the member countries. Electronics and car industries are a good case in point. The import quota on Japanese cars for instance is to remain in force until late 1990s. There is also the problem of local content, which has worried especially the US-built Japanese cars (see chapter 4).

Given this situation, the main competitors of the EC companies in Japan and the United States have enhanced their presence inside the Community. Major Japanese car manufacturers have set up new plants and/or increased investment in their existing subsidiaries in the United Kingdom and other member countries, and plan to be 'good Europeans'.

Many foreign companies view the market as yet another opportunity to be exploited. A survey conducted by the Bank of Boston in 1989 showed that 85 percent of the 1,200 US chief executives questioned regarded the single market as an opportunity and 50 percent were actively restructuring to take advantage of it (*Executive Post*, 27 September 1989). (See also Box 8.)

The EC and the less developed countries

The European Community's policy towards development in the LDCs consists of a combination of trade concessions and aid which are granted to certain less developed countries, especially the former colonies of major European nation states. Most of this policy is conducted at the national level and through bilateral agreements.

Like all industrialized countries, the Community operates a generalized system of preferences (GSP) in favour of those less developed countries which are members of the United Nations' Group of 77. The GSP was introduced in 1971 and is variable in its generosity, covering a limited range of industrial and agricultural products, and incorporating tight rules of origin and quotas and exceptions for important goods such as textiles and agricultural products covered by the EC's Common Agricultural Policy. Furthermore, under the GSP it is possible for the Community to withdraw preferential access, which it has done at various times of perceived threat from imports from the newly industrialized countries (Lintner and Mazey, 1991). The main beneficiaries from the Community's GSP have in the past been Yugoslavia, Malaysia, Hong Kong, South Korea, and Brazil, although the overall impact of the system has been rather limited (Hine, 1985).

The most important and systematic part of the Community's Third World policy has, however, been conducted through the Lomé Convention, named after the capital city of Togo in which it was signed. The Convention covers a group of sixty-six African, Caribbean, and Pacific (ACP) countries, which have diverse languages and cultures, political and economic systems, and different sizes of population. Their one common denominator is that they were all once European colonies.

The Lomé Convention operates on several economic levels. It provides aid, which for example in the period between 1985 and 1990 amounted to around $9.4 billion (*Europe*, March 1989). The Convention also provides trade concessions that permit most

Box 8   *Corning Inc. and 1992*

Generally best known for its Pyrex and Vision household products, Corning Incorporated is no newcomer to Europe. The US based world-wide glass and ceramics producer has been involved in glass manufacturing in the UK and France since the early 1920s. Today, these European operations have been joined by a plant in Germany, manufacturing extruded ceramic supports for car catalytic convertors.

The Corporation operates four broad business sections – speciality materials, consumer products, laboratory sciences and telecommunications. In addition it has a significant presence through its equity bases, participation and joint venture companies.

Europe division
As part of a move towards total integration with the Single Market, Corning has recently formed a European Industrial and Speciality Products Division (ISPD) which handles the sales and marketing operations, with world-wide sourcing for a large part of the speciality materials sector.

ISPD is designed to provide the maximum flexibility to handle a variety of products ranging from ceramic metal filters to video components. As such, it serves a broad range of industries and aims to provide an integrated approach throughout the EC while retaining the essential element of local national contact.

Its small multinational team is emphatically European in outlook. Regional and sales managers frequently have a Europe-wide responsibility for particular products for different sectors, as well as local responsibilities.

The General Manager of ISPD Europe is confident of significantly increased business with the formation of ISPD Europe. 'Increased integration of industries such as automative components and electronics means that a national approach only is inappropriate. The new move towards the single market convinces me that, with its wide product base, Corning is right to adopt an integrated approach', he says.

Trade barriers
Another single market move which the General Manager sees as a positive plus for Corning is the easing of customs regulations, which will speed up transit of goods through Europe. 'If goods are moved within a country it takes no longer than a day', he explains. 'However with the substantial paperwork that customs regulations involve, movement of goods takes much longer country to country. As 1992 approaches we should have to deal with far less paperwork.'

ECU based prices
Corning operates a system of 'Landed ECU' based prices on certain products within ISPD. This means that all transport costs are included within the price. In the case of Corning's metal filter business which

serves automative foundries throughout Europe, the ECU system has simplified movement of products and cut delivery time, which in its turn increases efficiency and profit. 'The old concepts of "home and export" no longer have any validity in the Europe of the 1990s', emphasizes the General Manager.

Language barriers
Corning's managers undertake intensive language training before taking up a new post within the Group. Also, each European office employs a Customer Services Assistant who speaks a minimum of three languages – English, French and German.

As far as labelling and literature are concerned, the Corporation has a multilanguage policy. Their literature is translated centrally from the UK. Their labelling originates from each individual country. The latest Corning Pyrex brochure has been written in English, French, German, Spanish and Italian. It originated from the UK and has been translated by each country concerned.

The General Manager says, 'I believe that Corning is now seen as a European and international organization rather than a local national supplier.'

Source: *Single Market News*, 10, Spring 1991

industrial products from ACP countries to enter the EC without tariffs or quotas, and with no reciprocity requirements.

These trade concessions have been, on the face of it at least, quite liberal. Critics of the Lomé trade concessions point out, however, that they have tended to be liberal only where this was compatible with the Community's interests. The regime for industrial products is put into perspective, for example, when one realizes that most ACP countries are in no position to take advantage of these concessions, since they do not have industrial products that can compete with those of the Community (Lintner and Mazey, 1991). When a competitive threat is posed, the Community has tended to negotiate voluntary export restraint (VER) agreements to limit trade (Stevens, 1984).

The concessions for agricultural products have been even less favourable, with restrictions on products that compete with those produced in the EC member countries.

The European Free Trade Association

The creation of EFTA was a direct reaction to the establishment of the European Economic Community, and the failure of the negotiations conducted within the framework of the OEEC to set up a free trade area among all the members of that organization (Robertson, 1973).

These negotiations resulted from the concern felt by those countries which did not intend to participate in the Common Market as regards the effect which the latter would have on their trade. In July 1956, the Council of the Organization for European Economic Cooperation appointed a special Working Party to study this problem and to consider possible methods of association between the European Economic Community and other members of the OEEC. The British government proposed that this association should take the form of a free trade area between all member states. This, as was discussed earlier, would mean that internal tariffs would be abolished between member countries but that each country would remain free to regulate its external tariffs as it wished with the rest of the world.

After a series of negotiations and set-backs, the Convention for the European Free Trade Association was signed in 1959. The signatories were the United Kingdom, Denmark, Norway, Sweden, Austria, Switzerland and Portugal. Later, Liechtenstein (associate member), Finland and Iceland were also admitted to the Association.

The main objective of EFTA was to establish a free market between its members by abolishing tariffs and other obstacles to trade in industrial products. The reduction of tariffs was to be progressive over a period of years. As Robertson (1973) points out, one of the problems which may arise in a free trade area which is not also a common market is that goods from outside the area might enter a low tariff country and then be shipped on to another country with higher tariffs and thus by-pass the incidence of the latter. To counteract this danger, the Convention contains a number of rules of origin. The basic principle is the so-called '50 percent rule', according to which goods are considered as being of EFTA origin if the value of any material imported from outside the area is less than 50 percent of the export price of the goods. This permits a country inside EFTA to ship its manufactured goods duty free to another EFTA country provided that at least 50 percent of the export value is the result of the manufacturing process or other charges (including profit) incurred in its own territory.

EFTA and the European Community
Since its creation, EFTA was considered largely as a temporary measure designed to fortify its members in their negotiating

positions for entry into the Common Market. But after the breakdown of Brussels negotiations for the enlargement of the European Community in January 1963, which meant refusal to entry, EFTA took on a new meaning and started to develop on its own. Collectively, EFTA countries constituted one of the three great trading groups of the world, along with the United States and the European Community. Its foreign trade was indeed greater than that of the United States and almost as great as that of the Common Market (Lange, 1973).

Since 1973, however, the situation has changed again. The United Kingdom, Denmark and Portugal have left EFTA and joined the European Community. Austria has already applied for EC membership, and Norway and Sweden are seriously considering a similar move.

In recent years, there has been renewed pressure for full membership of the European Community in some EFTA countries. To ease this pressure, the president of the EC Commission launched a plan in January 1988 for the creation of a 'European Economic Space' (EES), later renamed European Economic Area (EEA). Starting in January 1993, this would link the EC to the seven nations of EFTA. The Association, according to this plan, would have a say in 'decision shaping', but not decision making, on the laws affecting the EEA. After 18 months of preparatory work the two sides began formal negotiations in 1990.

The EEA accord, which was finally signed in October 1991, will create a market of 380 million consumers stretching from the Arctic to the Mediterranean. The bloc currently accounts for more than 40 percent of world trade (*Financial Times*, 23 October 1991).

The key points of the EC–EFTA treaty are as follows:

- Free movement of products in the EEA from 1993.
- EFTA and the EC must agree on a system for classifying which goods will be regarded as originating from within the EEA.
- Special arrangements will cover food, fish, energy and coal and steel.
- EFTA will assume EC rules on company law, consumer protection, education, the environment, research and development and social policy.
- EFTA will adopt EC competition rules on anti-trust matters, the abuse of a dominant position, public procurement, mergers and state aid.

- An independent joint court will deal with EEA-related disputes and all appeals on competition policy.
- From 1993 individuals should be able to live, work and offer services throughout the bloc. There will be mutual recognition of professional qualifications.
- Capital movements will be freed up but there will be restrictions on investment in some types of EFTA real estate and on some direct investment.
- EFTA can maintain domestic farm policies, rather than join the EC's Common Agricultural Policy.

There will be reviews every two years – the first at the end of 1993.

EFTA states will not be taking on the entire EC single market programme. The issues of harmonization of indirect taxes and of alternative controls on people, animals, plants and goods – all related to the removal of border checks within the EC – will not apply, because EFTA states will maintain controls on frontiers with the Community. Nor does the EEA affect EFTA's relations with the outside world.

The EEA turns the EC–EFTA zone into a highly sophisticated free trade area, but not into a customs union with a common external tariff that would force EFTA into following the EC on trade sanctions and anti-dumping measures against third countries.

An EC–EEA joint committee will be in charge of the formal transformation of EC laws into those of the EEA's. Each side is intended to maintain autonomy over its decisions. This means that, as the *Financial Times* points out, if they cannot reach a consensus on a law for the EEA, the European Community will go ahead with its own law which EFTA need not apply. In their turn, EFTA states can opt collectively, rather than individually, out of, say an aviation regulation; but if they do, the Community has the right to 're-balance' the agreement by, if necessary, subtracting the whole transport sector from the EEA.

At the highest level, there will be a joint bench of EC and EFTA judges who will rule on EEA issues, while leaving to the EC Court of Justice the sole right to interpret EC laws.

As for the deal's economic implications, increasing by only 10 percent the number of people covered by the EC single market will not produce dramatic results overnight. Also, it seems that, according to a study, the EEA's effects are overwhelmingly more important for EFTA than for the EC. The major impact will come in EFTA's small home markets with a relatively low degree of competition. EFTA states can expect to pay less for such services as banking and air transport (*Financial Times*, 23 October 1991).

The impact on the EC is likely to be more localized. Hamburg and Copenhagen will benefit from the EC internal market being extended to Norway and Sweden; likewise southern Germany and northern Italy should benefit from closer links with Austria and Switzerland (*Financial Times*, 23 October 1991).

As was mentioned earlier, the European Economic Area was conceived as a way of easing the pressure in some EFTA countries to apply to join the EC. But the EEA accord has in fact settled the vast majority of economic issues which could have been the stumbling blocks to EFTA states' membership of the Community.

Moreover, as EC–EFTA negotiations got under way, EFTA members began to realize they were taking on economic obligations without political rights. Austria and Sweden decided this was an unsatisfactory half-way house and applied to join the EC. So did Finland. Even in Switzerland the new government said its goal was EC membership (*Financial Times*, 23 October 1991).

The Americas

American free trade areas

In recent years the United States has been engaged in a series of negotiations to establish bilateral free trade areas in the American continent. The first of these came into being in the late 1980s between the United States and Canada. In 1990 preliminary discussions began between Mexico and the United States on establishing a similar free trade area. A year later, the US president announced his plan to create a North American free trade pact among the US, Mexico and Canada. This three-nation pact is intended to create the world's largest tariff-free trade bloc, with 360 million consumers and a combined annual output worth almost $6 billion (*Time*, 25 February 1991). The pact would echo some themes of the US–Canada deal, which phased out tariffs and removed restrictions on foreign investment.

The agreement, although it will benefit the three countries overall, could have some disadvantages, especially for the United States and Canada. With the Mexican minimum wage at $4 a day, versus $4.25 an hour in Canada (as of 1991), the appeal of Mexican labour is causing anxiety among Canadian union leaders, who consider job losses inevitable if the three-way arrangement goes ahead. In the United States, some industries would be hurt by the new trade scheme. The United States fruit growers, textile producers and household-glassware manufacturers could be hurt by lower-cost Mexican competitors (*Time*, 25 February 1991).

Some trade experts are also concerned that the US free trade area plans run the risk of undermining the multilateralism that is at the heart of the world's free trading system. The programmes could have the effect of dividing the world into large trading blocs, even though that is not the intention of the North American trading partners (see chapter 7).

The United States has also signed 'framework agreements' with Chile, Colombia, Bolivia and Ecuador, which establish committees that will 'pursue the goal of open markets and negotiate agreements'. Similar pacts are being considered with Argentina, Brazil, Uruguay and Paraguay, which are now trying to create a common market of their own by 1992 (*The Economist*, 13 October 1990).

These agreements can both help Latin American economic reform and be of great benefit to the United States (*The Economist*, 13 October 1990). Latin American rules on foreign investment could be relaxed, and loose Latin American treatment of intellectual property could be tightened.

Each Latin American country is also seeking something specific in return. Chile, for example, wants a free trade agreement that would lift the seasonal restrictions on import of Chilean apples into the United States market, and put an end to quotas on textiles, cheese and powdered milk. Bolivia hopes for trade concessions on products that it does not yet make – in the hope of attracting desperately needed foreign investors to make them.

Colombia wants the United States' trade concessions in return for its efforts to combat drug trafficking, but is less keen on a free trade area throughout the Western hemisphere because it does not think it can compete. Argentina wants free trade with the United States, but is giving priority to its agreement with Brazil, because it sees Brazil as less of an economic threat to its own industries.

The Central American Common Market

The CACM was established in 1960. It has five members: Costa Rica, El Salvador, Guatemala, Honduras and Nicaragua. The principal aim of the CACM is to liberalize trade between members and to establish a customs union. Ideological differences between members and the general political turmoil of the region have prevented any obvious advance. In 1984 ministers of member countries agreed on a programme to reactivate the CACM which by then had lost most of whatever impetus it had.

The Latin American Integration Association

In 1960 a Latin American Free Trade Association (LAFTA) was established which by 1980 had collapsed. The Latin American Integration Association was formed from the ruins of the LAFTA, in Montevideo in 1980. Its members are Argentina, Bolivia, Brazil, Chile, Colombia, Ecuador, Mexico, Paraguay, Peru, Uruguay and Venezuela.

The LAIA is a deliberately loose and pragmatic association in contrast to its predecessor. It is intended to establish economic preferences and regional tariff preferences, and takes into account the different sizes and stages of development of the member countries.

The Treaty of Montevideo which created the LAIA envisages outward agreements between member states and non-members. Its piecemeal, pragmatic approach is a recognition of the great differences between the members and the impracticability of trying by means of such an association to achieve too much too quickly (Arnold, 1989).

Asia and the Pacific Basin

Unlike other parts of the Third World such as Africa, and to a lesser extent Latin America, which between them have spawned a large number of regional organizations, Asia and the Pacific have relatively few economic and trade groupings and pacts. Large countries such as China and India are more likely to create spheres of influence around their peripheries than feel the need to join regional groups for purposes of economic or political cooperation. Moreover, the size of these countries inhibits smaller neighbours from entering associations with them if they believe that such associations will be dominated by the larger power (Arnold, 1989). One of the relatively few groupings of nations in the region is the Association of South East Asian Nations.

The Association of South East Asian Nations

Formed in Bangkok in 1967, the ASEAN's principal aims are: to achieve regional peace and greater stability in the region and to advance the security of the member states (ASEAN was created at the height of the Vietnam war); and to assist the economic development of its members and to encourage economic cooperation between them.

The original members of the Association were Indonesia, Malaysia, the Philippines, Singapore and Thailand. Brunei joined in 1984 shortly after achieving independence and Papua New Guinea has observer status. Its first summit met in 1976.

The preferential trading arrangements between the ASEAN's members, however, cover only 15,752 items and account for less than 1 percent of the members' trade (*The Economist*, 9 March 1991).

Malaysia has recently proposed a new grouping, the East Asian Economic Group, which would include Japan, South Korea, Hong Kong and Taiwan as well as the ASEAN countries. The model for this group would not be the EC or American free trade areas, because there would be too much disparity in its members' wealth for it to be a completely free trade area. The proposed group instead would function as a forum where members can consult each other and arrive at a consensus before negotiating with Europe or the United States in, for example, GATT. It remains to be seen whether the proposal will get off the ground.

The South Pacific Bureau for Economic Cooperation

SPEC was established in 1973 to assist cooperation and consultation between members of the South Pacific Forum (see below), in matters of trade and economic development, transport, tourism, and so on. It first met in 1971.

The South Pacific Forum (SPF) is essentially a political grouping, consisting of Australia, New Zealand and eleven other independent and self-governing territories in the South Pacific. Its terms of reference covers political problems and issues of the region. In 1983, for instance, it called upon France to give greater autonomy to New Caledonia and to speed up the advance towards independence. The Forum has also repeatedly opposed the French nuclear tests in the Pacific. SPEC can be considered as the economic sister organization of the SPF.

The Organization of Petroleum Exporting Countries

The creation of OPEC was in response to a series of falls in the price of oil in the late 1950s. The fall in the price of the Persian Gulf crudes in 1959 especially affected adversely those Middle Eastern countries whose budgets depended upon oil revenues. As a result, in September 1960, following another oil price reduction, ministers from five major oil producing countries – Iran, Iraq, Kuwait, Saudi Arabia and Venezuela – met in Baghdad where they decided to establish a permanent body to act in the interests of oil producers. The emergent cartel, the Organization of Petroleum Exporting Countries, is intended to promote stability in international oil prices through control of the production and price structure. In the following thirteen years, the original five were joined by eight other countries – Algeria, Ecuador, Gabon, Indonesia, Libya, Nigeria, Qatar, and the United Arab Emirates (UAE).

The Organization attracted little public attention and was virtually ignored by international oil companies for the first decade of its existence. But a series of OPEC-induced price rises, oil production cut backs, boycotts and increases in taxes levied on oil companies in the 1970s brought it into prominence and gave the members an unprecedented power.

In the 1970s the oil producers were able to build up huge cash surpluses in a very short time which gave them a powerful bargaining weapon *vis-à-vis* the West. The OECD's estimates for 1973 to 1977 suggest that OPEC 'recycling' (spending the surpluses to purchase Western goods and industrial expertise) was equivalent to creating about 900,000 jobs in the industrialized countries over this period. This, was the basis of OPEC's power (Arnold, 1989).

The oil power thus allowed a small group of developing countries to dominate much of the international politics in the mid-1970s. It also gave great hope to the entire Third World for a short time that a more balanced new world order could be established. It created a fear in the West that the OPEC countries might decide to reduce the oil output to just enough needed to finance their own development projects. However, as Arnold (1989) notes, the West's fears and the Third World's hopes did not materialize. The OPEC members used their surpluses to purchase Western goods and placed much of the balance in Western banks or invested it in Western businesses.

The 1980s saw a rapid demise of OPEC as an effective cartel. Its ambition to control production and prices was shattered by enmity and mistrust, and two of its best endowed members, Iran and Iraq, engaged in an eight-year brutal war.

OPEC has been unravelling throughout the early 1990s too, its discipline undermined by evaded quotas, declining output and internal strife. Iraq's invasion of Kuwait, a fellow-member, which followed disputes over production and price policies as well as Iraq's historical territorial claims, almost put an end to the Organization's useful life.

There are also other factors which contributed to the weakening of OPEC's power in the international scene. These factors include a decrease in energy demand, conservation, worries about global warming and environmental damage, and alternative sources of energy, especially natural gas, wind and solar power. As a result, OPEC's share of the world oil production fell from 49 percent in 1979 to 37 percent in 1989 (*The Economist*, 18 August 1990). A boost to non-OPEC exploration because of the Iraqi action also may result in an overall reduction in demand for OPEC members' oil.

Africa

There are many technical or economic regional organizations in Africa (for example, the East Africa Community, the Economic Community of West African States, the Southern African Development Coordination). Between them they govern and regulate cooperation in agriculture, aid, the arts, economics, finance, education, government, politics, law, the media, religion, science, social services, trade, industry and transport. The most significant of these pan-African institutions is the Organization of African Unity.

The Organization of African Unity

In May 1963 the foreign ministers of thirty African countries met in Addis Ababa to prepare an agenda for a meeting of their heads of state. They discussed the creation of an Organization of African States which would be primarily involved in matters of collective defence, decolonization, and cooperation in economic, social, education and scientific matters. The meeting also dealt with apartheid in South Africa and racial discrimination.

Later that month the heads of state or government of the thirty countries met in Addis Ababa under the chairmanship of the Emperor Haile Selassie. They approved a Charter to create an Organization of African Unity. This Charter was signed by the participating countries on 26 May 1963.

The main objectives of the Organization as laid down by the Charter are to promote continental unity; to coordinate efforts to improve the life of the African peoples; to defend African sovereignty; to eradicate colonialism; and to promote international cooperation. The first Heads of State and Government Summit was held in Cairo in 1964.

As Arnold (1989) points out, it is not easy to assess the achievements of the OAU. It has, without doubt, helped shape the direction of the post-colonial African politics. 'Talking out' a crisis between its members is possibly its most important function. The OAU's insistence that its members accept the inherited colonial boundaries almost certainly lessened the possibilities of strife between member nations. Sometimes the OAU has achieved an impressive show of unity – over economic objectives or questions of race, for instance. Its role as a forum which enables every member country to put on record its views on continental problems is also important. But it suffers from certain defects. For instance, when such a major member as Morocco found itself at odds with the Organization over the question of its claims to Western Sahara, it simply withdrew from the OAU in 1984. Also, problems such as the civil wars which have wrecked Ethiopia and a few other member countries for years, and Africa's billions of dollars of debts still persist.

An important point to note in connection with unions and other regional cooperation groupings among African nations, and indeed many other less developed countries, is that these groupings often have purposes other than those officially stated. In many cases they represent the expression of a need – the determination to work together, to repudiate manipulation and interference from outside. This need exists mainly because many of these countries are economically, politically and militarily very weak.

Moreover, as Arnold argues, it is one thing to state an aim, such as greater unity or cooperation; but it is something quite different to achieve the objective. The slow progress and seemingly futile arguments about trivia which have characterized the history of the EC serve to remind us just how difficult almost any form of international cooperation is, especially where the main aim is to achieve closer integration of sovereign nations. Africa (and the less developed countries in general) is not different from the European Community or other groups that have been formed in the rich, economically advanced parts of the world. Unions are often not expected to work in the precise sense of two or more countries merging their sovereignty. They are rather expressions of the desire to work together.

PART IV

DOING BUSINESS WITH OTHERS

9

Socio-cultural Context of International Business

How would you feel if you became ill and were admitted to a hospital, and your manager came to visit you with a bouquet of flowers as soon as he or she could? Angry? Delighted? Or do you think your manager would never do such a thing? Yet this is precisely what some managers in Japan do and their subordinates approve of it too. Many people in some parts of the world might find this disturbing, to say the least, and assume that their manager is spying on them and wants to make sure that they are actually ill. These two different interpretations of the same action reflect different value systems, assumptions and meanings; in other words, different cultures (Tayeb, 1991a).

The present chapter explores the possibilities of cultural influences on organizations and on their members' relationships with each other and with the outside world.

Culture and its scope

Culture is a 'woolly' concept which has aroused controversy and confusion among scholars as to its precise meaning. For instance, Kroeber and Kluckhohn (1952) cited 164 different definitions of culture.

For the purpose of the present chapter, we can make a distinction between two broad interpretations of the concept of culture, depending on the context in which it is discussed. In an anthropological and sociological context, culture refers to values and attitudes which are collectively held by the people who belong to a given society. Outside the academic world and in day-to-day life, culture is usually identified with the arts and artistic activities, such as literature, theatre, opera, painting, and music. This chapter deals with the first interpretation of the term culture, and examines its implications for business organizations.

Culture is defined as historically evolved values attitudes and meanings which are learnt and shared by the members of a given community, and which influence their material and non-material way of life. Members of the community learn these shared characteristics through different stages of the socialization processes of their lives in institutions such as family, religion, formal education and the society as a whole.

This is not to say that all members of a community think and behave in the same way or hold the same values and attitudes. There are, of course, variations even among people from the same culture. In other words, one can make a distinction between individual variations and the dominant general pattern in any society. But there is also a recognizable whole, a discernible collection of values, attitudes and behaviours, which may differ from another recognizable whole in another place or time in significant ways (Tayeb, 1988). For instance, although not all Egyptians think or behave alike, we all agree that the Egyptians are very different from the Norwegians. The two peoples are different not only in their physical appearances, but also in their values, world views, and other invisible attributes.

There are a few important points about culture and its scope which should be borne in mind. First, the differences between cultures are of degree, not of kind. For instance, sexual discrimination against women is a socio-cultural dimension common to almost all societies. However, the extent of this discrimination varies from one society to another. In other words, cultural characteristics of a people should be considered in relative terms, in comparison with others.

As was mentioned earlier, cultural traits have their roots in history, and are often centuries old and change very slowly. The high degree of individualism attributed to present-day English people is an example of cultural traits. The origins of the English individualism can be traced at least as far back as the thirteenth century (McFarlane, 1978). Social taboos, such as the stigma attached to joblessness, attitudes to homosexuals, and cohabitation of unmarried couples, which change relatively faster over time and are replaced with other taboos, are also considered as cultural characteristics. There are differences in taboos between societies which reflect their cultural differences. In contrast, other social characteristics (such as opinions) are less-deeply rooted and are short lived.

Cultures are different one from another, but they are not

better or worse than each other. For example, the English in general may be more reserved, the Americans more open, the Indians more emotional, the Japanese more hard working and the French may have a finer taste for clothes and food than many other peoples. None of these peoples is either superior or inferior to the others because of these attributes.

In a world where interactions among people from diverse cultural origins are increasing all the time, the recognition of cultural differences between different peoples is essential. This recognition helps us understand the motives and behaviours of those with whom we interact, and avoid unpleasant and even harmful consequences, both socially and professionally.

Take, for example, the Americans and the Japanese. Behaviour which most Americans consider trustworthy is often precisely that which most Japanese associate with devious characters – and vice versa (*The Economist*, 24 November 1990). To most Americans, people who pause before replying to a question are probably dissembling. They expect a trustworthy person to respond directly. Most Japanese distrust such fluency. They are impressed by somebody who gives careful thought to a question before making a reply. Most Japanese are comfortable with periods of silence. Many Americans find silence awkward and like to close any conversation gaps.

The cherished American characteristics of frankness and openness are also misunderstood. Most Japanese think it is sensible, as well as polite, for a person to be discreet until he or she is sure that a business acquaintance will keep sensitive information confidential. An American who boasts 'I'm my own person' can expect to find his or her Japanese hosts anxiously counting the chopsticks after a business lunch. As the Japanese see it, individualists are anti-social. Team players are sound.

The origins of culture

It is difficult to pin-point the origins of culture accurately, even more so because of the interconnectedness between various institutions and factors, which are said to be responsible for the creation of a culture, and the two-way reinforcement processes between these institutions and culture itself. Of these institutions and factors the following play the most significant role in these processes.

Ecology, physical environment

The climatic and other physical conditions of the environment within which a community lives may have some bearing on the way they evolve as a culturally coherent group. For instance, suppose the climate of a country is harsh and hostile, with severe cold or hot seasons, land is difficult to cultivate, and other natural resources are not easily accessible. You might expect people who live under these conditions to be aggressive, tenacious, resourceful and hard working. In contrast, people living in fertile lands, with mild climates and abundant natural resources, might be passive, easy-going and non-violent.

India and Iran can be cited as an example to illustrate the influence of ecological conditions on culture. Throw your mind back a few thousand years, where politics, especially modern international politics, did not play much of a role in people's lives. Aryan tribes migrated from Central Asia to, among other places, India and Iran. In India, they found a fertile land with plenty of water and rivers and a relatively mild climate. In Iran, they faced harsh variable seasons, salt deserts and very few rivers. It was not perhaps an accident of history that Hinduism, a religion noted for its non-violence and passivity, found roots in India and that the country was so frequently invaded and ruled by others. The same race, when they settled in Iran, became an aggressive nation, fought other nations, conquered their lands and built up the Persian Empire which ruled over a vast area for centuries.

Family

What one learns at one's parents' knees might have a lasting effect on one's life, in terms of basic values and attitudes. It is here where most people start learning how to relate to others: attitudes towards powerful and experienced seniors, hier-archical relationships, the opposite sex, moral standards, expected behaviours in various situations, and so forth.

The present author conducted a comparative study of English and Indian cultures and organizations a few years ago. At the same time as I was collecting my data, a colleague of mine completed her study of English, Asian and West Indian children's play behaviours. Her sample consisted of a group of pre-school children who lived in Birmingham. Mine consisted of English and Indian adults who lived and worked in their respective countries. It was very interesting to note how similar the attitudes and values that the adult sample expressed in my survey were to those observed by my colleague among Indian and English children. In both studies, the English placed a higher value on independence, individual territory, and privacy; they were more aggressive, and showed less respect for and fear of people in senior positions than did their Indian counterparts (for details see Child, 1982; Tayeb, 1988). These similarities demonstrate how early in life basic cultural characteristics are formed and how they persist across generations and even across physical boundaries.

Religion

Religion, whether or not one is a believer, plays an important part in shaping one's basic value system. A code of conduct – what is right and what is wrong – is set out clearly in every religion. There is, for instance, nothing inherently or naturally wrong in stealing your next door neighbour's belongings; all other animals are doing it all the time. But most people do not go about killing, or stealing, or cheating, or whatever. This is because their upbringing and their society's values, which are in turn heavily influenced by the precepts and dictates of their religion, regard these actions as wrong and immoral.

The power relationships that one develops with others in the society, might also have their roots in religion. For example, your God, if you are a Muslim, is the Almighty who commands from on high, whom you should obey and fear, and who, although He loves you, would demand loyal submission to His will. A God–human relationship such as this is characterized by inequality of power between the two sides concerned, an inequality which is justified and legitimized on the basis of the unquestionable power of God over human beings.

In contrast, the Christian God is a symbol of love and humility. Christians believe that God came down to earth and lived alongside ordinary men and women. Here the emphasis is on the likeness and more or less equal nature of the relationship between God and human beings.

The powerful–powerless relationship and the role pattern which is thus originated in religious teachings may be mirrored in other aspects of social relationship and permeate in the society as a whole. In Muslim societies (for example, Saudi Arabia) one expects to observe more respect and even fear of authority than one does in Christian societies (for example, the United States).

Education

Formal education, especially in those societies where there is a well-developed educational system, contributes to the formation of culture, both through the value system and the priorities on which it is based and the teaching practices and styles.

In Britain, for instance, the educational system subscribes to so-called white middle-class values, such as resourcefulness, sacrifice of present interests for future ambitions, discipline and self-control. Teaching of applied science and commerce is given a lower priority and status compared to that of pure science and arts subjects. This contrasts sharply with Germany's greater emphasis on and prestige for technological courses and the United States' far better treatment of commerce and business in educational institutions.

As for teaching practices and styles, in some societies learning is through one-way teaching (from lecturer to students), memorizing textbooks and accepting 'facts' without a serious challenge. In others, students may be encouraged to participate in the teaching–learning process by engaging in discussions, arguments, experimentation and self-discovery. The implications of these two different styles of teaching practice for interpersonal relationships, especially in terms of power and authority, and ability to stand on one's own feet in life, are obvious.

Political system

The political system of a society, like other social institutions, creates and is created by the culture of that society. When the system is the outcome of historical and cultural evolutionary processes, it is compatible with the local culture, and it therefore survives and indeed flourishes. In some countries a certain type of political regime might be imposed on people by foreign powers or through military coups, and which could be incompatible with the local culture. Such imposed regimes will either collapse after a few years, or will lose much of their initial characteristics and be modified to allow for local preferences.

The short-lived Greek military government which was replaced after a few years by a democratic parliamentary regime in the 1970s, and the rejection in 1989 of over forty years of rule of Communism, which was imposed by the Soviet Union on the peoples of East European countries, are examples of this kind.

Indian democracy is another example of an imposed political structure, in this case by the outgoing British colonial rulers,

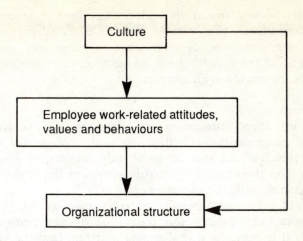

Figure 9.1 *The cultural model of organizations*

which has changed in fundamental ways since it was first installed. The new features are much more in line with other socio-cultural characteristics of the country as a whole (see, for instance, Segal, 1971).

A democratic political system usually develops and flourishes in cultures where people believe in sharing power and responsibility. In these cultures consultation and respect for other people's opinions are considered as strength rather than weakness. People demand to be consulted with and regard themselves as equal to those in positions of power. These values and attitudes are, in turn, reinforced and perpetuated by the political climate that they have helped to create. An opposite and contrasting picture is the case in an autocratic regime.

Culture and organizations

Culture can influence organizations either from without, through social and political institutions, or from within, through employees' work-related attitudes and values (Tayeb, 1991a). Figure 9.1 illustrates this argument.

Influence of culture on organizations from without

There are many institutions and factors outside an organization which are influenced or created by culture and which in turn have implications for the organization, in varying degrees of significance. It should be pointed out that some of these institutions and factors are heavily 'mixed up' with politics, both at national and international levels (for example, the role of the superpowers in suppressing economic developments in some less powerful countries). The overarching role of culture in the process must therefore be treated with caution.

Technology

There are three fundamentally different philosophies of humans' relationships with their physical environment on the basis of which all cultures can be broadly categorized. These are mastery over the environment, subjugation to the environment and harmony with the environment.

The first philosophy, which underlies most of the Western civilizations, emphasizes the power of human beings over 'nature'. It is basically a challenging and non-fatalistic view of the world. Natural resources are there to be exploited; animals to be tamed, and forests to be felled to provide us with more land and timber. The kind of technology that one expects a culture based on such a philosophy to 'produce' is inherently an aggressive one, and is a tool in the hands of human beings to conquer the world out there. It is therefore not surprising that major technological innovations, especially in the past 200 years, originated in Western cultures.

The second philosophy, that of subjugation to the environment, regards human beings as less powerful than, and at the mercy of, the elements. Some cultures which have fatalistic religions are generally based on this philosophy. Natural forces, symbolized in the will of God, are too powerful to master. The extremely low level of technological innovations in these cultures seems to reflect this type of worldview.

A third view, which has been developed in recent years, and is gaining in support, argues that the survival of human beings in the long run depends on a benign and sustainable relationship with their environment. Unless they harmonize their activities with those of nature, this life-support system will be irrevocably damaged, with disastrous consequences. The type of technology which the proponents of this view envisage to develop is one which will economize on the use of non-renewable natural resources and will allow nature time to recover from the effects of exploitation.

Economic advancement

The level of economic advancement and industrialization of a country may also reflect the cultural attitudes and values of its people. For instance, it has been argued (Weber, 1930) that the driving force behind capitalism and indeed the Industrial Revolution in the eighteenth century in England was the English people's high degree of individualism, which encouraged and was reinforced by Protestantism.

In a technologically and economically developed country, business organizations have better access to advanced technical know-how and infrastructures. They can recruit from a pool of professional managers and a highly skilled labour force, which could be utilized to create and maintain a competitive edge in international markets over those in the less developed societies.

Trade unions

Free and independent labour movements and trade unions are institutions which are encouraged and flourish in many democratic cultures (for example, Germany). In some cultures they are rubberstamping puppets of the regime (for example, the pre-1989 East European countries, China). In yet others they are either non-existent or repressed (for example, some countries in the Middle East).

The nature of the ideology and activities that unions might adopt also differs from one society to another. For instance, in France unions are highly political and tend to engage in class struggles. The Polish trade union, Solidarity, and the Siberian miners of the Republic of Russia in the former Soviet Union are other examples of highly politicized labour movements. In Britain, trade unions are more pragmatic and have no intention of overthrowing or challenging the authority of the management or the government. They fight for their jobs and for better working conditions. Trade unions in the United States are even less militant and more pragmatic than those in Britain.

There are differences, too, in the nature of industrial relations in different countries. In Britain the management–workers relationship is hostile and is characterized by a 'them and us' division. In Japan the unions, which are company-based, recruit both management and workers. The two sides of the industry cooperate with each other and see themselves as striving to achieve the same goals. The Japanese culturally rooted national unity and consensus are clearly reflected in that country's industrial relations practices (see also chapter 12).

Pressure groups

Pressure groups other than trade unions can also in some cultures be more successful than in others, both in terms of their numbers and of their influence on government policies, which in turn have implications for business organizations. Pressure groups can aim their activities at various levels: national, regional, local, industry and firm.

Anti-pollution and other environmental organizations, for instance, may try to influence governmental policies through changes in legislation, or even through direct action (for example, Greenpeace). Some pressure groups may focus their attention on increasing the awareness of the general public about certain issues, such as the harmful effects of some food additives on health, the dangers associated with the nuclear power industry, and the contamination in egg production.

The changes thus caused in the legislation and consumers' awareness force companies to adopt new policies and take appropriate actions.

Influence of culture on organizations from within

Culture is a social construct, and manifests itself in the context of social interactions. In an organization culture comes into play at the point of the interaction among members and between members and the organization. The decision-making process in organizations may be an appropriate point to look for such interactions (Tayeb, 1988).

The decision-making process is viewed as a base on and around which the organization is built. In other words, behind every action which takes place in an organization lies a decision or decisions. An organization comes into being when a person or a group of persons decides to achieve certain goals in collaboration with one or more persons. Decisions are then made on the ways and means by which these goals are to be achieved – what and how to produce, what kinds of employees are needed to carry out the business of the organization, who the likely customers are, what geographical markets to serve, what pricing policy to adopt etc. The death of the organization too is the outcome of a decision.

A decision-making process in an organization involves power and authority relationship, risk taking and coping with uncertainty, delegation, dedication and commitment, motivation, communication and exchange of information, consultation, control and discipline, and rules and regulations.

The attitudes and values that managers and other employees hold with respect to these issues and relationships determine to a large extent the form that the decision-making process takes.

These are attitudes to power and authority, the ability to cope with uncertainty and ambiguity, trust – or lack of it – in others, honesty and trustworthiness, choice of mechanism for control and discipline, attitudes to participation in collective activities and consultation with others, and expectations from a job. It is here that culture enters the 'picture'.

Attitude towards power and authority
In a culture where people respect their seniors and/or are even afraid of people in positions of power, it is less likely that as employees they challenge their superiors. Decisions tend to be taken by a few senior managers and carried out by subordinates. Iran is an example of this type of culture (Tayeb, 1981). In cultures where people are brought up to share power with others, organizations may also be more decentralized, managers may delegate their authority lower down the hierarchy, and there will be more consultation and communication among employees. The United States and the United Kingdom belong, to a large extent, to this last cultural category.

Tolerance of ambiguity and uncertainty
This cultural dimension is especially relevant to the risk taking aspect of decision making in an organization. Social institutions such as family, religion and education could encourage or discourage risk taking and accepting responsibility for one's own actions. Thus, the ability or inability to cope with uncertainty can be inculcated in people as a cultural trait. This trait may then be reflected in their behaviour in work organizations.

Employees who have less tolerance of uncertainty and are unwilling to face ambiguity and risk are more likely to avoid making decisions on their own and without direction from above, in the form of procedures and regulations. Alternatively they may like to share the responsibilities with others. Hofstede (1980) attributes the Japanese organizations' practice of collective decision making, *ringi*, to the Japanese people's high uncertainty avoidance. Fromm (1942) argues that the rise of Nazism in Germany earlier this century was because of the German people's relatively low degree of tolerance for ambiguity. Even now German organizations are more centralized than those in many of their fellow European countries (see for instance Child and Keiser, 1979; Maurice et al., 1980). However, the German political system is very decentralized. For example the power of the *Länder* is much greater than that of the local authorities of English regions. Also, in the business sector the top five

German retailers are far more decentralized than their UK or Dutch equivalents. This is because there are other factors beside culture which influence specific organizations (for details see Tayeb, 1988).

Individualism, collectivism

These concepts do not easily lend themselves to clear-cut definitions. Individualism, for instance, can be interpreted as self-interest and selfishness, and collectivism as self-sacrifice (Tayeb, 1988).

The view taken here is that an individualistic culture is generally characterized by a high value placed on one's independence, autonomy, and privacy, a belief in one's own worth, confidence in one's own ideas and opinions. In a collectivist culture the group to which one belongs, such as family, community, or even work organization, takes priority over one's individuality. England and many Western European cultures are considered individualistic cultures, as defined here, and India and Japan as collectivist ones.

The relationships between employees and their work organizations reflect their cultural backgrounds in this respect. Japanese employees, for instance, consider their workplace as an extension of their family and are highly committed to its goals and objectives. Their commitment is reciprocated by the organization. The managers, for example, may become involved in their employees' personal difficulties and try to help them out when in trouble. In an individualistic culture, such as Britain, this is far from the case, and may in fact be regarded by employees as intrusion in their privacy by managers (Tayeb and Smith, 1988).

In individualistic cultures the relationships between employees and work organizations are on the whole less emotional and are sometimes even downright hostile. For instance, compare the industrial relations scene in Britain with that in Japan. The former is characterized by apparent mutual hostility and distrust and the latter by apparent harmony and cooperation.

Interpersonal trust

Some cultures are characterized by a high degree of honesty and mutual trust and some others by a high degree of distrust. Organizations can reflect these traits. In low trusting cultures, such as Iran, decisions are more centralized, key positions are allocated to trusted people, usually friends and relatives of the owners and senior managers, control and discipline are tight, and rules and regulations are accompanied by close personal supervision (Tayeb, 1981). In high trusting cultures, such as Britain, there will be a relatively higher degree of delegation and control is more impersonal and less severe.

The discussion above leads us to the conclusion that cultural attitudes and values play a significant role in shaping the management style of work organizations and the leadership behaviour of their managers.

In some cultures, people value other people's opinion, believe in information sharing, recognize the rights of others to be consulted with, and can trust others. In these cultures business organizations are likely to have a more participative and consultative management style than in cultures with opposite values.

Leadership behaviour may be considered as having two aspects. The first is the **genotype** or the core intention of an action or behaviour. The second is the **phenotype** or the manner in which that intention is expressed (Misumi, 1985). For instance, almost all employees prefer a considerate and employee-oriented manager. This is the genotype, universal aspect of a leader behaviour. But how this employee orientation manifests itself or is perceived by employees in the workplace, the phenotype aspect, depends largely on the specific cultural backgrounds of the employees. A Japanese manager who goes to a hospital to visit his or her sick subordinate may be seen as a considerate manager by the Japanese employee, but as a nosy distrusting one by a British employee. The latter might perceive a manager who provides him or her with a personal computer or other equipment to assist him or her at work as a considerate or employee-oriented manager.

Table 9.1 summarizes some of the cultural characteristics which are most relevant to work organizations. The arrow in each row denotes a continuum on either end of which extreme values of a cultural characteristic are placed. The example for each trait illustrates the nation which is considered to be high or low on that trait. Various societies can be located along each of the continua to show the degree to which a characteristic is present or valued in those nations. For instance, Iran can be placed somewhere in the middle of the individualistic–collectivist continuum, and Japan nearer the right-hand end of the low–high tolerance of ambiguity continuum.

Table 9.1 *Nations and work-related attitudes and values*

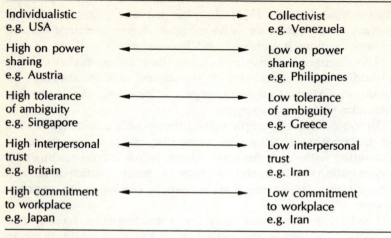

Individualistic e.g. USA	Collectivist e.g. Venezuela
High on power sharing e.g. Austria	Low on power sharing e.g. Philippines
High tolerance of ambiguity e.g. Singapore	Low tolerance of ambiguity e.g. Greece
High interpersonal trust e.g. Britain	Low interpersonal trust e.g. Iran
High commitment to workplace e.g. Japan	Low commitment to workplace e.g. Iran

Sources: Hofstede (1980); Tayeb (1979, 1988, 1990b)

Managers and culture

If you were a manager of a multicultural organization or a company in a country other than your own what would you do? How would you handle the issue of culture?

One option for a manager placed in this situation is to ignore employees' diversified cultures and treat them as if they were from a homogeneous background. He or she can concentrate instead on issues such as market share, competition and technological changes, which have more immediate relevance to the organization's success. To do this might indeed be easier, but it may not necessarily be a more useful course of action, in terms of, for instance, employees' satisfaction and productivity. There is evidence that some cultural characteristics such as attitude to power and authority can be dysfunctional in work organizations (Kakar, 1971). It has also been argued that some cultures set limits to the extent that organizations can respond and adapt to their environmental demands (Tayeb, 1979).

A second option is to take employees' different cultural backgrounds into consideration when devising authority structures, control strategies and inducement policies, and to recognize and utilize the employees' diverse attitudes and behaviours. This could in turn result in higher satisfaction for employees and more effective management of organizations. For instance, employees may come from a culture where people generally work better under constant direction and guidance from superiors than when they are left alone with only overall objectives of the tasks at hand. In situations such as this their managers could design a system which would facilitate the flow of detailed information and instruction between superiors and subordinates. Or, alternatively, these types of employees could be assigned the tasks which are routine and predictable and for which a manual of detailed instructions can be prepared.

A third course of action would be to create a cultural synergy (Adler, 1981). There are many aspects of cultures which can be incorporated and utilized in the management style of a multicultural organization and which would benefit it. For instance, group-orientation of employees from a collectivist cultural background could be turned into a high degree of commitment to the workplace. Or employees who come from a trustworthy culture could be put in charge of the jobs which by their nature cannot be subjected to constant direct supervision by senior managers.

A fourth way of dealing with employees' diversified cultural backgrounds is to build up a strong organizational culture and create a more or less homogeneous value system to which employees will be encouraged to subscribe. Formal and informal communication channels can be utilized to foster the company's own philosophy and 'way of life'. Selection procedures can be devised to recruit new employees with the kinds of values and preferences that are compatible with the organization's prevailing culture (for a detailed discussion on organizational culture see Schein, 1985).

Transfer of management practices between cultures

Many countries, especially the less economically developed ones, in an attempt to upgrade their organizational systems and to improve their performance, import various management techniques from the more advanced industrialized nations. It is, however, important for the managers from the less developed countries to be aware of the socio-cultural and technological characteristics which are unique to their own societies, and to recognize the implications of these characteristics for their work organizations. This will help them to utilize their employees' values and attitudes more fully, and to devise management systems which are more authentic and appropriate to their own particular circumstances. The managers should avoid importing and applying without modifications management practices from countries with different sets of values, socio-economic conditions and political ideologies. If these imported techniques are not modified and adapted to the local conditions, both in cultural terms and in terms of the availability of human skills, the transfer process will almost certainly fail.

In this connection, Hofstede (1980: 300) compares Japan, (once a developing country) and Iran (still a Third World developing country) with respect to the adoption of Western-style leadership practices, and points out the dangers of ignoring culture in the process:

> Attempts at the transfer of leadership skills which do not take the values of subordinates into account have little chance of success. . . . . Technologies are not neutral with regard to values: in order to work, they assume that certain values are respected. Making these technologies work means that people in the receiving countries must learn new leadership and subordinateship skills, change old institutions and shift their values. . . . Cultural transposition, in the ideal case, means finding a new cultural synthesis which retains from the old local values those elements deemed essential but which allows the new technologies to function. Probably the country which has most successfully done this so far is Japan; a country where it has clearly failed is Iran.

There are aspects of work organizations which can be sealed off, so to speak, from the cultural surroundings, and are therefore more receptive to imported technologies. As Kiggundu et al. (1983: 79–80) argue:

> Whenever the organization can function as a closed system – either because of the nature of the practice involved or because the managers succeed in sealing its core technology from the intervention of 'outside' actors – then what we know about organization from North America seems to work fairly well. Whenever the organization interacts with its environment, however, the resulting behavior cannot be understood without significant adjustments to the theories developed in industrialized nations.

The question of level of technical skill and know-how is however relevant here. No amount of sealing off of technological core from the social setting within which the organization operates can make the adoption of foreign technology successful if the company does not have sufficiently skilled employees to operate it.

Box 9   *England and India - a comparative cultural picture*

Primary institutions

Family is much more extended in India than in England. A traditional Indian family normally includes three or four generations, whereas an English family generally consists of parents and children, and the children usually leave their homes even before they set up their own families. The structure of family is less hierarchical and more egalitarian in England than in India, and the members' roles are less rigidly defined in the former than in the latter. Relationships between the members of the family are more emotional and dependent in India than in England. Child-rearing practices in the former encourages conformity, collectivism, and obedience to seniors; in the latter independence, individualism, and challenge.

Religions in both societies are, in theory at least, tolerant of other religious beliefs and practices, but they are more so in England than in India. In England, religious tolerance is manifested in many different denominations which come broadly under Protestantism. In India, Hinduism consists of numerous forms of worship and ritual. Hinduism emphasizes reincarnation, and is, as far as this life is concerned, a more fatalistic religion than Protestantism. The latter emphasizes 'free will' and encourages individual action, individualism and mastery over the environment.

Secondary institutions

Teaching practices in Indian educational institutions are largely based on a one-way relationship between teachers and pupils, and learning is generally through passive acceptance of facts and memorizing text books. In England, learning is largely based on self-discovery, experimentation, games, discussions and arguments.

Social stratification in England is based, primarily, on economic factors, such as occupation, the ownership and control of the means of production, and wealth. On this basis, the society is broadly divided into two large middle and working classes, with small 'upper' and 'under' classes at either ends of the social hierarchy. In India, social stratification is based, primarily, on caste. The caste system is sanctioned by Hindu precepts, and caste membership is determined by birth and, in turn, determines, to a large extent, a person's occupation as well as social standing. Class membership in England is to some extent subjective and the system is much more flexible than is the Indian caste system. In the former, an ex-working class person can consider himself or herself as a member of the middle class once his or her occupation and economic conditions change from a working-class type (such as, manual work) to a middle-class type (such as, managerial work). In India, social stratification is very rigid: a person is born into a caste, no matter what professional and economic position he or she may come to occupy later in life, he or she will remain a member of the caste of his or her birth.

Table 9.2 *Indian person–English person*

An Indian person is:	An English person is:
• more emotional	• less emotional
• fearful of people in positions of power	• respectful of people in positions of power
• more obedient to seniors	• less obedient to seniors
• more dependent on others	• less dependent on others
• more fatalistic	• less fatalistic
• submissive	• aggressive
• more open to bribery	• less open to bribery
• less able to cope with new and uncertain situations	• more able to cope with new and uncertain situations
• less concerned about others outside own community	• more concerned with others outside own community
• accept responsibility less	• accept responsibility more
• less disciplined	• more disciplined
• more modest	• more arrogant
• less reserved	• more reserved
• more collectivist	• more individualist
• caste conscious	• class conscious
• law-abiding	• bends the law if necessary
• opposed to change	• opposed to change
• less self-controlled	• more self-controlled
• less trustworthy	• more trustworthy
• more friendly	• less friendly
• less tenacious	• more tenacious
• more clan-oriented	• less clan-oriented
• less willing to take account of other people's views	• more willing to take account of other people's views

See note on page 138.

The **economic systems** in both countries are based on a capitalistic mode of production, with both private and public enterprises. However, Indian capitalism is much more protectionist, and the government is involved in direct intervention in the economy to a larger extent. Local industries are protected against foreign competitors through the government's strict import policies. English capitalism, especially under a Conservative government, is based on a minimal government intervention, and on stimulating industries through monetary policies which aim to facilitate the free play and interaction of market forces. In the pursuit of this aim, there is very little control over imports, and, as a result, manufacturing companies face fierce competition from foreign firms.

Trade unions in England have lost much of their powers in recent years because of job insecurity under the conditions of high unemployment, loss of membership due to mass redundancies, and

Table 9.3   *Indian employee–English employee*

An Indian employee:	An English employee:
• perceives to have less power and autonomy at work	• perceives to have more power and autonomy at work
• has lower tolerance for ambiguity	• has higher tolerance for ambiguity
• is individualistic	• is individualistic
• is more satisfied with own work organization	• is less satisfied with own work organization
• has the same degree of commitment to work organization as an English employee	• has the same degree of commitment to work organization as an Indian employee
• has the same degree of trust in colleagues as an English employee	• has the same degree of trust in colleagues as an Indian employee
• considers freedom and autonomy, belonging to a group, learning new skills and status as more important than other aspects of a job	• considers job security and good pay and fringe benefits as more important than other aspects of a job
• has a more negative attitude to the nature of human beings	• has a more positive attitude to the nature of human beings
• believes less in sharing information with others	• believes more in sharing information with others
• has a more positive view about participation for all	• has a more negative view about participation for all

anti-union legislation. In India, the organized sector is relatively very small compared to the total workforce, but the government's industrial relations acts are 'pro' workers and the unions have more power compared to their English counterparts.

Political regimes in both countries are based on parliamentary democracy, and freedom of expression and other individual and collective civil rights are respected in both systems. However, in practice Indian democracy is less 'democratic' and more centralized than the English democracy. Opposition parties are weaker and much more fragmented in India. Since the Independence, except for a brief period in the late 1970s and in 1991, only one party, the Congress, has been in power. Frequent irregularities during elections have also led many observers to have reservations about the extent to which democracy is practised in India.

Table 9.4 *Indian organization – English organization*

In an Indian organization:	In an English organization:
• there is less delegation	• there is greater delegation
• operative decisions are more centralized than financial and strategic decisions	• financial and strategic decisions are more centralized than operative decisions
• unallocated items and capital items are more centralized than allocated items and revenue items	• unallocated items and capital items are more centralized than allocated items and revenue items
• less communication and consultation take place	• more communication and consultation take place
• degree of specialization is the same as in an English organization	• degree of specialization is the same as in an Indian organization
• degree of formalization is lower	• degree of formalization is higher
• less use of job descriptions	• greater use of job descriptions
• more subordinates report directly to chief executive	• fewer subordinates report directly to chief executive
• same number of levels in the hierarchy as an English organization	• same number of levels in the hierarchy as an Indian organization

• dual control strategies:
  – managers and other members of staff are controlled by target setting and performance monitoring
  – manual workers are controlled by productivity measurements, close supervision, time-keeping, and other external measures
	• dual control strategies:
	  – managers and other members of staff are controlled by target setting and performance monitoring
	  – manual workers are controlled by productivity measurements, close supervision, time-keeping and other external measures

Note: Tables 9.2, 9.3, and 9.4 are not stereotypical. They have been compiled on the basis of the findings of extensive empirical surveys carried out by the present author in England and India.

Sources: Tayeb (1987a, 1988)

10

East European Countries

The political and economic reforms which have swept through the Soviet Union and East European countries since 1989 have attracted the attention of academics, politicians and businesspeople everywhere. These reforms have tremendous implications not only for the ex-socialist countries but also for the rest of the world. The present chapter concentrates on the implications of these reforms for East European societies, for their companies, and for the international firms which intend to have business with these countries.

Since 1989 substantial changes have taken place in the way that many business organizations situated in these countries are managed and structured. At the time of writing this chapter (May 1992) the political and economic situation across the socialist world was in a state of flux and unpredictability. Whereas the arguments and principles presented here may stand regardless of the pace of the changes (for example, the problematic nature of privatization of state-owned companies), some of the speculations as to what might happen in the process of transition from one system to another might well have been overtaken by events within a few months.

In their attempts to join in the world community after decades of near-isolation, East European countries face an immense challenge. They endeavour first to dismantle the system with which they were saddled for over forty years, a centrally planned Communist structure. They then aim at replacing it with one form or other of a decentralized market-based capitalism that may suit their individual circumstances best.

An appropriate point to start the discussion on the task facing the East European countries and their businesses is to examine the system from which they are emerging and the system which they may be aspiring to acquire.

Socialist and capitalist systems

The two systems stand in sharp ideological and institutional contrasts. There are at least five major aspects on which capitalist and socialist societies differ fundamentally one from another, and which have significant implications for work organizations. These are: dominant ideology and value systems, the ownership and control of the means of production, management of the economy, class structure, and the role of the state (Child and Tayeb, 1983; Tayeb 1991b).

Dominant ideology and value systems

The capitalist system is based on an essentially individualistic philosophy, where economic advancement of the society as a whole is achieved through the pursuance of individual initiative and interests. Adam Smith's notion of the 'invisible hand' is an embodiment of this principle.

In a pure *laissez-faire* capitalist economy the more competitive, competent and capable an individual is the more he or she will prosper, but life can be very harsh for the less competent and the losers. However, in practice all capitalist countries have some form of national welfare state in order to provide a minimum standard of living for the less capable individuals.

A socialist system, notably of the kind which existed in the former Soviet Union and East European countries, and still exists in China, Cuba and North Korea, places a great emphasis on the collective interests, with the Communist Party as the bastion of the interests of the working class as a general collective. There is in general a national psychology unwilling to allow some people to get rich faster than others.

These two different broad ideologies underlie much of the political, social and economic institutions of the two systems.

In a capitalist society, in principle at least, the political system reflects the respect for the right of the individual to express his or her views, to be consulted with and to participate in the running of the country, and to hold elected political leaders accountable for their actions. In reality, however, there are many capitalist countries which do not live up to this ideal. In a socialist system very few, if any, of these rights are respected.

Ownership and control of the means of production

In capitalist systems, the ownership and control of the means of production is mixed, though the proportion of private and state sectors varies a great deal from one country to another. For instance, France's state-owned businesses account for about one-third of the nation's GNP. State-owned manufacturers and banks alone employ about one million people. In Italy the state sector produces just as large a proportion of GNP – and the three biggest state holding companies, IRI, ENI, and EFIM, together employ 550,000 workers. Spain's state companies account for about 9 percent of its GNP. Its biggest industrial holding company, INI, has 150,000 staff (*The Economist*, 17 November 1990).

Under socialism the means of production is formally socialized in the hands of the state (Giddens, 1973). The means of production are not owned by any social class, in the sense of exclusive rights to enjoy and to dispose of assets; no identifiable group of persons may enjoy a source of income from the proceeds of ownership. Investment, production and the appointment of leading personnel of industrial enterprises in state socialist societies are firmly controlled by industrial ministries, and the possibilities of any group consistently extracting an economic surplus as a factor source of profit are extremely limited (Mandel, 1969).

However, many socialist countries, even those, such as China, which have so far opposed recent reforms in the Soviet Union and Eastern Europe, allow private ownership of enterprise, but its extent and role in the economy are negligible. For instance, in Hungary in 1984, before the recent reforms, the state sector employed almost 70 percent, non-state cooperatives 26 percent and the formal private sector 4 percent of all active income earners (Carroll et al., 1988).

Management of the economy

In capitalist societies, the market economy operates to maximize profits which in turn maintain a bourgeois class.

A distinctive feature of the socialist societies is the absence of a market economy. The economy is planned and controlled by the state. The centralization of planning and control in most socialist countries contrasts with the decentralization inherent in the use of market mechanisms.

A planned economy, also known as command economy, involves centralized controls over many aspects of the economic life: prices and wages, investments, products, the choice of production technologies, suppliers of raw materials, and foreign trade. Most enterprises are nationalized and do not need to exercise effective financial control over their own activities; neither do they need to market, distribute and develop their own production lines. Market forces, such as supply and demand, are for the most part irrelevant and play little role in guiding economic growth.

Planned economy and state intervention in economic and business activities, however, are not unknown in capitalist countries, especially those in the Third World. India is a good example of a capitalist country with extensive socialist policies and a planned economy, where targets for, among other things, growth in GNP and in employment, and schemes to relieve poverty are set by central planners. Singapore, South Korea, Taiwan and other East Asian NICs are other examples.

Even in some rich and advanced capitalist countries, such as Japan, the state plays an active role, in the form of industrial policies, to facilitate economic activities and to support industries.

Class structure

Capitalist societies are characterized by an antagonistic class structure with an inherent conflict of interests and inequality between the dominant owning and/or controlling class and the working class.

Socialist societies are not classless, but they are, in theory at least, not antagonistic class societies either. They are designed to be single-class societies or workers' states. The working class is the dominant class for whom and on whose behalf the state, or the administrative class, rules. At the same time, however, they have an essentially non-egalitarian or bourgeois system of distribution of wealth – expressed through the price and wage system (Lane, 1977). In other words, although the production of wealth is based on socialist principles (in terms of ownership and control), its distribution is not. Compare the empty shops in Moscow outside which ordinary working-class people queued for hours to buy foods, with luxury *dachas* and exclusive holiday resorts in which senior members of the Communist Party enjoyed themselves.

Role of the state

Under capitalism the type of activity performed by the government must of necessity be limited, whereas this is not the case under socialism. In the latter, the formal political apparatus is responsible to a much wider extent in determining who gets 'what, when and how': the political process decides the distribution of resources between various social groups and interests (Lane, 1977).

Table 10.1 summarizes major differences between capitalist and socialist systems.

Table 10.1   *Capitalism versus socialism*

Characteristics of capitalist systems	Characteristics of socialist systems
• private or mixed ownership of the means of production	• state ownership and control of the means of production
• multi-class, dominance of owning/controlling class	• single class, dominance of working class, workers' state
• emphasis on individual initiative and interests	• emphasis on collective interests
• market economy	• planned economy
• minimal state intervention	• state in full control

Source: Tayeb (1990a)

Organizations in capitalist and socialist countries

Capitalist organizations

In capitalist societies, the external environment of private enterprises is, in general, characterized by competition, both over suppliers and customers; fluctuating interest rates and currencies; pressure groups; no helping hand from the state; and, in short, the principle of 'the survival of the fittest'. As a result, successful firms have sophisticated production technologies, competent operators, and well-developed marketing skills.

Internally, the companies set their own objectives, which are mainly profits, growth and market power. Managers, having an eye on the shareholders' interests, acquire and allocate their resources, and plan their strategies and policies. Issues such as production targets, prices, the number of employees, the markets to serve, suppliers, and distribution, are all decided upon within the organizations.

The management style and structure of the organizations are devised by managers and their employees. Workers' participation in decision-making processes, although it is not always institutionalized, is present in varying degrees.

Trade unions are independent of the state and play a major part in many democratic capitalist countries. It has to be noted that in many countries, such as Britain, participation of trade unions in the management of the company is not obligatory by law, and it is rather based on the goodwill on the part of the management. In some countries, such as Germany and Norway, workers' participation is required by law.

Socialized organizations

In socialist societies, planning, resource allocation and control are far more centralized than they are in the capitalist countries. The centrally-planned economy forces state enterprises to focus on their quotas rather than on other indicators of success in their operation, such as sales and turnover. The measurement of an enterprise's performance is largely based upon the assigned production goals. Profits earned by enterprises are appropriated by the government and used to reimburse those units that suffer losses.

An enterprise usually does not perform marketing functions such as advertising, consumer surveying and selling on its own. Instead, over 90 percent of commodities are priced and distributed through channels set by the central planning system. The majority of consumer goods are sold in state-owned department stores, where prices are fixed. Under this kind of system, there is not much a supplier can do to control profitability.

Since there is no relation between companies' economic performance and their fortune, they tend to be inefficient, their technology is obsolete by Western standards, the quality of the products is generally poor, and managerial skills are underdeveloped.

Organizational objectives are decided by the state and are of a non-monetary and social kind, such as keeping people in employment. As a result, many companies suffer from over-manning. In other words, social welfare has been built into the mechanisms of production of goods and services. In capitalist societies these functions are separated, and an elaborate system of taxation channels part of the created wealth to the needy via national welfare institutions.

Investment is centrally decided and allocated in real terms while finance is provided automatically and interest-free from the state budget to investors. Trade credits between enterprises is forbidden.

Some socialist enterprises have a parallel Communist Party structure alongside the managerial authority structure. This parallel hierarchy reports directly to the local and central party organizations. The party is considered as having a legitimate role in the hierarchical structures of organizations. The dual authority system is intended to ensure that the party line is followed. This parallelism does not exist in capitalist organizations. The managerial hierarchy is accountable to the shareholders, and political parties, regardless of their ideologies and beliefs, have no control over it.

Table 10.2 *Capitalist organization versus socialized organization*

Organizations in capitalist countries:

- profit, growth and market power as primary objectives
- objectives set by the organization (owners, managers)
- decentralized approach to planning, resource allocation, control and other strategic decisions
- market-allocation mechanisms for resources and employment
- independent trade unions' action and voice in enterprise policy making, where it affects them
- investment fund raising in private sector is the organizations' responsibility
- single hierarchy structure
- structure and leadership style decided by managers and other employees within the organizations
- employees' participation in decision making is not institutionalized to any significant degree, especially in strategic areas
- bureaucratic and non-bureaucratic forms of structure

Organizations in socialist countries:

- full-employment, social welfare, redistribution of wealth as primary objectives
- objectives are set by the central state
- centralized approach to planning, resource allocation and control
- state is responsible to raise investment funds
- major decisions taken above the organizations
- dual hierarchy structure, party parallel hierarchy
- workers' participation is institutionalized to a great degree, e.g. worker directors, workers' committee
- bureaucratic structure

Source: Tayeb (1990a)

Free and independent trade unions did not exist in most of the socialist countries before the recent revolutions, and still do not exist in China and other Communist countries. The workers who organized themselves as such were quickly suppressed and dispersed by the ruling party (for example, Solidarity under Poland's former Communist government). However, as was mentioned earlier, workers' participation in management decision making is legitimized and practised in socialist societies much more widely than it is in the capitalist countries.

The former Yugoslavia's self-management with worker directors was the most extensive form of workers' participation. The future of self-management, like so much else in that country is uncertain, if not already destroyed. The country has virtually disintegrated. Three of its constituent republics – Slovenia,

Croatia and Bosnia-Hercegovina – have declared, and received recognition for, their independence. The self-management system has already disappeared from factories and workshops in Slovenia. The other two republics' declaration of independence was followed by a bloody civil war between major ethnic groups which destroyed, among other things, much of their economic infrastructure and many of their businesses.

Table 10.2 summarizes major characteristics of work organizations in capitalist and socialist countries.

Political and social reforms

The political and social revolutions that have occurred in East European countries since 1989 have significant implications for these countries, and indeed others, at several levels.

Political level

The reforms have swept away one ideology without replacing it with another which is as clearly defined. Democracy and a free market economy may be common and desirable goals, but history, geography and national psyche will be influential factors in determining how quickly, if at all, they are achieved. Hungary and Poland, for instance, are keener and have been quicker to take necessary measures to install a market economy. Others, such as Romania and Bulgaria, are more cautious. Czechoslovakia is somewhere in between. Albania's political freedom from the communist rule was eventually achieved in March 1992, and the country has only just begun its long road to economic freedom.

These countries have tried, with varying degrees of success, to bring about changes in their social and economic fabric through a change in their political system, shifting from a one-party totalitarian system to a multi-party democratic one. It will be many years, however, as Wallace (1990) states, before it will be possible to say that the political change has been completed, and that representative government in a reasonably effective form has come to stay in Eastern Europe.

Economic level

In the economic sphere, a shift to a free market system is difficult and has, in the short term at least, painful consequences for businesses and customers alike.

On the customers' side, the new regime means steep price

rises, and a sharp drop in the standard of living. On the enterprise side, a hands-off economic policy means the withdrawal of state subsidies and support for loss-making companies, the disappearance of interest-free loans, state-provided investment funds, price control, and guaranteed suppliers of raw materials and components. Managers will set their own goals and objectives, which will primarily be profit making, higher productivity and efficiency. This will inevitably bring about laying off of the excess manpower, leading to high rates of unemployment.

The most severe consequence of the free market policy will be fierce competition from domestic and foreign producers – something that the managers were not used to prior to the change of the regime and do not have the required skills to cope with, (for example, marketing, distribution, retailing, financial control and production design and development). Mechanisms for gathering, processing and transmitting information were also underdeveloped under the previous regime (Mcdonald, 1990). High rates of bankruptcy will weed out the less fit companies.

So far, Poland has been the only country which has applied what commentators call 'cold-shower treatment', proposed by Dr Jeffrey Sachs of Harvard and others,

> plunging directly into the harsh realities of competitive capitalism. As a result, an internal free market has opened up in many commodities, prices have sky-rocketed, wage increases have been pegged to productivity – and living standards have dropped. (*Time*, 7 May 1990: 16)

Other East European leaders have moved more cautiously. For instance, while the Czechoslovakian government was sketching out a new economic programme, subsidies remained in place for a wide range of goods, and opening a private business remains a cumbersome process. Even in Poland, the signs of slowing down the pace of reforms were being observed by early 1992 (*The Economist*, 22 February 1992). (See Box 10.)

Russia and some of the other former Soviet republics started their shock treatment much later than other ex-socialist countries, on 2 January 1992, with the lifting of price subsidies. A major reason for the delay was the internal political upheavals that they experienced for some two years prior to that date. These upheavals, as mentioned in chapter 2, led to the disappearance of the Soviet Union and the formation of the Commonwealth of the Independent States.

Box 10   *Poland – a year later*

Polish reform has had its faults. Privatization has been too slow. The dominant state industry still awaits a proper shake-out. Inflation remains 5 percent a month, a great improvement on a year ago but still worrying. Life has certainly been tough in Poland over the past year. But has it really been tougher than before?

Official figures greatly exaggerate the drop in industrial production (which is said to have fallen by almost a third last year). One reason is that previous years' figures were bloated by communist managers with an interest in padding their production numbers to get bonuses or promotion. Performance was measured against the plan, not the market. Now, in contrast, managers are tempted to under-report their performance, to avoid taxes.

One steel factory in Silesia found that it could no longer afford to make the heavily subsidized, high-quality steel it used to produce before the new budgetary regime, so it began to make smaller quantities of low-quality steel, which it found could be exported to Germany at a profit.

Factories reducing production in order to change their technology or improve quality – even factories going bankrupt – are excellent signs of industrial restructuring. But what really distorts the official statistics is that they are based almost entirely on the state economy. They fail to account for the boom in private enterprise. Any visitor to Poland immediately sees what the figures fail to reflect. Every Polish town now has its street market, where everything from imported toothpaste to once unavailable Polish ham can be bought. Queues have virtually disappeared.

The Polish government's statistical office believes that the output of private industry (excluding farming) grew by 50 percent over the past year, and that it now accounts for 18 percent of national income, up from 11 percent in 1989. The number of people employed in private enterprise, the government's statisticians estimate, grew by more than 500,000 in 1989, bringing the total to between 1.8 million and 2 million people.

There is a sharp increase in unemployment figures, but it appears to be in part because of the hidden unemployment in the communist era. Many people, such as housewives, who did not have any job before, signed up to get unemployment benefit. Traders and other entrepreneurs also signed up in order to supplement their unregistered incomes.

Polish housewives no longer have to spend 2 hours a day in queues, and they can choose between fifteen brands of mineral water, when once only one diesel-flavoured Polish brand was on offer.

Source: *The Economist*, 25 January 1991

Privatization of state enterprises is another major step in the implementation of a market economy, and has proved to be a formidable task. Most of these firms were antiquated and unprofitable. But even the healthy ones did not sell easily. In Poland, when shares in a profitable import–export company were offered to the public in 1990, only 20 percent were purchased (*Time*, 11 June 1990).

Moreover, these countries did not have capital and stock markets under the communist regime. Also, since the bookkeeping practices were not geared to Western-style profit and loss statements, it would be very difficult to determine the value of the enterprises and their assets.

In the midst of the uncertainties surrounding the ex-socialist economies, the one certain aspect is that it will take a long time for the reforms to come to fruition. After all, the capitalist economies of the West grew organically over centuries. It is totally unrealistic for anyone to expect that Eastern Europe could demolish the communist system and build free market democracies in two – or even ten – years (*Time*, 17 February 1992).

Social level

At the social level, there will be inertia as well as willingness to change. There is, for instance, as Wallace (1990) points out, an army of civil servants at every level who will resist change to protect their own jobs, and a widespread attitude of public lassitude that will lend them tacit support. In addition, those in industry and agriculture who have grown accustomed over several decades to taking orders from above will find it more than a little difficult to show personal initiative and to accept responsibility. Also, many sections of the population, however anxious to exercise their votes, may resist any attempt by their new representatives to cut back on the welfare provision to which they have become accustomed under communism.

Many East Europeans, though they renounce socialism may find unfettered capitalism, especially its class structure, equally repugnant (*Time*, 15 January 1991). These countries are single-class societies or workers' states, where the working class is the dominant class for whom the state rules. The fundamental principle underlying the capitalist society, on paper at least, is to each according to his or her work; under communism, to each according to his or her needs; and under both, from each according to his or her ability. A change from a communist to a capitalist system will bring its inherent conflict of interests and inequality between the dominant owning and/or controlling class and the working class (Tayeb, 1991b).

There are already signs of resentment towards this prospect among people. The ex-East Germans, accustomed to a non-assertive collectivist system, are worried about being over-run by aggressive individualistic behaviours inherent in capitalism. In the former Soviet Union people are reluctant to allow some to get rich faster than others. In Hungary, there is a growing disgruntlement at the disparity in life-styles between the small class of entrepreneurs who have sprung up in the past decade and the still poor majority. The government is willing to keep uneconomic industries and businesses running in order to protect jobs. In Czechoslovakia, a worker backlash against the government may occur when economic reforms begin to bite. According to a report (*Time*, 17 February 1992), almost half the population in that country was dissatisfied and non-supportive of economic reforms. The hardship was almost at the crucial point where it could turn to aggressive opposition to reform. In Bulgaria, conflict between rural and urban areas was slowing down the pace of reform (*Time*, 9 July 1990).

Class politics and personal ambitions can threaten economic reforms in all these countries. The prospect of job losses, of disparity between the rich and the poor may trigger a worker backlash against the governments. The workers may rally round a party that promises job security regardless of the larger economic consequences (*Time*, 9 July 1990).

It should also be noted that an important factor which has contributed to the slow pace of reforms in most of the ex-socialist countries is conflict and political struggle between various factions in their respective parliaments which constantly pull and push the reforms in opposite directions.

As was mentioned earlier, the ex-socialist countries approached the implementation of their reforms somewhat differently one from another. For instance, the former East Germany, after unification with West Germany, had the benefit of the latter's support of all kinds, from financial to managerial and technical know-how. The others had to rely on their own internal resources, and external assistance was far from being taken for granted, as was the case for East Germany.

In the case of the former Soviet Union, because of the constituent republics' military and other strategic significance, the West, especially the EC, embarked upon a more or less concerted effort to assist the emerging democracies. A fear of the return of communism, and possibly another spell of 'cold war', was perhaps a major deciding factor.

Reforms and international business

East European countries need to attract foreign investment to build their economies. Foreign companies and the ancillary industries which they will subsequently create have enormous implications for the economy and the country as a whole. For instance, these companies will bring with them their capital, sophisticated technologies and managerial skills and know-how. In addition, in order to facilitate the movement of their supplies and products, they will act as the impetus to building a better infrastructure in the host countries.

Foreign investments are therefore encouraged, and conditions for them made much more attractive. The investors are also lured by low wage rates, an educated labour force and a potential market of nearly 140 million consumers in the heart of Europe. However, the investors cannot count on wages remaining low for a long time, given the expected high inflation rates.

Moreover, investment in Eastern Europe can ensure a greater foothold in the post-1992 Western Europe. For instance, General Electric's acquisition of a majority stake in Tungsram (in Hungary) increased its 1 percent share of Western Europe's lighting market to 9 percent. That share could prove particularly valuable if the European Community decides to impose quotas on non-EC products after it becomes economically unified in 1992 (*Time*, 2 July 1990).

But foreign companies also face serious obstacles. The infrastructure, such as road and railway transport and telecommunications, is far inferior compared to that in Western and other advanced industrialized countries. Essential services, such as the supply of water and the availability of waste disposal, are also poor, and financial services are underdeveloped.

One of the major problems is the lack of the business environment to which businesspeople in the West are accustomed. There is also the problem of inconvertibility of East European currencies to dollar or other hard currencies. The Western companies must often take their profits in bartered goods, such as clothing or foodstuffs, which can subsequently be sold in other Western countries (*Time*, 2 July 1990).

Also, foreign firms will need to retrain the local workforce to learn new skills, such as Western-style bookkeeping, and working with complex high technologies.

The process of privatization of the ownership of property and means of production is not as yet completed. Also, many of the East European countries are reluctant to allow foreign companies into their economies as the sole owner and controller of whatever enterprise they want to set up or take over. As *Time* (2 July 1990) puts it, while most East Europeans welcome the torrent of Western investment, they often have mixed feelings about the changes that it brings. Some fear that the capitalist invasion may replace communism with a new and more subtle form of economic domination. There are doubts in many people's minds about selling off parts of their national patrimony to foreigners.

These doubts and fears appear to be well-founded, in some cases at least. For instance, according to a recent report published by the Organization of Economic Cooperation and Development (OECD, 1990b), Eastern Europe risks being asset-stripped by Western investors rather than receive the long-term investment it needs. The OECD warns the emergent democracies that there will also be a substantial lag between pledges of direct investment and funds coming on stream. Large-scale onward investment is seen to depend on the pace of reform, especially in the area of property and ownership rights.

Given the extremely imperfect asset markets in the region, there is a risk that private foreign direct investment into these economies will be characterized by predatory manoeuvres rather than longer-term development considerations. The OECD also notes that the need in some countries for hard currency and inadequate information about the value of state assets makes them vulnerable to transfer-pricing practices.

11
Developing and Newly Industrialized Countries

A major proportion of the foreign direct investment of multinational companies is concentrated within industrialized countries, but the trend to move to less developed countries and the newly industrialized nations is on the increase. The reduction in the cost of production in an increasingly competitive world is more than ever becoming a significant determining factor in the choice of location for offshore plants. Less developed and newly industrialized countries are more likely to offer a competitive tender in this respect.

These two categories of countries both offer opportunities and pose constraints and challenges to multinational companies which have business dealings with them.

Less developed countries

What are less developed countries? This is a problematic question for various reasons. First, there is the problem of appropriate criteria by which a country can be defined and judged as a developing one. Economic criteria such as per capita income and gross domestic product (GDP) do not reflect the real amount and distribution of wealth. Black economy and wide income disparities, for instance make these yardsticks meaningless. Health care, infant mortality rate, per capita calorie consumption, life expectancy and literacy may be better criteria. But these are difficult to measure accurately for many countries because of inadequate and unreliable data. Infrastructure and electricity consumption are other aspects of a country which can be used as a measure of development. As we saw in chapter 2, many of these countries compare much the worse on many of these criteria with more advanced nations.

Secondly, the sheer number (approximately 140) and the diversity of the so-called developing countries in terms of the above-mentioned criteria make it almost impossible to put them together under one category. According to the World Bank

(1991), between 1950 and 1989 real incomes per head in Asia went up, on average, by 3.6 percent a year. During the same period in Latin America, they went up only one-third as fast, at 1.2 percent a year. Sub-Saharan Africa fared even worse: its real incomes went up by 0.8 percent (and during the past two decades actually fell). In fact, some of these countries, (for example, Cambodia, Ethiopia and Sudan) are not developing at all, and are either stagnating or indeed going backward.

Within various regions, there are even greater disparities. Asia has South Korea and Taiwan at one extreme, and Bangladesh at the other. Latin America has both Bolivia and Argentina.

Thirdly, people and institutions that are one way or another involved in developing countries – such as politicians, industrialists, academics, the UN, the IMF and the World Bank – do not seem to agree on the terminology by which to refer to these countries: 'Third World', 'South', 'undeveloped', 'under-developed', 'less developed', 'not-so-developed', 'developing', and 'industrializing', and so on.

Be that as it may, let us arbitrarily decide that there is a cluster of countries which have a sufficient number of features in common to be cautiously grouped together, and to be called less developed countries (LDCs). Observations by Hernando de Soto, who is an authority on developing countries and is an adviser to the Peruvian president, is interesting in connection with these common characteristics. He is quoted as saying that as he circles the world on business, he is struck by the similarity in the problems that emerging countries face. In Sri Lanka, he delivered a speech in which he used the problems of Peru to illustrate his points. 'When I got down, people came over and said, "That was very clever the way you criticized our leaders here without using their names". They thought I was talking about their country' (*Time*, 9 September 1991: 73).

The following sections discuss some of these common features and their implications for international business.

Common characteristics of the LDCs

Economic objectives
The genesis of the LDCs lies in the fear of domination. Almost all of them, except for a few countries such as Iran, were until a few decades ago the colonies of major imperial powers. Because of this, they see themselves as exploited by their former rulers. For this reason they consider economic growth and

industrialization as one of their top priorities. These objectives, however, have not yet been achieved in many of the LDCs.

Level of GNP

A comparison between LDCs and the industrialized countries is revealing. In terms of GNP, Britain ranks fifth in the Western world after the United States, Japan, Germany and France. Yet Britain has a GNP equivalent to one and one-third times the combined countries on the African continent. The United States' GNP is about eight times that of Britain (Arnold, 1989).

The African LDCs are in the worst situation. According to a World Bank report the gap in per capita income between sub-Saharan Africa and the rest of the LDCs keeps widening. In 1988 the contrast was $330 versus an average $750 for all developing countries. The nations of black Africa, home to 470 million people, together have the purchasing power of Belgium, a country with the population of only 10 million (*Time*, 21 May 1990).

Political instability

Much of the LDCs' development is characterized by violence. In 1988, a rough count showed that about forty wars, revolutions or guerrilla confrontations were taking their toll in the LDCs. Of the major ones nine were in Africa, eight in Asia, five in Latin America and three in the Middle East (Arnold, 1989).

Poverty

More than 1 billion people living in developing countries are in poverty, according to the World Bank – the poverty line being $370 per person a year in these countries (at 1985 prices). On this definition, more than half of the world's poor live in South Asia and well over one-third of them in India alone. For the developing countries as a whole, two-thirds of the people are above the poverty line (*The Economist*, 21 July 1990).

Latecomers' advantage

Developing countries start their industrialization and economic development from an advantage point. They have the opportunity to learn from the experiences of pioneer countries such as the United Kingdom and the United States. Dore (1973) calls this the 'late development syndrome'. Mistakes can to some extent be avoided and rules of the game are there to be mastered and modified to the individual needs of LDCs. In Britain, where the Industrial Revolution originated, industrialization was a long drawn-out slow process which started in the mid-eighteenth century and spread over a period of 200 years. Whereas the LDCs can 'jump' – as did Japan, a country which was an LDC until the Second World War – from a feudal form of corporatism to a modern form of enterprise. Modern management techniques and practices, and advanced technologies are available for the LDCs to pick and choose from and to adjust to their requirements. As Dore (1973: 416) puts it, corporations in the contemporary late starters,

> sending their personnel officers to business schools in Europe and [the United States], begin with industrialization under the influence of human relations theories and 'Y' theories, and theories about the virtues of consultation with workplace representatives.

This late development syndrome has also shortened the length of time needed for a country to move from a state of underdevelopment to a highly advanced one. Britain needed roughly 60 years to do this after 1780 (the early years of the Industrial Revolution), the United States nearly 50 years after 1840, Japan about 35 years after 1885, and South Korea did so in 11 years after 1966 (*The Economist*, 13 July 1991).

Role of the state
A major characteristic of less developed countries is the all-pervasive and crucial role that their governments play in the management of the economy as well as in politics. Almost all the LDCs pursue protectionist industrial and economic policies. And the vast majority of them have centralized non-democratic governments.

Protected industries
One of the major consequences of protected internal markets in LDCs is that business firms do not face any serious competition, especially from abroad. This, in turn, means large market shares and therefore a lack of incentive to spend financial and other resources on research and development activities.

In a comparative study of English and Indian firms, the present author (Tayeb, 1988) found that the English electronics companies which participated in the research had a market share of not larger than 3 or 4 percent, thanks to their German, American and Japanese rivals. But their Indian counterparts had between 50 and 90 percent share of their domestic market in the absence of foreign competitors. As a result, the English companies had specialized departments for R & D in order to meet the challenges posed by their competitors. But none of the Indian firms felt the need for such a specialist function. At the most, they would send their senior managers to attend international exhibitions and conferences in order to learn and come back with new ideas.

Social welfare through industrial policies
Almost all these countries lack an extensive and well-developed national welfare state. People largely depend on their families and other relatives for help when they get old, or are sick or are without a job. Social issues such as poverty, unemployment and even ethnic problems are tackled through economic plans via business organizations.

In India, labour-intensive technologies are encouraged in order to increase the level of employment. Quotas are set for the companies to recruit workers from among lower castes and migrants from rural areas. There are minimum wages regulations and measures which make it almost impossible for managers to sack their manual workers or deduct from their wages even if they do not carry out their tasks properly. This is because, given the tradition of extended family in India, the livelihood of so many depends on the head of the household's earnings that to sack him may mean starvation for several people (Tayeb, 1988).

In Nepal, as in many other LDCs, the government encourages regional economic development and job creation plans by luring industries to the backward areas and by giving industries concessions such as financial help, tax relief and low-cost land (Render et al., 1985).

LDCs and international trade

As we saw in chapter 2, less developed countries are at a disadvantage in international markets compared with their more advanced trade partners. There are many reasons for this. A major reason lies in the nature of what they sell and what they buy. Advanced countries (ACs) export largely finished or semi-finished manufactured goods, the LDCs export mainly raw, non-processed primary commodities. The production and price of manufactured goods can be easily controlled in response to fluctuations in demand, but it is not so easily done for primary commodities. For instance, a car factory can switch from one model to another depending on what customers want. But a farmer producing coffee, whose production depends heavily on climatic conditions, is far less able to control his or her supplies.

Furthermore, the income elasticity of primary products is low, but that of manufactured goods is high. As people's income increases, they can buy more manufactured consumer goods: radio and television sets, music systems, compact discs, washing machines – the list is virtually infinite. But there is only a limited number of lamb chops and cups of coffee that people can consume in a day, regardless of the level of their income.

Also, the cost of manufacturing goods in the ACs has greatly increased in past decades, perhaps because of high energy costs, among others. At the same time, there has been a drastic fall in the price of commodities that the LDCs export. This means that the LDCs earn *less* from their exports while they have to pay *more* for their imports – a poverty trap.

The ACs have a comparative advantage over the LDCs not only in manufactured goods but also in a large number of primary products, mainly because they employ sophisticated advanced technologies and processes. In addition, they are able to control fluctuations in the supply by storing their surplus, for example butter or grain, in modern well-equipped warehouses which are not always available to farm producers in LDCs.

Moreover, ACs impose restrictions, such as quotas and tariffs, on the import of LDCs' semi-finished and processed goods and products, in order to protect their own domestic manufacturers and producers.

As was discussed in chapter 2, there is also the legacy from colonial rule that many of the LDCs have to live with. The colonial powers used to force the LDCs to specialize in primary products for at least two reasons: to provide cheap raw materials for their industries (for example cotton grown in India to supply the mills in the North of England); and to have markets in the LDCs for their manufactured goods. This process prevented the LDCs from producing either for their own food consumption or engaging in industrialization.

But changes have been taking place in recent years. The ACs are gradually losing their markets in the LDCs because the latter now manufacture some of the goods themselves ('import substitution') or import them from other LDCs (for example, the ASEAN trade agreements).

Also, because of the protectionist measures taken by the governments of LDCs, instead of directly exporting their goods to these countries the ACs are having to set up production units in the former. This, as was mentioned earlier, also has the added attraction of availability of cheap raw materials and a low-waged workforce.

For instance, in Sweden the volume of foreign direct investment by manufacturing companies, mainly in LDCs, increased by 12–15 percent a year over the past decade, while manufacturing investment in the internal market was lower in real terms in 1985 than in 1975 (*The Economist*, 21 June 1986). Major Japanese companies in car, shipbuilding, mining and steel industries are shifting production overseas, especially to the South East Asian countries.

Because of their cost advantage over ACs, the less developed countries are more competitive in the areas where they produce similar industrial goods to those produced by the ACs, and the LDCs are making inroads in the latter's market territories. For example, Switzerland, which was once the watchmaker of the world, made only 10 percent of the watches produced in 1985, whereas Asian countries other than Japan produced 50 percent (*The Economist*, 17 May 1986).

The way ahead for LDCs

An examination of the past performance of LDCs shows a trend towards an increase in the production of goods and economic growth. Japan, once a developing country, has grown into the ranks of highly industrialized countries since the Second World War. Japan is certainly not a one-off phenomenon. That country's 'leap forward' from a state of Third World country to one of the most advanced nations may well be repeated by other developing countries in the future. This is already happening in many cases.

Within the last three decades or so the East Asian Five Dragons have achieved spectacular economic growth. In South Korea between 1962 and 1976 the GDP grew at an average rate of 10 percent and the industrial production at 18 percent. Malaysia, Singapore, Taiwan and Thailand have also achieved similar economic success. Brazil too has enjoyed an average growth rate of 7 percent in the past 25 years, and is now the world's ninth largest producer of cars and the seventh largest in steel production. In agriculture it ranks among those right on the top (Tayeb, 1987b). These countries are certainly knocking on the doors of the developed nations.

Some 25 years ago India was perceived as economically backward, with rapid population growth and starvation staring it in the face. It is now the ninth most industrialized country in the world and is self-sufficient in many respects. India, a heavily populated country, has successfully utilized its human resource assets in the realm of software development, among other things, and has exploited this niche with increasing success. There is no reason why the expansion of LDCs' economies should not continue. African countries appear to be at the stage where India was three decades ago (Harrison, 1987). These countries currently have immense problems, including not being able to feed themselves, but there are indications that solutions for these problems are to hand and that an agricultural base may be established from which an industrial base could be developed.

Many of the LDCs have rich and extensive reserves of minerals and other natural resources (for example, oil in the Middle East, rubber in Malaysia, timber in the tropical forests of Latin American countries). Many of these countries, which were colonies in the past, have now more control over their resources and increasingly use them in their own manufacturing sectors. Also, because of the largely non-democratic and non-accountable political regimes in the majority of these countries, they are less constrained by the general public and pressure groups, and are therefore freer to extract and use their virgin raw materials.

One of the main obstacles to the LDCs' rapid economic development and progress is poor infrastructure and a shortage of capital, but these countries are being assisted by multinational companies in this respect. Considerations such as relative freedom of action, cheap labour, close geographical proximity to raw materials, and tax concessions have attracted the multinationals to locate their processing and production units in the LDCs. In doing so, these companies have spawned both capital and infrastructure in the host countries.

The LDCs' growth could also be accelerated dramatically by advanced techniques such as computer integrated manufacture (CIM). As was mentioned earlier, less developed countries do not have to go through the long-drawn out process of developing new technologies. They can employ the most advanced production techniques readily available to them, and take it from there. The main advantage of new technologies, such as CIM, is that they come as a package with a built-in management control system, they are adaptable, and can be handled with minimal know-how and industrial expertise. This suits the conditions prevalent in most LDCs.

A major issue confronting the aspiring LDCs is to choose the best way to promote growth in their economies. Is it better to encourage trade, exposing domestic producers to foreign competition; or to discourage it, shielding producers until they can compete?

Liberal traders such as Hong Kong, Taiwan, South Korea and Singapore have achieved startling rates of growth. Followers of the protectionist model – including, until recently, Mexico, Brazil and Argentina – have grown far more slowly. A study by the World Bank looked at thirty-six reform programmes in nineteen countries. It concluded that the successful programmes were those that had moved away from quotas as a way of controlling imports, were strong and radical, involved a devaluation of currency and avoided loose fiscal policy (*The Economist*, 27 October 1990).

Since the early 1980s many LDCs, especially those that had debt problems such as Mexico and Peru, have had to undertake structural adjustment measures to open their external trade systems in order to obtain loans from the World Bank and the IMF. The process entails taking steps to rationalize public sector enterprises, to make the tax system more efficient, to ease restrictions on foreign investment, and to deregulate specific economic activities. Trade liberalization is intended to reduce the coverage of import licensing and tariffs. The same pressure has also been exerted on the sub-Saharan African LDCs (Zaïre, Benin, Gabon, Ivory Coast, Tanzania, Zambia) by the IMF to liberalize their economy and to introduce democratic political systems. However, it remains to be seen how far such processes can be implemented and sustained.

Opportunities and constraints for international business

Cheap labour, untapped markets, abundant raw materials, tax concessions, and strategic locations are some of the major attractions of LDCs for international companies.

Constraints are mainly caused by limitations and shortcomings in infrastructure such as transport and telecommunications. Then there is a marked shortage of know-how, technological support and back-up services in most of these countries. A further constraint is found in the government bureaucracies. As was mentioned earlier, in many of the LDCs the initiative to plan and implement industrial and other economic changes and 'leaps forward' is, understandably, taken by their respective governments. This, in many cases, has resulted in huge bureaucracies which are too deeply caught in the web of procedures and rules to be able to move fast enough to do what they were set up to do in the first place (Luck and Tayeb, 1985).

In some of these countries if, for instance, you want to set up a business, or export your products, or import your badly needed capital goods, you need to climb a bureaucratic 'mountain' to get a licence. You have to find your way through a lengthy and frustrating series of rules and regulations and will be pushed around by officials between various governmental departments for many months. National and regional development plans more often than not get 'bogged down' in paperwork, endless committee meetings and referral back to and from higher up officials.

Parallel economy and black money are another all pervasive and tremendously influential factor in the socio-economic life of many of the LDCs. In India (Mehta, 1989), for example, this great money power is used to create and finance pressure groups. It also provides political finance for elections and other such activities. Therefore, it is not possible to judge government policies by stated goals and priorities alone.

Vietnam is a good example of an LDC which offers opportunities and poses challenging constraints to the international managers dealing with it. This country, with its GDP officially estimated at $120 a head, is one of the world's poorest nations and is ruled by a communist party which is determined not to go the liberalizing way of Eastern Europe. The country's new Prime Minister, however, is believed to have 'liberal' economic views and is keen to open up the economy to some extent.

But Vietnam is in the right place – the centre of the world's fastest growing economic region (*The Economist*, 7 April 1990). It has many unplundered natural resources, from timber to coal, plus the possibility of large oil and gas reserves. Its 65 million people work for low wages: average pay in a foreign-owned low-tech factory is $30 a month, half that in nearby Thailand.

Another lure is Vietnam's open approach to foreign investment. Foreign companies can repatriate all of their profit at the official exchange rate, which is now based on a more realistic black-market rate. For the first four years those profits will not be taxed.

However, most of the joint ventures are cautious about doing business in Vietnam. Its infrastructure is woeful, especially in the North, and its bureaucracy oppressive. Foreign investors face other problems as well. After years of economic management by a communist government, Vietnam has no laws to regulate free markets. Emerging entrepreneurs, foreign or local, are left at the mercy of local officials. Furthermore, the rules governing what is allowed or forbidden change very frequently. Bribery is often the only way to make life predictable.

Newly industrialized countries

The newly industrialized countries (NICs) of South East Asia are becoming an increasingly competitive and formidable force to be reckoned with. They have made inroads in the markets which have hitherto been regarded as the domain of Japanese and Western companies.

The South East Asian NICs are former LDCs that have achieved their aspirations through mainly export-led development and openness to foreign direct investment. They are Hong Kong, South Korea, Taiwan, Singapore, Indonesia, Thailand and Malaysia. They are sometimes referred to as the Asian Dragons or Asian Tigers, and are included in various combinations in wider regional clusters such as the Pacific Rim, the Asia–Pacific and the ASEAN.

There were several factors which gave these countries a comparative advantage in many manufacturing and service areas and contributed to their spectacular economic take-off.

First, they achieved their growth through export. Taiwan and South Korea, for instance, have few natural resources, little arable land, and the highest population densities of any country save Bangladesh and the city-states of Hong Kong and Singapore. The one policy that both have pursued is to be export oriented. This simply means that they did not handicap their exports in world markets. As we saw earlier, almost all developing countries do this, by bans, quotas or tariffs on imported goods. One of the disadvantages of trade restriction is that it both makes the home market more attractive to a would-be exporter, and also raises the cost of their imported input, so hampering them if they try to sell abroad.

In partnership with the Japanese, South Korean and Taiwanese firms have penetrated new markets. In the period from 1989 to 1990, when the value of world trade expanded by an annual average of 13 percent, Thailand increased its exports by 31 percent, Malaysia by 23 percent and Indonesia by 15 percent (*The Economist*, 8 September 1990).

Secondly, some, but not all, of the NICs adopted an open approach towards foreign direct investment. Unlike many of the LDCs, they actively encouraged foreign direct investment

Box 11   *Indonesia's magnetic pull*

The rise in foreign and domestic investment in Indonesia over the past three years has been little short of phenomenal. In the past three years, foreign investment approvals represented almost half of the total 1,795 projects, worth $38.7 billion.

Mr Sanyoto Sastrowardoyo, chairman of Indonesia's Investment Coordinating Board (BKPM), says there are many reasons for the investment increase. But he highlights Indonesia's deregulation and depreciation policy, the country's competitive advantage, abundant and diversified raw materials and the absence of foreign exchange controls. To these might be added perceived political stability and a large but underdeveloped domestic market.

While higher domestic investment levels reflect growing confidence in the local economy – somewhat tempered recently by high interest rates – the most important factor explaining the rise in foreign investment is probably Indonesia's competitive advantages – a magnetic pull which attracted waves of foreign investment, particularly from Japan and Asia's newly industrialized countries in search of cheaper manufacturing bases for their exports. 'In the last three years most of the new foreign investment projects have been export-oriented', says the BKPM chairman.

Indonesia's low wage rates and the country's favoured status under the US Generalized System of Preferences are critical factors. Officially, the average hourly wage rate in Indonesia is about 23 cents, compared with 50 cents an hour in Thailand, $3.45 in South Korea and $2.60 in Japan.

Indonesia is fast becoming the offshore manufacturing base of choice for Japan and other industrialized nations. It may even be poised to outflank its chief rivals in the region, Malaysia and Thailand.

Predictably, Japan headed the list of Indonesia's foreign investors in 1990 followed by Hong Kong, South Korea and Taiwan. Singaporean investments are also rising, quadrupling in the last four years and totalling $265 million in 1990 alone. Mr Barry Desker, Singapore's ambassador to Indonesia, says the increase shows that economic deregulation measures taken by Indonesia since 1984 'have begun to bear fruit' and that the exchange rate devaluations and depreciation together with reforms 'sharply increased the incentives to export'. Unlike some of its regional competitors, Indonesia does not give tax breaks to foreign investors. 'It seemed to us that tax privileges were not the primary reason for investment here', says the BKPM chairman.

Nevertheless, Indonesia has established an investment framework which has proved very attractive.

In particular, Indonesia has no foreign exchange controls; tariff barriers have been lowered and import duty concessions are available for machinery and raw materials; bonded free trade zones have been established in Jakarta and Batam; new investment protection accords have been signed with several countries, most recently South Korea; immigration rules for expatriate workers have been eased and foreign joint venture companies producing for export have been allowed greater levels of foreign ownership.

Moreover, the procedures for applying for investment permission have been simplified and streamlined. In May 1989 long-standing barriers to foreign investment were eliminated by replacing a complex list of areas open to investors with a simple 'negative list' specifying just nine areas in which foreign investment is totally prohibited and a further sixty-six areas where it is permitted only if production is earmarked for export.

There are, however, constraints on Indonesia's future direct investment potential. Chief among these are infrastructure problems.

Indonesia's telephone service is notoriously unreliable, electricity is in short supply, ports are congested and efforts to attract investment to 'go east', away from overcrowded Jakarta and Java, have been stymied by inadequate road and transport systems. In addition, while Indonesia's 78 million workforce is adept at learning new skills, some employers complain that professional managers, accountants and others are in short supply.

Many of these problems are as pressing in other rapidly industrializing countries in the region, particularly Thailand. They will need addressing if Indonesia is to continue to attract more foreign investment to develop its economy and provide new jobs and training opportunities.

Source: Financial Times, 22 March 1991

without foreign ownership in their economies. Singapore's offer of generous tax breaks to foreign investors three decades ago lured major oil refineries. These have made the country the world's third largest refining centre, after Houston and Rotterdam, even though the island republic produces no petroleum of its own and consumes only 10 percent of its refinery output (*Time*, 30 July 1990). This policy is still pursued to date.

The primary attraction of Thailand, Malaysia and Indonesia for foreign investors was these countries' low-cost production sites and a highly skilled workforce.

South Korea, however, only recently decided to open up its territory to foreign direct investment and to allow a very limited entry as of January 1992. No single investor can hold more than 5 percent of a South Korean company, and total foreign ownership in any company is limited to 10 percent. Major industries such as steel, electricity and finance are closed to foreign investors altogether.

Thirdly, cultural, political and economic characteristics, such as a strong commitment to public education and a neutral role for religion have been major reasons behind the success of Asian Dragons and their would-be imitators in the region (Schlossstein, 1991). These countries have highly skilled, committed and loyal workforces which are prepared to sacrifice themselves for the good of the company to a far greater extent than are their counterparts in other LDCs (and indeed in Western advanced countries). As West (1989: 5) puts it,

> East Asia can point with pride to the more accurate measure of economic vitality, their increasing rates of productivity. Here we confront the East Asia edge as a reflection not of trade surpluses but of ideas about work, loyalty to their country, and notions about the future. East Asia cultures have turned on its head the long-held claim that successful modernization was somehow linked to the 'particularistic' values associated with Western thought.

Herman Kahn stated it boldly in 1979 when he said the Confucian ethic was playing a 'similar but more spectacular role in the modernization of East Asia than the Protestant ethic played in Europe' (see also Weber, 1930). These 'non-Confucian countries', Kahn (1979: 185) added, 'now outperform the West'.

Fourthly, as industrialists, these nations are very entrepreneurial, aggressive and competitive, and keep an eye for new opportunities and new markets. For instance, Thailand, which has the region's most flexible and vigorous private sector, was very quick to react to the Persian Gulf crisis in late 1990 and early 1991. With a characteristically sharp eye for the main chance, the country's Prime Minister exhorted Thai businesspeople to sell fruit juice to Coalition soldiers stationed in the Persian Gulf (*The Economist*, 8 September 1990).

Fifthly, as late developers, the NICs utilized modern techniques and high technology in their efforts to pursue their policies and to achieve their economic objectives. Singapore is typical of the Asian Tigers. Lacking in major natural resources, Singapore must trade to survive. The information technology industry makes a crucial contribution to those export efforts and, in the process, it has modernized the entire business infrastructure. Indeed, Singapore owes its strategic position in the international trading network to its electronic links to global markets. To capitalize on the full potential of information technology, Singapore formed a National Computer Board in 1981. Its objective was to establish Singapore as an international computer software services centre. Singapore has also poured millions of dollars into its utilities and infrastructure (for example, modern highways, an excellent underground system) and has under-written R & D and office/science parks.

Finally, political stability in these countries in the past three decades or so has also played a significant role in their economic success. Their governments have pushed through development policies single mindedly, resisting pressures from special interest groups. Land reforms, for instance, were carried out in Taiwan by a dictator (Chiang Kai-shek), and in South Korea by a government carried along by a wave of public anger at collaborators with the Japanese colonizers.

These countries, even though they have the appearance of a democracy, and now respect civil liberties, have pursued an authoritarian regime throughout the period of their industrialization and economic take-off. It was only in 1987 that the South Korean street riots drove the military out of office. Taiwanese gradual political reform started in the early 1980s and culminated in the end of martial law and a much freer electoral system as recently as 1988. Singapore is still a virtual 'benign autocracy'. It is interesting to note that political reforms in these countries began only after they had achieved a high level of prosperity and growth.

There is, however, a shadow of political instability hanging over Hong Kong, which is currently a British colony and which is due to be handed over to its original owner, China, in 1997. Given the sharp contrast between the political and economic systems of Hong Kong and China, there is no absolute guarantee that the highly liberalized and entrepreneurial economy of Hong Kong will be allowed to continue unabated, in spite of all the official assurances. Many entrepreneurs and skilled men and women have left the country or are in the process of doing so. The future for this Dragon remains uncertain.

12
Japan

The success of Japanese managers in the past few decades has encouraged many businesspeople to attempt to reorganize their companies' management structure on a Japanese model, in part at least. Concepts such as quality circle, teamwork, and just-in-time, which are associated with most Japanese organizations, are becoming the in-words in business circles.

There is a school of thought which argues that we have now entered a post-modern era as far as the management of work organizations are concerned. A major characteristic of this new era is that such Western-inspired management principles as specialization of functions and roles, hierarchical structure, promotion on the basis of performance and so forth, are increasingly being replaced by Japanese-style management practices (Clegg, 1992).

Many academic researchers have been (and are) engaged in studying Japanese organizations in an attempt to establish whether or not Japan's distinctive culture accounts for the success of Japanese companies.

In view of the significant role that the Japanese economy plays in the international market and the increasing attention which is paid to Japanese management practices, this chapter is devoted to Japanese culture and Japanese organizations and explores the extent to which their management styles can be employed elsewhere.

Major features of Japanese organizations and their management practices which have captured the attention of Western researchers and managers are: flexible working arrangements, an emphasis on high product quality and low wastage, long-term planning, collective decision making, concern for employees' well-being, lifetime employment, a high degree of employee commitment and loyalty, teamwork and enterprise–union contracts.

What makes Japanese organizations so different in many respects from their Western counterparts? Is it their culture? Can Western companies adopt Japanese management styles successfully? An appropriate starting point would be to explore the salient characteristics of Japanese culture, especially those which are related to workplace behaviour, and then to examine the extent to which they influence Japanese organizations.

Japanese culture

Collectivism

Japanese society is characterized by a strong sense of group and community. A typical Japanese person's loyalty is to his or her own group or team, and has no great willingness to accept influence from those outside it (Nakane, 1973). The scope of one's own group, or what Triandis (1981) calls 'in-group', includes not only one's family, relatives and friends, but also, it seems, one's work organization.

The extent of Japanese collectivism can be illustrated by comparing the in-groups in individualist nations such as Britain or the United States and even in a collectivist culture like that of India, with that in Japan. The in-group in Britain or the United States includes only the immediate nuclear family – spouse, children and sometimes parents. In India, in-groups not only include the immediate family, but also the extended one – grandparents, brothers, sisters, uncles, aunts, nephews, nieces and close friends. In Japan, there is an additional member in the in-group: the company for which a person works.

One of the paradoxes that every Japanese person has to face is how to be a winner in a society that encourages group loyalty and discourages individual assertiveness (Buruma, 1985). The Japanese in school, business and industry have long known the answer to this problem: compete as a member of a group, rather than as an individual.

Endurance

The concept of endurance is fundamental to the Japanese, and owes much to their notion of *bushido* or the way of the warrior. To follow in the footsteps of their illustrious ancestors, the Japanese must be exponents of *seishinshugi* – the victory of spirit over material things. *Seishinshugi* or *konjo*, as Buruma (1985: 139) explains, 'involves a Zen-like suppression of reason and personal feelings, a blind devotion to direct action and an infinite capacity for hardship and pain'.

While most Japanese only aspire to *seishinshugi*, many are masters of *gaman*, the modern equivalent, which involves the resigned acceptance of hardship without complaint. Complaint is anathema to the Japanese: not only does it show the wrong spirit, but it also involves the kind of blunt communication they prefer to avoid (Briggs, 1988).

Indebtedness

The Japanese have a strong sense of duty and indebtedness, *on*. Ruth Benedict (1946) identifies two types of *on* repayment: *gimu* and *giri*. Each of these can be broken down into a number of obligations, some of which are: duty to one's work; duty to one's superiors; duties to non-related persons because of the *on* received; and one's duty to oneself – to admit no failure or ignorance, no loss of face.

This sense of obligation and repayment of *on* can sometimes span generations. The present author was once told by a Japanese acquaintance that his great-grandfather had helped build a house for a neighbour. Generations later, the great-grandson of that neighbour helped my Japanese friend financially to complete his studies at university.

Absence of horizontal social groupings

Japanese society, unlike many other modern countries, is not stratified horizontally by class or caste. The overall picture of the society is that of vertical stratification by institution or group of institutions. For example, a shopfloor technician does not identify him- or herself with all the technicians in the country or with the working class in general. He or she identifies him- or herself with his or her work organization and all those people who work below and above within it.

Japanese enterprise unions are a manifestation of this vertical structure. As Nakane (1973: 90) puts it,

> even if social classes like those in Europe can be detected in Japan, and even if something vaguely resembling those classes that are illustrated in the textbooks of Western sociology can also be found in Japan, the point is that it does not really reflect the social structure. In Japanese society it is really not a matter of workers' struggles against capitalist or managers but of Company A ranged against Company B.

Observance of social status

The absence of a Western-type class structure, however, does not mean an absence of status differentiation and of its acknowledgement. Status is clearly signalled in other ways, such as the extent to which one bows when meeting others, sitting arrangements at tables, order of serving meals, the time given to people to speak in groups, and the terms one uses to address people of different ages and professions.

Japanese language itself is such that the relative status of any two speakers is signalled immediately (Briggs, 1988). The correct behaviour is so important that if they do not know each others' professional status, on being introduced to one another they immediately exchange business cards to know where everybody stands.

The present author's experience at work with a Japanese colleague a few years ago is quite revealing in this respect. We used to share an office for a short while. I was much younger than he was, and, at the time, junior to him professionally. Moreover, since I am a woman, he regarded me as inferior to him anyway. As a result, he never addressed me by anything other than 'eh', 'oy', or 'you'. Also, he always expected me to offer him a cup of coffee whenever I made one for myself, but he never did the same for me! It was interesting, however, to note his extreme deference to and respect for my senior male colleagues.

The business climate

Industrial structure

One of the features of Japanese economy is the large families of firms with interlocking stakes in one another, known as *keiretsu*, which have long dominated the business environment. Six prominent *keiretsu* (a network of firms centred on the Mitsui, Mitsubishi and Sumitomo trading groups and the Fuji, Sanwa and Dai-Ichi Kangyo banking empires) group together 12,000 companies which between them have sales equivalents to a quarter of Japan's GNP (*The Economist*, 5 January 1991).

The origins of the *keiretsu* go back to the rise of Japan's great banking families in the nineteenth century. By the 1930s the country's bankers had built vast mining-to-manufacturing conglomerates, known as *zaibatsu*, which became the driving force of Japanese militarism. After the war, American occupation authorities disbanded the *zaibatsu*, but many of these companies later regrouped themselves after the Americans had left and restrictions on cross-holdings and other ties were relaxed.

Today *keiretsu* companies often coordinate their investment plans, employment practices and even political donations. The old-style conglomerates based around a bank which emerged from the pre-war *zaibatsu* differ markedly from newer groups that have spring up since the Second World War. The former tend to be more loosely affiliated and more diversified. The latter are more specialized, and usually based on a single large manufacturer. The predominance of *keiretsu* groups often acts as a brake on competition in Japan (*The Economist*, 5 January 1991).

Subcontracting relationships

Japan has 6.5 million businesses, excluding agriculture. Of these only 46,000 can loosely be described as large corporations. The rest are small- to medium-sized firms. The vast majority of these – some 5.6 million firms in all – are in services and other tertiary fields. The remaining 900,000 have traditionally been the loyal burden-sharers for Japanese manufacturing (*The Economist*, 27 October 1990).

The subcontracting relationship spreads down a tiered structure, with the principal firm at the apex, followed by a small number of large subcontracting firms, then a tier consisting of a large number of smaller firms, and so on. The number of tiers in each set of relationships could be as large as seven or eight. Figure 12.1 illustrates this tiered structure.

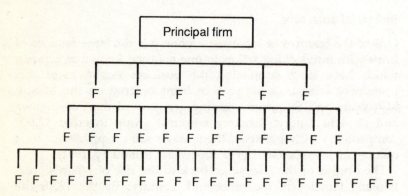

F   subcontracting firm

Figure 12.1   *Japanese subcontracting structure*

These small subcontracting firms supply components to large manufacturers, and are highly dependent on their more powerful partners for business. In the times of poor trade and economic downturn, the large firms usually protect themselves by squeezing their subcontractors for lower prices and by exporting any adjustment of employment to them. In other words, the large firms take their subcontracted work back in-house and small subcontractors are made to absorb the unemployment costs, by making some of their workforce redundant.

This situation is gradually changing. A recent study by the Ministry of International Trade and Industry (MITI) shows that the ratio of smaller firms operating as subcontractors declined in 1987 to 56 percent. A few years before, 65 percent of Japan's smaller firms earned their living out of subcontracting. Probably less than half do so today (*The Economist*, 27 October 1990).

Enterprise unionism

Trade unions in Japan are company-based. For example, Toyota has its own union, Nissan its own, and Hitachi its own. Compare this with Britain, where unions are craft-based, that is, transport and general workers have their own union (T & GWU), coal miners their own (NUM), teachers their own (NUT), and so on.

In a Japanese company there is only one union. Again compare this with a typical British manufacturing company, whose workers are represented by a number of unions, depending on the number of crafts or professions that the workers and employees perform.

The principal characteristics of enterprise unions are that membership is limited to regular employees, temporaries and part-timers being excluded; both white and blue collar workers are organized into the same union; union officers are elected from among the workforce, retaining employee status but being paid by the union; and most are affiliated to some external federation, but retain almost exclusive sovereignty locally.

Shirai (1983) reckons that the origins of enterprise unionism go back to the 1920s, and they are sustained to date because workers prefer this form of representation to any other on offer. This is principally due to their enterprise consciousness, itself brought about because of Japan's heavy dependence on imports of energy, raw materials and food. This has made, he argues, most union leaders acutely conscious of the competitiveness and productivity of their industries. Most of them believe that in the long run the employment security and improvement of working and living conditions of their members crucially depend upon how their industry improves its position in changing world markets. As a result, the enterprise unions generally have a cooperative attitude toward management, although in substantive terms they appear to serve their members well.

The character of unions and management is moulded by the company culture, and the relationship between the two sides, if they can be described as two sides, are based on cooperation and harmony. *The Economist* (25 March 1989: 94, 96) illustrates this point well:

> In the ritual *shunto* (spring labour offensive) the unions will demand a 6–8% pay rise. Equally ritually, Nikkeiren (the Japan Federation of Employers) will say that wages can go up by no more than 3%; and that any cut in working hours must come from improved productivity. Given last year's record profit (up 23% over 1987), the two sides will haggle, the unions will apologize, go on strike for five minutes and then split the difference with the employers, settling for a 5–5.5% rise plus a modest reduction in working hours. All very civilized.

Management practices

The ringi *method of decision making*

This involves a great deal of informal consultation and problem solving, leading to the preparation of a written proposal which is circulated first to those who would be affected by the implementation of the proposal and then to senior management. *Ringi* methods are very time consuming and are thus increasingly used only for more important decisions (Misumi, 1984).

Employees, especially at the operating level, are also encouraged, indeed expected, to take part in the decision-making processes by putting their suggestions for improvement or new ideas into a suggestion box located prominently in the company premises. Some companies, Toyota for instance, have a very high weekly rate of suggestions (Kamata, 1983). Some attribute this to the fact that the shame for each individual is considerable should he or she fail to make the requisite number of suggestions, and that this might be exacerbated by the introduction of group pressure, and the consequent danger of 'letting one's colleagues down' (Briggs, 1988).

Most ideas, however, never make it as far as the top senior managers and are quietly shelved by middle managers unwilling to risk offering their own endorsement. The new ideas that do get through this process are put into effect with speed.

Quality circles

A quality circle, which is a vehicle for employee participation, is a small-group activity in which ordinary blue- and white-collar workers, usually employed on broadly similar work and led by their supervisor, volunteer to participate. Such volunteers are trained in problem-identification and problem-solving techniques. Quality circle members may identify problems to solve themselves, or these may be suggested by others. Either way it is generally the members who select which specific problem to work on. Applying the training they have been given, they analyse the problem and try to arrive at solutions to it. The circle formally presents its analysis and findings to management who may accept or reject the recommendations. If its proposals are accepted and implemented, the circle will monitor progress for a period of time, making adjustments where appropriate, before moving on to another project (Hill, 1987).

Inherent in a quality circle programme are the characteristics which have been related to the interest in the work and to job satisfaction. These are: the opportunity to apply a wider range of skills and abilities on the job; the opportunity for additional training and learning; wider scope for creativity; greater responsibility for one's own work; and more control over working methods (Mento 1982).

As Strier (1984) points out, it is important to note that the success of the Japanese quality circle technique is sustained by certain other management practices, such as: lifetime employment, which in the large industrial conglomerates creates a stable work environment with virtually no fear of unemployment; the seniority wage system, which encourages loyalty to the firm; and a higher propensity to invest in the extensive training which the Japanese consider is required to prepare employees for meaningful participation in an initiative such as quality circles.

Lifetime employment

Lifetime employment, or *nenko*, is not a matter of law but normal practice in all major enterprises. In its pure form this would mean that employees are hired on leaving full-time education and remain with the same company for the duration of their working lives, undertaking a range of jobs and in many cases progressing up the hierarchy.

However, *nenko* is operated only by large firms, and therefore applies to no more than one-third of Japan's labour force (Oh, 1976). Many of the large organizations employ large numbers of temporary employees who are not entitled to membership of the company union, nor to any of the other benefits extended to permanent employees (Collick, 1981). Also excluded from lifetime job contracts are women employees (see below, p. 178).

Seniority wage principle

Workers join the company at a relatively low starting salary, related to age and educational standard, which then rises gradually and by increment until retirement. The wage itself is not dependent upon the level of work done. It is the award of bonuses which relate to individual performance and the company profits, and thus provides an additional monetary incentive since these can in total add about a third of the earnings (Briggs, 1988; OECD, 1977).

Employee commitment to company

The Japanese see the company as a family which is primarily a social entity though operating in an economic environment. This contrasts with the West where a firm is overwhelmingly an economic entity (Sasaki, 1981). This unitary ideology of 'the company' is reinforced by the system of lifetime employment, linked to a seniority system, which determines progress up the status/wage scale, and to the company benefits to which the employee is entitled. Moreover, employees are explicitly rewarded for 'desirable' behaviour, and ostracized should they display attitudes not in keeping with the company philosophy. In other words, all of the workers understand the need for loyalty and obedience to the firm (Briggs, 1988).

However, economic facts of life have eroded much of the employee long-time commitment to company. A combination of a very low unemployment rate, 2 percent, and shortages of skills has resulted in fierce competition between employers for qualified employees in recent years. As a consequence, technical high flyers and new mid-career recruits are indifferent to corporate traditions, and few of them care about dedicating the rest of their lives to the company. Equipped with technical, linguistic or artistic skills that older workers never acquired, younger workers are changing jobs more frequently. By instinct, they are job-hoppers, part-timers, moonlighters, and even telecommuters (*The Economist*, 4 March 1989 and 10 August 1991).

There are some executives who try to reinforce corporate loyalty by building ever more luxurious company-owned housing, sports centres and resorts for staff. Such perks are difficult to give up even for the promise of a higher salary. Moreover, employers appear to have fostered loyalty so well that even though job-hopping is increasing, only 3.5 percent of workers in 1989–90 switched companies (*Financial Times*, 20 February 1991).

Teamwork

Teamwork and a consensus style of management are often regarded as a distinctive characteristic of Japanese companies. Employees are said to view themselves as members of a community rather than hired labour (Marchington and Parker, 1987). Many other observers (for example, Bradley and Hill, 1983; Ouchi, 1981; White and Trevor, 1983) also stress the importance of consensus and teamwork, of managers attempting to seek the approval of their subordinates in reaching decisions, and in the processes attached to discussions between workers and their foremen.

Wickens (1985) argues that the early morning meetings held in Japanese companies are not for their obvious media description as fitness and exercise sessions, but for their team building aspects. Employee involvement at the task level is seen as a normal feature of affairs, as too is a commitment to the team. Japanese managers are able to harness this group-orientation, one obvious example being the quality circle.

One of the factors which contributes to the cohesion among team members is their strong sense of obligation, not only to each other but also to their immediate supervisor. In turn, the supervisor's debt to his or her workers develops as a result of their contributions to his or her success. A senior member of staff who attains promotion will not forget the junior member whose contribution was so valuable. It is seldom that a favour will go unacknowledged (Briggs, 1988).

This system clearly helps to bind a working team together; so much so that it is often assumed that Japanese workers are exceptional in the extent to which they develop close personal ties with their colleagues. However, research does not always support this viewpoint (Lincoln et al., 1981).

The just-in-time practice

The *kanban* method of production, or just-in-time, involves a finely tuned scheduling system, where stocks are supplied only when needed, and work in progress is closely controlled. The system also encourages a modular organization of work, where members of a team are responsible for the completion of any one stage in the production process.

The success of module production is dependent on a social organization for the production process intended to make workers feel obliged to contribute to the economic performance of the enterprise and to identify with its competitive success (Turnbull, 1986). The Japanese are clearly masters at fostering this sense of obligation.

Another important factor contributing to the success of the just-in-time practice in Japanese companies is the special subcontracting relationships that exists among large firms and their 'satellites', whereby the companies involved synchronize their operations. As a result, delivery times are met, and components and other input materials arrive just in time to go on to the production line.

Just-in-time techniques are an integral aspect of controlling materials and inventory costs. Developing appropriate management techniques to implement just-in-time would encompass not only setting up manufacturing and computer systems for the purpose of control, but staff education and the integration of information systems as well. The implicit intent of just-in-time is to reduce waste and cost.

Women in Japanese companies

Women in Japan face discrimination in almost all areas of employment (Taylor, 1983). Companies almost always expect women to retire upon marriage, and those women who fail to find a husband within a 'suitable' period following graduation will find few companies willing to consider offering promotion. Even within occupations such as kindergarten and primary school teaching, considered traditional for women, employment contracts are often offered on a yearly basis, and can be terminated without notice (Briggs, 1988).

The content of work is another area in which women are discriminated against. Despite the passing of equal opportunities laws in 1986, most companies make only token efforts to recruit women on the same basis as men. Even women admitted into previously male-only management streams often feel they are treated as second-class citizens. Women's wages are on average about 50 percent of men's, compared with 65 percent in the United Kingdom (*Financial Times*, 20 February 1991).

A shortage of male recruits is forcing new companies, including many foreign-owned groups, to give women responsible posts. But in conservative organizations, progress is slow, given the innate belief of many male managers that a woman's job in the office is to run errands. According to a *Financial Times* commentator Japan has some of the world's most highly-qualified tea ladies. On a recent visit to Mitsubishi Bank, he was offered a drink by a female graduate management trainee who spoke four languages.

Leadership style

It is widely held that managerial practices in Japan are more employee-centred than those in the West, that is, more reliant upon collective decisions made with the interests of the worker uppermost. Moreover, because of a commitment to training and (where possible) lifetime employment, Japanese employers are believed to treat their workers as a valuable resource (*The Economist*, 25 March 1989).

The principle of job rotation also contributes to a better management–employee relationship. Managers are recruited straight from university and trained in-house by rotation between different departments, dealing with specific company problems. The early stages of rotation involve experience of working on the shopfloor, which improves communications and reduces 'them and us' attitudes.

However, as was discussed above, while there is evidence that decision making is more diffuse within Japanese companies (Pascale, 1978), there is little reason to suppose that the managers themselves are more human-centred in their outlook (Briggs, 1988). Mouton and Blake (1970), for instance, found that after five-day workshops, Japanese managers were more prone to characterize themselves as 9,1 (production-centred, scoring 9 on production and 1 on concern for employees) than were managers of most other nationalities. Hofstede's (1980) characterization of Japanese managers as 'masculine' and Bass and Burger's (1979) and White and Trevor's (1983) portrayal of the 'task-centred' management that they found in Japanese companies fit the same picture.

But, some argue that the Japanese management looks task-centred when seen by Western eyes, or by Japanese who have been influenced by Western concepts (Smith, 1984). But even so, employee relations has never been ranked by the Japanese firms higher than third or fourth in priority – after market share, new product development and finance (*The Economist*, 10 August 1991).

Classless organizations

Japanese companies operate a rigidly hierarchical system (Smith, 1984), but the barriers between blue- and white-collar workers are not synonymous with class, as in Britain (Dore, 1973; White and Trevor, 1983). Class markers such as different dining rooms, segmented car parks, and others are absent. Open-plan offices accommodate directors and other senior managers together with the rank and file employees under the same roof. This illustrates the 'egalitarian' nature of the Japanese management system. However, Briggs (1988) argues that the absence of these class markers is misleading, since status is so clearly signalled in other ways. For instance, the finely graded hierarchy which exists within the organizations is explicitly mirrored in the language, and is thus apparent to all.

Recent trends in management practices

Japan's largest companies have long nurtured, and one might even say exploited, almost feudal reserves of loyalty, devotion and dependence in the core group of technical and managerial workers who have been most responsible for their country's competitiveness. This approach proved phenomenally successful when Japanese companies were concerned largely with making or processing things, especially in the steel, chemical, shipbuilding and motor industries.

However, for the past decade Japanese manufacturers, like their competitors in the United States and Europe, have been shifting much of their attention away from honing their production processes to applying new information-processing technologies and competing fast-growing service businesses.

With a chronic shortage of labour, the biggest problem for Japanese companies is not closing down old smoke-stack businesses but retraining spare manufacturing hands to become skilled knowledge workers, and retaining their technical 'job-hopping' high flyers.

Such changes are forcing Japanese managers to rethink many of their time-honoured practices, including rigid, seniority-based pay systems; regular job-rotation; consensus-forming rituals; and their choice of university graduates. For example, in order to compete in businesses that require more individual initiative and less teamwork, Japanese firms are looking for a new breed of manager. In the past the ideal managers were those who were not necessarily strong leaders but simply good coordinators. Now they have to be far more entrepreneurial and innovative as well. Also, diversified companies such as Nissan, offer employees a chance to move from their more traditional divisions to fast-growing parts of the company such as mobile telecommunications, regardless of their seniority (*The Economist*, 10 August 1991).

How Japanese are Japanese organizations?

There is clearly considerable coherence and continuity between many of the Japanese management practices discussed above and the culture of Japanese people in general. But we need to examine whether such practices, even if typical of many, especially large organizations, are either inherently Japanese in origin, or are indeed exclusive to Japan.

The heavily culturalist interpretation of Japanese management practices has certainly been disputed (Child and Tayeb, 1983). For instance, Japan's so-called lifetime employment might have an element of cultural continuity within Japan. But it has also at times been instituted by large Western oligopolistic firms in the light of political economy factors, notably in the first half of this century. In a period of growing labour militancy and high labour turnover, these firms would attempt to secure labour commitment through offering job security and regular promotion (Littler, 1982; 1983).

Moreover, the contemporary Japanese industrial relations have been developed within a limited segment of the Japanese labour market during a limited period of the country's industrializing history (Shirai, 1983).

It is also well known that practices such as quality circles were introduced into Japan by Americans such as Deming and Juran who helped bring about the post-war production miracle. Finding that their ideas about total quality management evoked little interest in the United States, they discovered more fertile ground elsewhere (Hodgson, 1987). However, it is worth noting that it was the particular Japanese culture that could accept and use these US-grown ideas. One could argue, for instance, that one of the prerequisites for the successful implementation of quality circles is a high degree of commitment by employees to their company and its goals – a characteristic that is attributed to most Japanese employees.

The just-in-time practice is another aspect of Japanese management style which may not necessarily be inherently Japanese. It is true that this practice depends heavily on the subcontracting relationships that exist between Japan's large firms and their smaller business partners. It is also true that this kind of relationship does not exist in most other countries to the same extent as it does in Japan. But there is little or no reason why other countries cannot reorganize their industrial structure to enable them to take advantage of just-in-time practices. In other words, the distinctive Japanese culture does not appear to be a pre-condition for the successful operation of just-in-time.

It appears, therefore, that there is little inherently Japanese about many of the characteristics of Japanese organizations, but they may be due to other less culturally specific factors which are applicable to companies elsewhere.

Japanese companies' strategic decisions, which are foundations for their economic success, reflect hard-nosed policies more characteristic of a capitalist approach to business rather than of a cultural uniqueness. The way in which some Japanese companies responded to the high rate of their currency a few years ago (*The Economist*, 4 March 1989) is a case in point. The main response to the high yen by large exporters was to ship capital abroad instead of cars, video recorders and copying machines. In other words, these companies turned themselves from exporters into multinationals. By this means exchange-rate risk was hedged.

For the lower end of their product ranges, many Japanese firms set up factories in the cheap-labour markets of South East Asia (Thailand, Malaysia and, increasingly, Indonesia). For engineering components and more sophisticated parts, they went to technically knowledgeable Taiwan and South Korea, where local firms act as original-equipment manufacturers, but stick the name-plates of their Japanese customers on locally-made products such as microwave ovens, hi-fi sets and video recorders before shipping them directly to Europe, the Middle East or the United States.

Then there are the car plants, and factories for making up-market consumer electronics equipment. These required investments of anything up to $600 million at a time, carefully trained local manpower, the best managers from head office, and two or three years to get full-scale production. The only place to locate them was close to the customers – in the United States and Western Europe.

Japanese companies abroad

Japanese firms are accused of not blending into their surroundings. They are run by Japanese, the important decisions are taken at head office, foreign employees have no chance of promotion. All the research and development and design work is carried out back at home, leaving the overseas factory as just an assembly plant for imported components. This is why Japanese car factories are known rudely as 'transplants': unnatural organs vulnerable to rejection by their new body (*The Economist*, 23 February 1991).

There may be cultural as well as organizational reasons for this. Take the *ringi* style of decision making for example. Decision making based on *ringi* is one of the Japanese management practices which is particularly problematic in Western subsidiaries, since non-Japanese managers may find it difficult to master its subtleties. In Yoshino's (1975) view, participation in the initial preparation of a *ringi* proposal requires a detailed knowledge of trends and policies within the organization as a whole. This can most readily be acquired through frequent face-to-face interaction and reading of cues which are subtle, discrete and indirect. A similar knowledge of the organizational grapevine is of course of inestimable value in Western organizations, but the point being made is that Western managers may have great difficulty gaining access to this information in organizations all of whose senior members are Japanese (Smith, 1984).

These assertions are given substantial support by studies of decision making within Japanese subsidiaries in Britain (Kidd and Teramoto, 1981; Trevor, 1983). A series of case studies confirmed that *ringi* decision making was often confined to Japanese nationals, and that this was even more true of the informal consultation (*nemawashi*) which preceded the actual formulation of a *ringi* proposal. Sometimes the non-Japanese managers in a firm were not even aware that the *ringi* system was being used.

There are, however, many other aspects of the Japanese management style which the Japanese have taken with them to their foreign-based subsidiaries. These are single-union agreements; breaking down physical barriers between management and employees, such as a single dining room for everybody, identical overalls, and open-plan offices; an emphasis on quality; and zero-rate reject and waste.

But some practices like quality circles and just-in-time have not been implemented successfully abroad, especially in the

West, and this is not for lack of trying. Rather, it may be for the lack of culturally-influenced employee loyalty and commitment in the individualistic nations of the West, and in the case of just-in-time as was argued earlier, for the absence of special subcontracting relationships among firms in these countries.

In chapter 1 the readers were introduced to Rainbow, which is a Japanese company operating in Britain, and whose management style was researched by the present author (Tayeb, 1990b). This company can be used here again as a good case to examine the way in which the Japanese run their subsidiaries in the West.

As was mentioned in chapter 1, Rainbow was originally a British-owned company which was acquired by the Japanese. They naturally wanted to run it their way and so started to introduce changes on several fronts.

To start with, they removed physical and tangible barriers between managers and workers, which they saw as symbolic of British class differentiation and an obstacle to better cooperation between the two sides. The walls between offices were knocked down to be replaced by an open-plan layout. The senior directors and other managers and members of staff shared the same large space on the ground floor. Small cabins and meeting rooms, with glass walls were placed in the same space as the employees' desks.

A single large canteen was allocated as dining hall/tea room for everybody, with managers, employees and workers standing in the same queues to be served the same wide selection of hot and cold meals. A blue overall to be worn by all members was introduced. In short, at the end of the day, everybody looked alike, and it was difficult to tell, from their appearance, a director from a lavatory cleaner.

The next move was to do away with multiple union contracts. All members were told they should be represented by only one union in their negotiations with the management. There was of course opposition to this plan by union officials. But they were told if they insisted on doing things the old ways, the company would shut the plant and pull out its investment. The prospect of workers losing their jobs and joining the already large numbers unemployed in the area deterred the unions from further resistance. The union with the largest membership in the company became the single union to represent all workers and other employees. Using the same tactic, Japanese managers signed a no-strike agreement with the union officials.

This left the British managers and some union officials

disgruntled, but the employees and workers were happy with the new situation as they had gained a great deal compared with the old days.

On the technical side, the Japanese managers placed a greater emphasis on quality than their predecessors. For instance, before the take over, the completed products would be placed in a special control room for six hours to undergo various checks. In the new regime, they would stay there for twenty-four hours. Additionally, quality control was built in throughout the production process. However, the Japanese were unsuccessful in setting up quality circles. They reckoned the long tradition of non-participation by the shopfloor workers in the running of their own sections, and the fact that they never saw the company's interests as their own, were responsible for their failure in setting up quality circles.

One of the ways in which senior managers tried to make employees more involved in the decision-making processes was to arrange regular meetings at the beginning of every shift and to invite the workforce to make suggestions to improve work performance and working conditions. However, in practice, the meetings were only a forum for the supervisors to tell the workteams what they were expected to do for the duration of the shift, rather than a vehicle for two-way communications between the management and workers. Also, the suggestions put forward by the employees were hardly taken note of, and therefore they were reluctant to make further efforts in this direction.

Another aspect of the Japanese management style which was unsuccessful was the practice of just-in-time. Suppliers could never be relied on to deliver the orders in time for the company to reduce the size of the input to the warehouse and to save time and money on this front. In Japan, the company had special mutually trusting relationships with small firms and subcontractors, as part of a network. Here, this kind of relationship did not exist, certainly not to the same extent.

In spite of some difficulties in applying the Japanese management style in its pure form, the company has been a successful concern since the new owners took it over and implemented the intended changes. Its products are of a high quality and incorporate the latest developments in the electronics field. The workers, with their jobs now more secure, are generally happier than they were before. The British managers of the company have also come to accept and indeed realize the merits of the new management style and organizational structure.

Box 12   *Saturn Inc. and Japanese management style*

Is this an American auto plant, or a factory from another planet? The company president walks around in a polo shirt with a pocket logo right out of *Star Trek*, allows workers to call him 'Skip' and describes his position as 'team member'. He and the union boss (who goes by 'Dick') have a strange, collegial relationship. As for the rank and file, they don't punch a time clock, and they get to handpick the people they work alongside. During off-hours they run around an outdoor obstacle course and engage in group hugging sessions. If they develop a bad attitude, they are paid to spend a day thinking about what's bothering them. . . .

Yes this is an American auto factory, one as far out as its name: Saturn. Situated 56 kilometres south of Nashville in the small town of Spring Hill, Tenn., the Saturn plant and its 3,000 team members represent a grand experiment in American manufacturing.

For General Motors, which has invested eight years and $3.5 billion to launch Saturn, the venture has a specific competitive goal: to build small cars as well as the Japanese do. . . .

Most important, as a working laboratory of labour relations and manufacturing know-how, Saturn will help answer one of the most pressing questions of the 1990s: Can the United States compete with the Japanese? . . .

Why is Saturn so revolutionary for American industry? Primarily because this attempt to reverse GM's industrial decline acknowledges for the first time on a large scale the real reason for Japan's manufacturing superiority over the past two decades. The secret is not advanced technology or low wages or some mystical Asian work ethic. Japan's most important advantage is its management system: the way it deals with employees, suppliers, dealers and customers, . . . [its] teamwork, efficient use of resources and a tireless commitment to improving quality. . . .

Saturn's best hope is that it represents a profound change in the way GM manages its people. But the difference is not technological. Saturn's cavernous, 1.6 kilometre long Tennessee factory is a medium-tech plant, as are many of the most efficient facilities in Japan. The core of Saturn's system is one of the most radical labour–management agreements ever developed in the US, one that involves the United Auto Workers in every aspect of the business. The executive suite in Spring Hill is shared by president Le Fauve and the union coordinator Richard Hoalcraft, who often travel together and conduct much of the company's business in each other's presence.

Beyond sharing power at top levels, the labour–management agreement established some 165 work teams, which have been given more power than assembly-line workers anywhere else in GM or at any Japanese plant. They are allowed to interview and approve new hires for their teams (average size: ten workers). They are given wide responsibility to decide how to run their own areas; when workers see a problem on the assembly line, they can pull on a blue handle

and shut down the entire line. They are even given budget responsibility. One team in Saturn's final-assembly area voted to reject some
proposed pneumatic car-assembly equipment and went to another
supplier to buy electronic gear that its members believed to be safer.
. . . the most radical feature of Saturn's labour–management agreement, one that is even more democratic than the Japanese model, is
the provision for consensus decision making. The Saturn philosophy
is that all teams must be committed to decisions affecting them
before those changes are put into place, from choosing an ad agency
to selecting an outside supplier. 'That takes a lot of yelling sometimes, and every thing takes a lot longer', says the union official Jack
O'Toole, who oversees Spring Hill personnel, 'but once they come
out of that meeting room, they're 100 percent committed.' . . .

Instead of hourly pay, the workers work for a salary, . . . 20 percent
of which is at risk. Whether they get that 20 percent depends on a
complex formula that measures car quality, worker productivity and
company profits. . . . If a team produces fewer defects than the
targeted amount, its members will receive 100 percent of their salary.
If they perform even better, they are eligible for a bonus.

But people skills are not Saturn's only strong point. Since they were
outfitting a plant from the ground up, Saturn's team members incorporated an array of new equipment and techniques. Their aim was
to achieve what an MIT study dubbed 'lean production', the Japanese
system that uses 'half the human effort in the factory, half the
manufacturing space, half the investment in tools, half the engineering hours to develop a new product.' At Saturn, team members
rejected the traditional US form of assembly line, where workers do
two things at once – toil and shuffle – as they struggle to keep up
with car bodies creeping down the line. On the Saturn 'skillet' line,
workers ride along on a moving wooden conveyer belt as they do
their jobs, which enables them to concentrate on their work. . . .

Source: Time, 29 October 1990

Western companies and Japanese management practices

Given the success of Japanese companies, many Western firms
are keen to emulate their style of management in the hope of
enhancing their performance, and achieving the same
competitive edge as their Japanese rivals in international
markets.

Japanization through the adoption of Japanese ideas and
methods can take place in five ways (Arthurs, 1987). First,
Japanese industry may be taken as a model, analysed in depth,
and coherent strategies developed in order to bring to Western
industry what are perceived to be the key elements of Japanese
economic success. Secondly, selective copying of particular

policies and practices can be carried out. They are not necessarily, as in the first step, part of a radical strategic appraisal, but none the less are carefully considered and based on detailed knowledge of Japanese developments. The danger of this approach for managements is that because they have been extracted from a different overall system, as well as a different culture, they will probably not yield the same benefits as in Japanese companies.

Thirdly, Japanese methods and practices may be cited, by management and by trade unions, simply to legitimate particular changes which are in their interests. Fourthly, managements, in some cases out of a desire to be seen to be doing something to improve matters, will pick up faddish, half-baked ideas from television, magazines, management conferences and visits to Japan. They will attempt to apply some of these to their firms without first making a detailed analysis of the ideas or of their relevance to industry.

Finally, Japanization may have an element of inevitability, if it takes place in response to the development of new technologies and changing world markets in all advanced industrialized countries. In this case it is not so much that Japan provides a model, but that it has been able to make the changes earlier than Western industry has been able to.

Japanization of Western companies has taken place only in some aspects. Japan appears to provide a model for a wholesale strategic change in manufacturing methods. But in such areas as personnel and industrial relations policies, and just-in-time, Western companies face far more constraints, and the model is applied only selectively.

In Britain, for example, the area in which the managers have perhaps been more keen to follow a Japanese model is management–union relationships, especially, the single-union and no-strike agreements. The managers aim to localize bargaining, as opposed to the usual national procedures, and to include white and blue collar employees in a single bargaining unit. The goal, as Arthurs (1987) argues, is almost certainly to develop enterprise consciousness and commitment, moving towards quasi-enterprise unionism in which bargaining takes place with union representatives who have few, if any, commitments, loyalties and resources beyond the boundaries of the company. They will be separated as far as possible from the influence of the external union movement and external labour market.

Overall information on this is brief, but according to the latest Workplace Industrial Relations Survey, in 1984 35 percent of manual workers and 61 percent of non-manual workers still had more than one union at their place of work, compared with 35 percent and 57 percent respectively in 1980 (Millward and Stevens, 1986). Most large plants are still organized by a cluster of separate, partly competing unions.

There is also a trend to harmonize the working conditions of blue- and white-collar employees, in terms of symbolic distinctions such as restaurants, car parks, toilets and dress. In a survey of British business, *The Economist* (20 May 1989) reported that many of the symbols of division between workers and managers – them and us – have been dismantled. Many firms have dispensed with their ranks of corporate dining rooms and substituted one modern single-status canteen. Some have got rid of their segmented car parks, where bosses were less likely than workers to get their hair wet in a rainstorm. This new trend, if trend it is, has affected most obviously the several thousand workers who are employed by Japanese firms operating in Britain.

The Japanese egalitarian and collective decision-making style has also been partially copied, especially in the British companies which are keen to follow the Japanese model.

Despite the belief that it will break down barriers and remove a source of demotivation, the approach to the Japanization of decision-making processes is far from the egalitarianism of Japanese companies described by Dore (1973). Little or no emphasis, for instance, is placed on those elements which might undermine managerial power (Arthurs, 1987).

PART V

THE INTERNATIONAL MANAGER'S WORLD

13
Management of International Firms

This chapter draws on some of the issues discussed in the previous parts of the book to highlight the global perspective of international firms.

Companies with ambitions to establish themselves internationally must examine fundamentally how they operate. Operating multinationally is much more than strengthening the export department, and replacing Joe Bloggs plc with Joe Bloggs International Group on the company's letterheads, to rephrase Vineall (1988).

A multinational organization differs significantly from a single-nation firm by virtue of having to operate in more than one country.

Activities such as formulating policies and strategies, dealing with competitors, responding to customers' needs, creating new 'needs' for customers, coping with pressure groups, complying with government policies and regulations, designing appropriate organizational structure, and operating with appropriate technologies, are among the normal preoccupations of managers in any company. But these are magnified and become far more complicated as companies stretch their boundaries to cover more and more countries. In addition, there are other challenges, opportunities and threats which are unique to multinational firms and require special skills to handle.

This is so because individual countries have their own more or less unique laws and regulations, political, social and cultural norms and practices, and their own economic and technological characteristics. These have implications for a vast majority of the activities of the multinational firms.

Multinationals in general face challenges in three broad areas of activities: those which are concerned with the strategic and

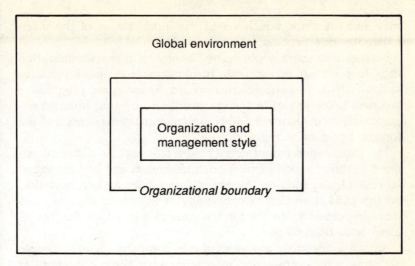

Figure 13.1 *Multinational companies' main areas of challenge*

planning aspects of their business; those which are related to their internal organization; and those which concern the interface between internal and external aspects of their activities, that is, boundary spanning functions. Figure 13.1 illustrates this point.

The common thread which runs through all three aspects of the business activities of international firms consists of opportunities and threats. Opportunities have to be recognized and exploited, threats should be avoided or reduced, or even be turned into opportunities where possible, and challenges have to be faced and met.

Planning and strategic activities

One of the major strategic decisions that companies may consider taking is whether or not to become involved in international business. This depends, among other things, on the size and nature of their domestic market, their production capability, and the financial and other resources which expansion into foreign markets requires.

The companies then, as was discussed in chapter 1, may decide on the form and the extent to which they wish to have business involvement with foreign countries. Importing, exporting, franchising and licensing are foreign business activities which do not involve direct investment in other countries, and may suit the firms which are at the initial stages of the internationalization process.

Further and more sophisticated stages of internationalization include portfolio investment, turnkey projects, joint ventures and wholly-owned subsidiaries abroad. These entail progressive business involvement in foreign countries, ranging from investment only to investment and complete managerial control of the foreign business of the firm.

The progression from foreign businesses with no direct investment to those which involve offshore investment and managerial control, depends on the firms' capabilities and competence, on the market and other conditions in the home country, and more importantly, on the foreign countries in which the investment is to take place.

Astra,[1] a Swedish pharmaceuticals company, is an example of firms which gradually internationalize their operation as circumstances become more favourable, and as they build up the competence and resources which are required to handle international operations.

The pharmaceutical industry is a high risk, high reward business. The cost of developing a new drug is very high. Much of this is the expense of meeting complex regulatory requirements. One consequence for companies developing and marketing their own patented drugs is that there is really no freedom in deciding whether to go international or not. The only way to survive is to address the global market.

In this industry the global market consists of Japan, the United States and Europe, which together bought 78 percent of the drugs sold in the non-communist world in 1986 (Scrip, 1988). That is not to say that drug companies do not go into Third World markets, but their strategies are determined by the characteristics of their main markets.

This requirement to address the global market poses special strategic problems for the smaller companies in the industry. They do not have sufficient in-house resources to carry products through the complexities of different regulatory procedures in several countries, nor the marketing force to sell them worldwide. Even for the medium-sized, better established companies, the challenges are considerable.

However, this has not prevented a number of small and medium-sized pharmaceutical companies from designing

[1] I owe this example to Dr D.J. Bower, a colleague at the Heriot-Watt University Business School.

strategies to enter this lucrative market. Using a complex web of licensing and joint venture agreements, younger companies plan from the earliest stages to bring their products to the international market. As they grow, they progressively aim to build their own marketing forces. This allows them to retain greater control over their products and to maximize their revenues.

Astra, which is one of the fastest-growing pharmaceutical companies at present, is a medium-sized company and was founded in 1923. From the earliest days it devoted a high proportion of its resources to R & D. It was closely involved in the development of penicillin, and has built up a high reputation for its research in an increasing number of product areas. In spite of this it grew rather slowly until recently, as it did not have a very strong strategic rationale.

Its first internationally-marketed product, the anaesthetic Xylocaine, was launched in 1948, but it was not until the company was reorganized to focus on its core pharmaceutical business that its profitability started to improve.

Initially the company had to rely on licensing arrangements for all non-Swedish sales. Between 1977 and 1987 it built up its own marketing organization in several countries including Germany and the Far East. In Japan, the first steps were made through a joint venture company, Fujisawa-Astra. At the end of 1988 it acquired Hoei Pharmaceuticals to improve its access to this market.

To gain entry to the world's largest pharmaceutical market, the United States, Astra signed a marketing agreement with the major US drug company Merck, Sharp, Dohme. Merck agreed to assist Astra in registering and marketing all Astra products (in development in 1982) under licence in the United States. Under the same agreement, if total sales in 1993–5 exceed a certain level (believed to be $500 million), the business will be transferred to a joint venture company. Thus, if the current batch of products are successful Astra will acquire a marketing operation in the United States. It will gain a high level of direct control and will greatly increase its returns. Merck's assistance will also smooth the slow and difficult process of obtaining regulatory approval for drugs in the United States.

At present its drug for gastric ulcers, Losec, is challenging the leading market position of Zantac, one of the most successful drugs of all time. Thus through the high quality of its proprietary products and through complementing its weaknesses with carefully planned joint agreements, Astra is within reach of its ambitions to achieve its own world-wide sales force.

If its growth continues at the current rate it may soon join the giants of the pharmaceutical sector.

As the example of Astra shows, international firms study and assess potential and actual opportunities and threats before making their move into wider global markets.

Opportunities

Opportunities can be found both within a company and outside it, especially abroad. Healthy finances and excess capital, managerial expertise, advanced production techniques, the growth and maturity stages in the product life cycle, and competitive advantages are among factors which may prompt a company to go international.

Externally, companies look where the most favourable and fertile grounds for their internationalization plans can be found. Some countries are eager, as was argued in chapter 1, for their own political and economic reasons, to attract foreign capital and expertise to their territories. They entice international firms by offering them tax concessions and grants, and by relaxing the licensing rules and procedures. Appreciating and high-income consumers, lax environmental regulations, accessibility to cheap raw materials, and a low-waged and/or skilled workforce are other factors which persuade firms to set up plants abroad. These considerations influence not only the type but also the location of the foreign investment by international firms.

Threats

Threats may come from individual firms and from foreign governments.

Domestic and foreign firms operating in similar lines of business are major sources of competition and threat to one another. For instance, Japanese companies, especially those engaged in car and electronics industries, pose formidable threats to the US and West European multinational firms. Their competing grounds include not only the domestic markets of the American and European firms but also the foreign markets of these firms in developed and developing countries.

Governments, you may remember from the discussions in chapter 4, can be a source of threat to foreign firms through protectionist policies and through more politically motivated actions.

Sometimes governments erect barriers against imports of certain goods and services from abroad for political and economic reasons, such as national defence needs, protection of domestic industries, restructuring and diversification of the economy, or even sanctioning an unfriendly country. They may also restrict the extent to which foreign firms can invest within their territories.

Protectionist measures such as import barriers can be turned into opportunities. Firms might decide to invest and manufacture their products in a country which used to be a market for their exports. They can benefit from already established brand-loyalty of their own customers in that country.

Restrictions on the extent of foreign direct investment can also be turned into an opportunity in the form of partnership in joint ventures. This has the added attraction of reducing the risk of nationalization.

Governmental actions, as was argued in chapter 3, sometimes may involve an overt interference in the business of an already operational foreign firm in their country. They may interfere with and even dictate the management policies and operational functions of the firm. It might be forced to take on board certain extra-organizational activities, for example constructing local amenities such as roads, houses for employees, hospitals and schools in the area where the firm's subsidiary is located.

There is also always a risk of nationalization and confiscation of the firm's assets when an unfriendly regime comes to power, especially through revolution or a *coup d'état*.

Wars between 'home' and 'host' countries, and regional conflicts can pose serious threats to the international firms concerned.

Wars, especially when they are over, can at the same time offer fertile grounds for opportunities which may not have existed before. The Persian Gulf war in 1991 is a good case in point. The reconstruction of Kuwait's infrastructure and the capping of its burning oil wells, and the demand on the part of Middle Eastern countries for intelligent missiles and smart bombs such as those used by the Coalition forces, were among the new opportunities which were created in the region by the war.

Some of the actions that governments take, either individually or in association with others, for example, in global and regional agreement, are double-edged, so to speak. These actions can be seen as opportunities by some international firms and as threats by others, depending on where the firms are.

Protectionist measures are a threat to foreign-based international firms, but an opportunity for the locally based ones. The

European single market is seen as a wonderful opportunity for international companies in the European Community, but viewed as a 'fortress' by some of their Japanese and American counterparts.

International companies based in advanced industrialized nations may find the outcome of the GATT negotiations beneficial to their businesses. But firms based in less developed countries might consider some of the decisions taken at the GATT Rounds as detrimental to their interests.

Boundary spanning and interface activities

International firms deal with their external environments through interface activities. These include activities concerning customers (for example, identifying and responding to their preferences and tastes, marketing and promotion channels), trade partners (for example, conducting negotiations with governments and firms) and the local public at large (for example, devising appropriate advertising policies).

Interface activities require not only business competence and negotiating skills, which are also the case with the single-nation companies. But they require, more crucially, the ability to cope with and handle the national and cultural diversities of the context within which the interface takes place.

Take marketing for example. International firms are faced with an array of countries to cope with. Different promotion channels may be called for in different countries. In some, sophisticated market research might be a suitable approach, in others, especially where there are no alternative products, successful negotiations with local governments may secure entry into a market.

Chapter 8 discussed some of the major regional trade and economic blocs, such as the European Community and ASEAN. In the current competitive and uncertain atmosphere, many countries increasingly tend to group themselves into blocs in order to protect their interests. Multinationals are accordingly having to shift their emphasis from single-nation marketing strategies to pan-bloc strategies.

Distribution systems, which vary dramatically from country to country, pose another challenge to multinationals. In Britain, for instance, household goods are sold through national chains specializing in so-called 'white' goods. In Italy white goods are sold through a profusion of small retailers, and customers haggle over price. Marketing 'tricks' learnt in one country are of little use in the other. (*The Economist*, 22 October 1988). Differing retail systems mean that distribution must be arranged separately in each country.

Cultural diversities among various nations have significant implications for the management of interface activities of multinational companies.

Take advertising for example. Sensitivity to the tastes and preferences of local people, which are largely rooted in their culture, is very crucial in the way companies sell their products. Benetton, an Italian multinational, has a very *avant garde* style of advertising its products. The images that it uses in its commercial posters and billboards are straight to the point but very striking in appearance, for example, a newly born baby with the umbilical cord still attached to it. The company uses the same images all over the world. The reaction to these images has, however, varied tremendously from country to country. Some countries have found many of the images distasteful and offensive, and have banned their appearance in the national press, and removed the billboards from public places. Some countries have welcomed the images, and others have been indifferent to them. Another advertisement by the same company shows a multicoloured collection of condoms. This may not be a great success in some Catholic countries such as Eire and those in Latin America.

In contrast, the producer of an aftershave adopted different approaches to advertising in different countries. In Western countries, the idea of a man using the company's aftershave before meeting a woman is conveyed in two bare arms and hands entangled with one another in a suggestive manner. In a similar advertisement for Muslim countries, the two arms are fully clothed, conveying an atmosphere of a formal and public occasion, and there is only a hint of the woman's fingers touching the man's coat sleeve.

Product specification is another area where local tastes and preferences are taken into consideration by many multinationals.

Pioneer, as an old established Japanese hi-fi company, has been in the UK market for many years. Early on it suffered from the inconsistencies of a series of importers and distributors but things improved dramatically when it set up its own branches in Europe. In spite of the fact that Pioneer can point to as wide a range of products as most of the Japanese majors manufacturers, historically it has been one outstanding item which brought it the most popularity and profit. Back in the 1970s countless hi-fi initiates entered the world of recorded music with the help of one of its turntables (the PL12). At one period a check on any university campus would have revealed dozens of them in student rooms. It seems that something similar has been achieved with a new amplifier (the A-400).

A few years ago Pioneer decided to increase its share in the UK hi-fi market by attracting a wider public through sensitive advertising and through producing equipment, particularly amplification, tailored to local requirements and to indigenous valuations of what is right and proper. To that end it examined some of the most widely accepted British-made products and noted their features and facilities. Pioneer also assiduously studied and digested British high fidelity magazines. Having filtered this mass of information to remove the grosser absurdities, the Company produced the A-400 amplifier.

One of the things that emerged from this research was the increasing dismay of the British consumers at products becoming overburdened with unwanted facilities at each annual update. The British do not want the elaboration of controls and the proliferation of coloured lights, all of which apparently are what appeal to the Japanese home consumers.

This is not to say that the A-400 amplifier could be seen as anything other than a Japanese product; but in spite of its standard black finish, the drum feet and classic layout, it has gained immeasurably in dignity by having only three rotary knobs and the company's tidy gold legends on the front panel. There is a headphones socket too, but no loudspeaker switching, no tone or loudness controls, and no muting or direct inputs (for further details see *Gramophone*, December 1990).

Sony, another Japanese electronics firm, has a similar culturally-sensitive approach to product specifications. An example of this is the TA-F540E amplifier, described by *What Hi-Fi?* (October 1991) as 'the latest in a line of creeping Anglicisations to join Japanese amplifiers'. It has been designed specifically for the UK market, with substantial and continued input from at least two members of the staff at Sony UK, who have been listening to prototype models for almost a year.

The emphasis on locally sensitive product specifications should not, however, overlook the fact that there are some products which can be produced in exactly the same standard form and be marketed successfully and sold in many countries. After all, one of the attractions of internationalization is the economies of scale. McDonald's hamburgers are an example of this kind.

Also, it is possible for companies to manufacture a large number of the components of their products using standard mass production formats, but some of the finishing touches could be made having regard to local tastes and preferences.

A multinational company manufacturing household appliances for the world-wide market, for instance, can create a world-scale business in white goods components as well as in the appliances themselves. Many of the differences between the machines sold across countries can be achieved by putting the same parts together in different combinations. This way it might manage to exploit the economies of scale in component production.

Countries have different laws, social structures, cultural norms and political systems. In the words of Hernando de Soto, the Peruvian President's adviser (*Time*, 9 September 1991), some nations bask in prosperity while their neighbours are perennially impoverished. Justice is even-handed in some places, capricious in others. Some governments can manage their resources and collect taxes without fuss; others see their economies slip beyond their control. Some cultures encourage success, while others hinder it.

For de Soto, communication and accountability are articles of faith. Different nations keep open the channels of communication via different means. In Japan, it is government bureaucrats, not elected politicians, who have the most influence in pressing for effective laws. In Germany de Soto credits the court system, not the legislative or executive branch, with fine-tuning laws to keep pace with changing public opinion. It is not important who gets the credit as long as problems are discussed and solved.

By contrast, in much of the Third World decisions are made by decree and published *ex post facto*. Debate of controversial issues is desultory, not to mention dangerous. The standards of public order of the developed world – property registration, law enforcement, impartial courts – must be bought with bribes, or may be unattainable at any price. Faced with 'ugly' circumstances they cannot change, citizens do not cooperate with the government. They ignore laws, evade taxes, run unregulated businesses and generally reduce the quality of life even further. In Peru, for instance, 60 to 70 percent of the population works outside the law. But that does not mean that they are outlaws; it means the law does not work. A case in point is the Upper Huallaga Valley, notorious for its coca crop, which is also ideal for growing coffee. Yet for years a coca farmer willing to switch crops had to prove he had been growing coffee beans for three years before he could sell them.

In many countries local people are in a position either to adapt to or to change the political and social circumstances of their countries, for example through election or revolution, or at the very least through breaking the law. But the choice for international firms is to 'take it or leave it'. They have either to adapt and take appropriate measures to suit local conditions, or not have any business dealings with them at all. There are, however, some powerful multinationals which are able, and have in the past done so, to influence local governments' foreign and other strategic policies (for example, Chile's entanglement with a powerful multinational company a few years ago). But these are by and large exceptions rather than rules.

The first step in the adaptation is cultural awareness and the recognition of the differences between nations. A need to understand the cultural differences between countries is therefore becoming increasingly important as the multinationalization of firms proliferates. But as Holberton (1990: 9) states, to acquire and master cultural awareness is not easy:

> Today's quest for the international manager echoes the mediaeval alchemists' search for a secret formula for changing base metal into gold; it is a venture which promises untold riches, but getting it right is awfully difficult.

Moreover, some international companies, especially those from more advanced countries, often resist adapting to cultural differences because they believe their own way of doing business is superior to that of others, is logical and works well, and perhaps because it is the only system they are familiar with.

For example, as Altany (1989) points out, foreign customs initially strike some American managers as strange or even backward, even though in most cases these have their own logic and benefits. Americans often feel that the European practice of meticulously cultivating personal relationships with business associates slows the expedient conduct of business. They argue that time is money, and the Europeans waste time. But to Southern Europeans, trust and long-term commitment – not legal contracts and short-term gains – are the heart and soul of a solid business relationship. And the European approach, slower though it is, usually leads to longer and stronger business alliances.

The development of these long-term alliances can bring rich rewards for European business partners:

> A European purchaser may sacrifice a few dollars in sticking with a familiar supplier, but these executives are more interested in linking up with companies that will make concessions over the long haul – for instance, to make a design change, or to hold the line on price increases in the event of a financial crunch. (interview with C. Valentine in Altany, 1989: 14)

International firms have to adapt to their hosts' way of doing business early on in negotiations to ensure their success. Language differences pose obvious hurdles for negotiators, but to a large extent these can be overcome with the help of a good translator. Many people, however, make the mistake of assuming that bridging the language gap is all that is necessary to communicate effectively with foreign business partners. Just as important to clear communications are the use of body language, expressions, and a knowledge of one's foreign associate's cultural background (Altany, 1989). As an example[2] one of the senior managers of an American company, who is French and was president of a French company bought by the American firm, is quoted as saying that American managers often make two mistakes concerning their European counterparts: first, they assume that Europeans are simply Americans who live in Europe, and secondly, they fail to understand or acknowledge the sometimes vast cultural differences found among Europeans.

From early adolescence we begin learning subtle ways to communicate – through our use of eye contact, hand gestures, tone of voice, and through our posture. These are very different for the people of different countries. For example, in Japan the depth of the bow people take when they meet indicates their status in relation to one another – the junior person bows deeper than the senior one. In Iran, in parties and social gatherings sitting or standing with one's back to others, especially older people, is very rude and is regarded as an insult, while in many countries this is not the case. In Buddhist East Asian countries, patting children on the head or extending one's feet towards another while sitting are deeply offensive.

Learning to adopt unfamiliar body language and to accommodate the cultural behaviour patterns of foreign businesspeople is important in establishing trust:

[2] I owe this item to my colleague Dr Alan Cheney.

We might meet someone from another culture, and because our antennas are searching around for understandable clues to their disposition and personality but can't find any, we get anxious. In this kind of situation we usually presume that the other person is untrustworthy. At the very least, we feel that doing business with that person is uncomfortable ... Two American strangers [, for instance,] can determine fairly quickly whether they are trustworthy and likable to each other or not. That is the key to doing any kind of business. This becomes much more difficult when you go outside your own culture. (interview with L. Griggs in Altany, 1989: 14)

Activities related to internal organization

Organization structure and management style

Operations which cross national boundaries will almost inevitably run with matrix structures, whether or not they are called that. Dotted lines; more than one boss; activity-based working groups whose members have a primary reporting relationship in many different parts of the organization; more time spent consulting and agreeing and building consensus than in issuing or receiving command-type instructions – all these will characterize the management style. Only thus, as Vineall (1988) argues, can the economies of cross-national operations be combined with the need to accommodate local market requirements, local employment systems and local governments.

As was discussed in chapter 9, the multicultural character of the employees of international companies should also guide the management style. For example, some employees may come from cultures which are receptive to a participative and consultative decision-making approach, others may not. Some may prefer to be left on their own to get on with their tasks and to use their own initiative, others may feel more comfortable and work better when they are frequently directed and guided by a senior manager. The management styles should therefore vary from one subsidiary to another, depending on the ability, willingness and other characteristics of the respective local employees.

In order to accommodate the needs and abilities of the employees from diverse cultural backgrounds, the managers should study and measure culture, or, more specifically, their own employees' work-related attitudes and values. Multinational corporations such as HERMES (pseudonym) (Hofstede, 1980) conduct periodic attitudes questionnaire surveys among their employees all over the world. This kind of survey can provide managers with the required information about the cultural and non-cultural characteristics of their employees. A simplified version of the work attitudes questionnaire employed in studies conducted by Tayeb (1988) and by Hofstede (1980) and similar projects could for instance be administered by a small team working in the organization's personnel department.

Personnel policies and human resource management

Operating internationally is much more demanding than operating within a national boundary. The quality of employees is a very important consideration here. Launching a product across several nations or devising an international buying strategy raises the level of competence required and calls for specific skills. In the words of Vineall (1988: 45), 'the second division player will find it more difficult to keep up'. Recruitment becomes more important than ever, and selection has to take account of the demands of international jobs. All this has to be achieved against a background of highly volatile external labour markets.

Operating a multinational is also about the whole orientation of a business – how the company sees its market opportunities, how it sees its sources of product ideas, how it sees its manufacturing potential and how it sees and organizes its management resource.

Creating a multinational management team is probably the most consistent thread running right through the process of internationalizing a business. Making multinational teams work at the level of the face-to-face group is important enough; a much wider range of expectations and assumptions about what is 'normal' is brought to such groups by members. Appreciating how wide that range can be and how easily one can miss realizing this fact is probably the crucial step for the individual in this whole matter (Vineall, 1988).

It is crucial for the employees and workteams to have a high degree of cultural awareness in order better to understand each other and to interpret correctly the meaning of each others' actions and behaviours.

As was discussed earlier, this high degree of cultural awareness is also necessary for the employees who participate in negotiations with foreign partners and conduct business deals.

Personnel selection criteria and training programmes, preferably followed by expatriation, are among the courses of

Table 13.1   *Characteristics of the international manager*

	%
Strategic awareness[1]	71
Adaptable in new situations	67
Sensitive to cultures	60
Able to work in international teams	56
Language skills	46
Understanding international marketing	46
Relationship skills	40
International negotiation skills	40
Self-reliant	27
High task orientation	19
Open, non-judgemental	19
Understanding of international finance	13
Awareness of cultural backgrounds	2

[1] Strategic awareness is defined as an executive's ability to take a global view of his or her contribution to the company.

Source: Holberton (1990)

action that firms can take to prepare their employees for the challenges of international business. Some multinational companies recognize the importance of these points, but they do not seem to incorporate them in their personnel policies.

In this connection, the Ashridge Management Research Group recently interviewed senior managers from forty-eight companies, both manufacturing and services, in fourteen countries (Barham, 1990; Holberton, 1990). Table 13.1 ranks the characteristics that personnel development specialists viewed as being most important for the international manager. Four of the top six could be called 'soft' skills. They emphasize the human skills involved in managing people in a foreign country and tap the manager's resourcefulness and sensitivity in coping with alien situations. But when one examines the criteria by which employees are selected, one notices that the possession of these skills by the candidates does not get the same priority among the job requirements.

Table 13.2 shows the selection criteria, ranked in order of frequency of citation, that companies apply to the executive targeted for a foreign posting. Here 'language skills' retains its fifth position, but the remaining five criteria are either 'hard' skills or relate to the executive's own development within the organization. The strategic vision has disappeared, and a new

Table 13.2 *Selection criteria for international positions*

	%
Technical skills and experience	85
Potential to develop in role	69
Knowledge of company systems	63
Understanding market and customers	48
Appropriate language skills	46
Posting necessary for career path	46
Support of spouse and family	38
Knowledge and understanding of host country	25
Good health	13
Age	8
Seniority	6
Gender	2
Proven expatriate record	2

Source: Holberton (1990)

item, 'technical skills and experience', has taken its place in the top position. Knowledge of procedures and systems is rated very highly. The soft skills which were seen as so crucial to the international manager are in practice relegated to eighth place and lumped together under 'knowledge and understanding of culture/norms of host country'.

Organizational versus national cultures

The shared values, the norms which are used to interpret experience and guide actions, and at a more visible level, 'the way we do things around here' vary considerably from one organization to another.

Many multinational companies such as IBM and Nissan, which deal with widely diverse cultures, build and foster a strong organizational culture consciously and as a matter of policy. This creates a more or less homogeneous atmosphere within which employees from different backgrounds can live together and understand each other.

Organizational culture can sometimes be used as a substitute for the local culture in an attempt to overcome some of its dysfunctions, for example, weak work ethic, corruption and dishonesty.

Particularly important, and not quickly achieved, as Vineall (1988) points out, is the right relationship between corporate culture and the national cultures in which individuals live. A wise company will not see its corporate culture as something which challenges or replaces, or even transcends, the local manager's identity as a German or Canadian or Nigerian. Ideally, managers should feel fully nationals of their own country, yet equally members of the corporate club.

The creation of a cultural synergy (Adler, 1981) enables senior managers to incorporate, where appropriate and possible, the company's own culture with the desirable aspects of the local national culture, such as group-orientation, commitment, honesty and hard work.

But can one change the cultural attitudes and values of employees? Is culture malleable? Attitudes theories suggest that people's attitudes and behaviour can be changed through communication and persuasion (Kleinke, 1984; Petty, 1981), cultural shock (Hofstede, 1978) and sustained discontinuity (Mangham, 1978). As Silverman (1970: 135) puts it, 'if the reality of the social world is socially sustained, then it follows that reality is socially changed – by the action of [humans].'

Bate (1982: 27) also argues in the same vein and offers a possible way to introduce the change:

> Perhaps the initial step would be for the change agent to attempt to raise the parties' awareness of their culture – the taken-for-granted meanings that they share and collectively maintain, and which inhibit the development of effective problem solving activities.

Cultural change and cultural synergy in an organization can be initiated, developed and maintained largely by the daily actions of those who run the business – by what they say, by what they do.

Training can also make a significant contribution in this area. A programme of central courses, focused on the needs of managers at particular career stages, can help to give cohesion to a group and provide focal points for the evolution of a culture, as well as for the development of individuals. The formation of the peer group on courses which bring together representatives from all parts of the organization, the choice of the right content and case material, the style of the courses and the messages they convey about the international orientation of the business – all these are important and productive.

However, as Vineall argues, training courses can do little on their own. If the messages are inconsistent with the way the corporation operates, they can do harm. But as a complement to an organization with a clear sense of direction and commitment to an international style of operation, their contribution is enormous.

Box 13 *An American in Europe*

France

A US manufacturing executive eager to expand into the European market arrives at a potential business partner's headquarters in France. He strides into the meeting room, enthusiastically wrings his host's hand and says, 'I've heard a great deal about you; please call me Bill.' Eager to show off his product, the American opens his brief-case and suggests getting right down to business.

By this point, if the French executive hasn't abandoned the meeting room with a strained look on his face, chances are he is either hiding his discomfort or is accustomed to American ill manners.

Ill manners? To the French, yes.

Regardless of how well-intentioned the American executive's greeting was, he did not take the time to research French business customs. Had he done his homework, he would have learned that the French are very formal and deliberate in the way they warm up to strangers. The American's friendly handshake and comment probably embarrassed his host, who is accustomed to a more formal handshake and greeting (first names are rarely used in France, even among colleagues).

French businesspeople similarly are uncomfortable launching directly into business matters, as the American urged. They first like to get to know prospective business partners to assess their personal compatibility and to build a mutual trust.

Spain

If an American businessman wants to be successful in Madrid, he has to learn to be patient, advises Robert John, the US commercial counsellor in Spain. A good appetite will not hurt either.

The business lunch is an integral part of conducting business in Spain, and Spanish businessmen conduct these meetings with great ceremony. In contrast to fast-paced American 'power' lunches, business lunches in Madrid typically stretch from 2.30 to 5.30 p.m.

Friendship is a more important part of business relationships in Spain than in the US. In the United States, business comes first, and friendship or pleasure comes later. But in Spain, knowing and liking a business associate is a *prerequisite* for the conduct of business. Lunches in Spain as such are used to develop these personal associations.

A lunch in Spain may include three to six courses, topped off by cognac, coffee and cigars. Business is not discussed before the drinks and the cigars are brought out, which signals the transition from personal to business matters.

Greece

Difficult though it is to comprehend, the United States' faltering federal bureaucracy moves with the swiftness of Mercury compared with Greece's formidable and slothful legion of civil servants.

Greece's government plays an unusually large role in the country's economy; about 70 percent of the national output is generated by the public sector. Consequently, conducting business – especially on a large scale – requires working through government channels.

Because of Greece's daunting bureaucracy, developing contacts within the country is crucial to establishing credibility when bidding for government contracts.

Business in Greece is very personalized – family connections, political connections, business connections, long-term relationships, and the quality of personal relationship is extremely important to the success of business partnerships in Greece.

In their style of speaking, American businessmen tend to be more blunt than their Greek counterparts. Ironically, this approach is often viewed with suspicion. When Americans are straightforward, businessmen in Greece often look behind the face value of what has been said for other meanings, when the Americans did not intend any other interpretations. Greeks are candid, but they take a softer, less direct approach.

Contracts are also handled differently in Greece than in the US. When an American businessman submits his 'best and final offer' for a contract, he is frequently unwilling to negotiate substantial changes in the proposal; Americans also will observe contracts to the letter regardless of changing circumstances. In Greece, however, negotiations are not finished even after a contract has been awarded. A contract in Greece is viewed as an *evolving* document of agreement.

Italy

Italian cars may not be the engineering envy of the world, but in their design and styling they have no rivals. This holds true beyond cars, as well: appearance and style are very important to Italian businessmen.

To Italian businessmen the appeal and polish of a presentation reflect the quality of the product or the company itself.

Every culture has its own soft spots and preferences. Americans look for price and reliability, Germans respect solid engineering, and the Italians the quality of design.

Italian businessmen are confident, shrewd, and competent negotiators. They commonly have the perception that Americans are interested only in making money. So the American who is conscious of style and expresses an interest in Italian art and culture can both disarm and charm Italian executives who accept this stereotype.

Italians take great pride in their business acumen. Most Italian businessmen eschew the advice of outside consultants and even in-house specialists, relying instead on the instincts of top executives. Italians take more pride in their individual expertise than in the reputation or size of the company to which they belong. As a result, they will judge another company by the expertise and polish of its executives and representatives, rather than by the company's size and reputation.

Germany

If you want to hear it straight, ask a German. German businessmen are technically oriented, disciplined, and orderly. In contrast to the majority of US executives – who usually have financial backgrounds – most German executives have degrees in engineering and the sciences.

To appeal to Germans' technical tastes, Americans should be direct and factual in manner. The use of excessive mannerisms such as backslapping are considered unbusinesslike.

Unlike businessmen in several Southern European countries, Germans generally do not emphasize the development of personal relationships with business associates. To the contrary, they value privacy and strive to keep their business and personal lives separate.

Most Germans are very methodical and conservative in their business approach, and are often repulsed by Americans' emphasis on making a 'fast buck' through financial gimmickry and risk taking. Because of these conservative business attitudes, women, and to a lesser extent young business associates, are frequently at a disadvantage in negotiations.

Britain

Whereas most Americans are eager to get the job done fast, the British are enamoured with conducting business matters 'properly', without offence or imposition.

The British are very civil and reserved; they do not admire overt ambition and aggressiveness, and are offended by hard-sell tactics. British businessmen are highly confident, but rarely flaunt their finances, or position.

This tone of understatement extends beyond self-characterization. British executives' speaking style is more subtle and indirect than most Americans', requiring some sensitivity and inference from the listener. When a British person subtly prefaces a statement with, 'It's a bit surprising that . . .' or 'Are you quite certain that . . .', his remark is probably meant to convey more of a critical or admonishing tone than most Americans will infer.

The British are good negotiators, but do not have a high regard for bargaining in general. Negotiations were not as prevalent in Britain's past as in other European countries' because businessmen operated within 'old-boy' networks and through gentlemen's agreements confined to the very few and well-connected. So a clear and reasonable approach to negotiations with the British is the best approach.

Source: Altany (1989)

Recommended further reading

Journals

The Economist and the international edition of *Time* cover a world-wide spectrum of social, political, economic and business events. They are a must for serious students of international business. The *Financial Times* and the *Wall Street Journal* are more specialized publications and give a good coverage of business events and company performances. The *Financial Times*'s occasional surveys on various countries are very informative.

Books and other academic publications

Abegglen, J.C. and Stalk Jr, G. (1985) *Kaisha, The Japanese Corporation*. New York: Basic Books.

Alhashim, D.D. and Arpan, J.S. (1992) *International Dimensions of Accounting*. Boston: PWS-Kent.

Arnold, G. (1989) *The Third World Handbook*. London: Cassell.

Bhagwati, J. (1991) *The World Trading System at Risk*. Hemel Hempstead: Harvester Wheatsheaf.

Enthoven, A.J.H. (1977) *Accounting in Third World Countries*. Amsterdam: North-Holland.

Evans, T.G., Taylor, M.E. and Holzmann, O. (1985) *International Accounting and Reporting*. New York: Macmillan.

Foreman-Peck, J. (1983) *A History of the World Economy*. Brighton: Wheatsheaf.

Greenaway, D. (1983) *Trade Policy and the New Protectionism*. New York: St Martin's.

Hofstede, G. (1980) *Culture's Consequences*. Beverly Hills, Calif.: Sage.

Industrial Relations Journal (1988) Vol. 19, which is devoted to Japanese culture and Japanese management practices.

Kamata, S. (1983) *Japan in the Fast Lane*. London: Allen and Unwin.

Lintner, V. and Mazey, S. *The European Community: Economic and Political Aspects*. Maidenhead: McGraw-Hill.

Male, S.P. and Stocks, P.K. (1991) *Competitive Advantage in Construction*. London: Butterworths.

Mueller, G.G., Gernon, H. and Meek, G. (1987) *Accounting: An International Perspective*. Homewood, Ill.: Irwin.

Porter, M.E. (1990) *The Competitive Advantage of Nations*. London: Macmillan.

Robertson, A.H. (1973) *European Institutions*. London: Stevens.

Schlossstein, S. (1991) *Asia's New Little Dragons*. Chicago: Contemporary Books.

Sen, G. (1984) *The Military Origins of Industrialisation and International Trade Rivalry*. London: Frances Pinter.

Smith, P.B. (1984) 'The Effectiveness of Japanese Styles of Management: A Review and Critique', *Journal of Occupational Psychology*, 57, pp. 121–36.

Smith, P.B., Peterson, M.F. and Tayeb, M.F. (1989) 'The Cultural Context of Leadership Action: A Cross-Cultural Analysis', in J. Davies, M. Easterby-Smith, S. Mann and M. Tanton (eds), *The Challenge to Western Management Development: International Alternative*. London: Routledge. pp. 85–97.

Szell, G. (1991) *Labour Relations in Transition in Eastern Europe*. Berlin: de Gruyter.

Tayeb, M.H. (1988) *Organizations and National Culture: A Comparative Analysis*. London: Sage.

Tayeb, M.H. (1990b) 'Japanese Management Style', in R. Daily (with contributions from T. Keenan and M. Tayeb), *Organisational Behaviour*. London: Pitman. pp. 257–82.

Wallace, C.D. (1982) *Legal Control of the Multinational Enterprise*. The Hague: Martinus Nijhoff.

References

Adams, J.D.R. and Whalley, J. (1977) *The International Taxation of Multinational Enterprises in Developed Countries*. London: Associated Business Programmes.

Adler, N.J. (1981) 'Cultural Synergy: The Management of Cross-Cultural Organizations', paper presented to the International Symposium on Cross-Cultural Management, Montreal, Canada, October.

Allen, G.C. (1972) *A Short History of Modern Japan*. London: Allen and Unwin.

Altany, D. (1989) 'Culture Clash', *Industry Week*, 2 October, pp. 13–20.

Arnold, G. (1989) *The Third World Handbook*. London: Cassell.

Arthurs, A. (1987) 'Japanisation and the Harmonisation of Employment Conditions', paper presented to the Japanisation of British Industry Conference, Cardiff, September.

Barham, K. (1990) *Making Managers International: A Preliminary Report*. Berkhamstead: Ashridge Management Research Group. Quoted in Holberton (1990).

Barret Brown, M. (1974) *The Economics of Imperialism*. London: Penguin.

Bass, B.H. and Burger, P.C. (1979) *Assessment of Managers: An International Comparison*. New York: Free Press.

Batchelor, R.A., Major, R.L. and Morgan, A.D. (1980) *Industrialization and the Basis of Trade*. Cambridge: Cambridge University Press.

Bate, P. (1982) 'Impact of Organizational Culture on Approaches to Organizational Problem-Solving', paper presented to the Conference on Qualitative Approaches to Organizations, University of Bath, 19–21 April.

Benedict, R. (1946) *The Chrysanthemum and the Sword*. Tokyo: Charles E. Tuttle.

Bhagwati, J. (1991) *The World Trading System at Risk*. Hemel Hempstead: Harvester Wheatsheaf.

Black, J. and Ackers, P. (1987) 'The Japanisation of British Industry? A Case Study of Quality Circles in the Carpet Industry', paper presented to the Japanisation of British Industry Conference, Cardiff, September.

Bradley, K. and Hill, S. (1983) 'After Japan: The Quality Circle Transplant and Productive Efficiency', *British Journal of Industrial Relations*, 21, pp. 291–311.

Briggs, P. (1988) 'The Japanese at Work: Illusions of the Ideal', *Industrial Relations Journal*, 19, pp. 24–30.

Buruma, I. (1985) *A Japanese Mirror: Heroes and Villains of Japanese Culture*. London: Penguin.

Carroll, G.R., Goodstein, J. and Gyenes, A. (1988) 'Organizations and the State: Effects of the Institutional Environment on Agricultural Cooperatives in Hungary', *Administrative Science Quarterly*, 33, pp. 233–56.

Chaudhuri, K.N. (1971) *The Economic Development of India under the East India Company 1814–1858*. Cambridge: Cambridge University Press.

Child, E. (1982) 'Individual and Social Factors Associated with the Behaviour of Children in a Play Setting'. Ph.D. thesis, Aston University.

Child, J. and Keiser, A. (1979) 'Organizational and Managerial Roles in British and West German Companies: An Examination of the Culture-Free Thesis', in C.J. Lammers and D.J. Hickson (eds), *Organizations Alike and Unlike*. London: Routledge and Kegan Paul.

Child, J. and Tayeb, M.H. (1983) 'Theoretical Perspectives in Cross-National Organizational Research', *International Studies of Management and Organization*, 12, pp. 23–70.

Clegg, S. (1992) Inaugural lecture, St Andrews University, 11 March.

Collick, H. (1981) 'A Different Society', in H. Smith (ed.), *Inside Japan*. London: British Broadcasting Corporation.

Dore, R. (1973) *British Factory – Japanese Factory*. London: Allen and Unwin.

Enthoven, A.J.H. (1977) *Accounting in Third World Countries*. Amsterdam: North-Holland.

Ernst & Young, (1990) *Scotland in the Single Market: Opportunities and Challenges for Scottish Business*. Glasgow: Scottish Development Agency.

Evans, T.G., Taylor, M.E. and Holzmann, O. (1985) *International Accounting and Reporting*. New York: Macmillan.

Foreman-Peck, J. (1983) *A History of the World Economy*. Brighton: Wheatsheaf.

Fromm, E. (1942) *The Fear of Freedom*. London: Routledge and Kegan Paul.

Giddens, A. (1973) *The Class Structure of the Advanced Societies*. London: Hutchinson.

Globerman, S. (1986) *Fundamentals of International Business Management*. Englewood Cliffs, NJ: Prentice Hall.

Greenaway, D. (1983) *Trade Policy and the New Protectionism*. New York: St Martin's Press.

Gunder Frank, A. (1967) *Capitalism and Underdevelopment in Latin America: Historical Studies of Chile and Brazil*. New York: Monthly Review Press.

Harrison, P. (1987) *The Greening of Africa*. London: Palladin Grafton.

Hill, F.M. (1987) 'What British Management Can Reasonably Expect from a Quality Circle Programme', paper presented to the Japanisation of British Industry Conference, Cardiff, September.

Hine, R.C. (1985) *The Political Economy of European Trade*. Brighton: Wheatsheaf.

Hobson, J.A. (1905) *Imperialism: A Study*. Revised edition. London: Constable.

Hodgson, A. (1987) 'Deming's Never-ending Road to Quality', *Personnel Management*, July.

Hofstede, G. (1978) 'Culture and Organization: A Literature Review Study', *Journal of Enterprise Management*, 1, pp. 127–35.

Hofstede, G. (1980) *Culture's Consequences*. Beverly Hills, Calif.: Sage.

Holberton, S. (1990) 'International Manager: When the Idea and Reality do not Match', *Financial Times*, 13 August, p. 9.

Hutton, J. (1988) *The World of the International Manager*. Oxford: Philip Allan.

IMF (1990) *One World, One Economy*. Washington: IMF Publications.

Julius, D. (1990) *Global Companies and Public Policy*. London: Frances Pinter.

Kahn, H. (1979) 'The Historical and World Context of East Asian Development', in R.H. Solomon (ed.), *Asian Security in the 1980s: Problems and Policies for a Time of Transition*. Cambridge, Mass.: Oegeschlager, Gunn & Hain. pp. 181–99.

Kakar, S. (1971) 'Authority Patterns and Subordinate Behavior in Indian Organizations', *Administrative Science Quarterly*, 16, pp. 298–307.

Kamata, S. (1983) *Japan in the Fast Lane*. London: Allen and Unwin.

Kemp, T. (1969) *Industrialization in Nineteenth Century Europe*. London: Longman.

Kidd, J.B. and Teramoto, Y. (1981) 'Japanese Production Subsidiaries in the United Kingdom: A Study of Managerial Decision-making', working paper no. 203, University of Aston Management Centre.

Kiggundu, M.N., Jorgensen, J.J. and Hafsi, T. (1983) 'Administrative Theory in Developing Countries: A Synthesis', *Administrative Science Quarterly*, 28, pp. 66–84.

Kleinke, C.L. (1984) 'Two Models for Conceptualizing the Attitude–Behaviour Relationship', *Human Relations*, 37, pp. 333–50.

Kroeber, A.L. and Kluckhohn, C. (1952) *Culture – a Critical Review of Concepts and Definitions*. Cambridge, Mass.: Harvard University Press.

Lane, D. (1977) 'Marxist Class Conflict Analyses of State Socialism', in R. Scase (ed.) *Industrial Society: Class, Cleavage and Control*. London: Allen and Unwin.

Lange, G. (1973) 'EFTA – some Reflections on its Origin, Foundations and Future', in *European Year Book*, XI, pp. 3–21. Quoted in Robertson (1973), p. 233.

Lenin, V.I. (1934) *Imperialism: The Highest Stage of Capitalism*. London: Lawrence and Wishart.

Levi, M.D. (1990) *International Finance*. Singapore: McGraw-Hill.

Lewis, W.A. (1978) *Growth and Fluctuations 1870–1913*. London: Allen and Unwin.

Lincoln, J.R., Hanada, M. and Olsen, J. (1981) 'Cultural Orientations and Individual Reactions to Organizations: A Study of Employees of Japanese-Owned Firms', *Administrative Science Quarterly*, 28, pp. 93–115.

Lintner, V. and Mazey, S. (1991) *The European Community: Economic and Political Aspects*. Maidenhead: McGraw-Hill.

Littler, C.R. (1982) *The Development of Labour Process in Capitalist Societies*. London: Heinemann.

Littler, C.R. (1983) 'A Comparative Analysis of Managerial Structures and Strategies' in H.F. Gospel and C.R. Littler (eds), *Management Strategies and Industrial Relations*. London: Heinemann.

Luck, G.M. and Tayeb, M.H. (1985) 'Operational Research as Organizational Intervention', in N.K. Jaiswal (ed.), *OR for Development Countries*. New Delhi: Operational Research Society of India.

McDonald, F. (1990) 'Eastern Europe and the UK Economy', *British Economy Survey*, 19, pp. 51–4.

McFarlane, A. (1978) *The Origins of English Individualism*. Oxford: Basil Blackwell.

McGovern, E. (1986) *International Trade Regulation*. Exeter: Globefield.

Maddison, A. (1971) *Class Structure and Economic Growth, India and Pakistan since the Moghuls*. London: Allen and Unwin.

Maizels, A. (1970) *Growth and Trade*. Cambridge: Cambridge University Press.

Mananyi, A. (1983) 'The World Bank: A Study of its Operations in Developing Countries'. MSc thesis, Heriot-Watt University.

Mandel, E. (1969) *The Inconsistencies of State Capitalism*. London: International Marxist Group.

Mangham, I.L. (1978) *Interactions and Interventions in Organizations*. Chichester: Wiley.

Marchington, N. and Parker, P. (1987) 'Japanisation: A Lack of Chemical Reaction?', paper presented to the Japanisation of British Industry Conference, Cardiff, September.

Maurice, M., Sorge, A. and Warner, M. (1980) 'Societal Differences in Organizing Manufacturing Units: A Comparison of France, West Germany and Great Britain', *Organization Studies*, 1, pp. 59–86.

Mehta, P. (1989) *Bureaucracy, Organisational Behaviour, and Development*. New Delhi: Sage.

Melvin, M. (1989) *International Money and Finance*. Second edition. New York: Harper and Row.

Mento, A.J. (1982) 'Some Motivational Reasons why Quality Circles Work in

Organisations', *Transactions of the 4th Annual Conference of IAQC*. Quoted in Hill (1987).

Millward, N. and Stevens, M. (1986) *British Workplace Industrial Relations 1980–84*. Farnborough: Gower.

Misumi, J. (1984) 'Decision Making in Japanese Groups and Organisations', in *International Yearbook of Organisational Democracy*, 2. Chichester: Wiley.

Misumi, J. (1985) *The Behavioral Science of Leadership: An Interdisciplinary Japanese Research Program*. Ann Arbor: University of Michigan Press.

Mitchell, B.R. and Deane P. (1962) *Abstract of British Historical Statistics*. Cambridge: Cambridge University Press.

Mouton, J.G. and Blake, R.R. (1970) 'Issues in Transnational Development', in B.M. Bass, R. Cooper and J.A. Hass (eds), *Managing for Accomplishment*. Lexington, Mass.: Heath.

Mueller, G.G., Gernon, H. and Meek, G. (1987) *Accounting: An International Perspective*. Homewood, Ill.: Irwin.

Mulhall, M.G. (1899) *The Dictionary of Statistics*. London: Routledge.

Nakane, C. (1973) *Japanese Society*. London: Penguin.

OECD (1976) *Declaration on International Investment and Multinational Enterprises by the Governments of OECD Member Countries*. Paris: OECD Publications.

OECD (1977) *The Department of Industrial Relations: Some Implications of Japanese Experience*. Paris: OECD Publications.

OECD (1990a) 'Economy-wide Effects of Agricultural Policies', *OECD Economic Studies*, 3. Reported in *The Economist*, 31 March 1990.

OECD (1990b) *OECD Economic Outlook*. Paris: Organization of Economic Cooperation and Development. Reported in *The Times*, 11 June 1990, p. 21.

Oh, T.K. (1976) 'Japanese Management: A Critical Review', *Academy of Management Review*, 1, pp. 14–25.

OOPC (Office for Official Publications of Communities) (1988) *Europe without Frontiers – Completing the Internal Market*. Luxembourg: OOPC.

Ouchi, W. (1981) *Theory Z: How American Business Can Meet the Japanese Challenge*. Reading, Mass.: Addison-Wesley.

Pascale, R.T. (1978) 'Zen and the Art of Management', *Harvard Business Review*, 56, pp. 153–62.

Patterson, G. (1966) *Discrimination in International Trade: The Policy Issues (1945–65)*. Princeton, NJ: Princeton University Press.

Petty, R.E. (1981) 'The Role of Cognitive Responses in Attitude Change Processes', in R.E. Petty, T.M. Ostrom and T.C. Brock (eds), *Cognitive Responses in Persuasion*. Hillsdale, NJ: Erlbaum.

Render, B., Robbins, S.H. and Paksoy, C.H. (1985) 'The Issue of Implementing Management Science in Nepal', in N.K. Jaiswal (ed.), *OR for Developing Countries*. New Delhi: Operational Research Society of India.

Robertson, A.H. (1973) *European Institutions*. London: Stevens.

Roemer, J.E. (1976) *US – Japanese Competition in International Markets*. Berkeley, Calif.: University of California Press.

Sasaki, N. (1981) *Management and Industrial Structure in Japan*. Oxford: Pergamon. Quoted in Black and Ackers (1987).

Schein, E.H. (1985) *Organizational Culture and Leadership: A Dynamic View*. San Francisco: Jossey-Bass.

Schlossstein, S. (1991) *Asia's New Little Dragons*. Chicago: Contemporary Books.

Scrip (1988) *The Scrip Yearbook, 1988*, Richmond, Surrey: PJB Publications.

Segal, R. (1971) *The Crisis of India*. Bombay: Jaico Publishing House.

Sen, G. (1984) *The Military Origins of Industrialisation and International Trade Rivalry*. London: Frances Pinter.

Sheridan, R.B. (1976) 'Sweet Malefactor: The Social Costs of Slavery and Sugar in Jamaica and Cuba 1804–54', *Economic History Review*, 2nd series, 29, pp. 236–57.

Shirai, T. (1983) *Contemporary Industrial Relations in Japan*. Madison, Wisc.: University of Wisconsin Press.

Silverman, D. (1970) *The Theory of Organizations*. London: Heinemann.

Smith, P.B. (1984) 'The Effectiveness of Japanese Styles of Management: A Review and Critique', *Journal of Occupational Psychology*, 57, pp. 121–36.

Stevens, C. (1984) 'The New Lomé Convention: Implications for Europe's Third World Policy', *CEPS Papers* (Brussels), 11. Quoted in Lintner and Mazey (1991).

Strier, F. (1984) 'Quality Circles in the United States: Fad or Fixture?', *Business Forum*. Summer.

Tayeb, M.H. (1979) 'Cultural Determinants of Organizational Response to Environmental Demands: An Empirical Study in Iran'. M. Litt. thesis, University of Oxford.

Tayeb, M.H. (1981) 'Cultural Influences on Organizational Response to Environmental Demands', University of Aston Management Centre working paper no. 215.

Tayeb, M.H. (1987a) 'Contingency Theory and Culture: A Study of Matched English and Indian Manufacturing Firms', *Organization Studies*, 8, pp. 241–62.

Tayeb, M.H. (1987b) 'New Technology and the Shape of Things to Come', paper presented to the 8th EGOS (European Group for Organization Studies) Colloquium, Antwerp 22–24 July.

Tayeb, M.H. (1988) *Organizations and National Culture: A Comparative Analysis*. London: Sage.

Tayeb, M.H. (1990a) 'Political Economic Environment of Organizations', in D. Wilson and R. Rosenfeld (eds), *Managing Organizations: Text, Readings and Cases*. Maidenhead: McGraw-Hill. pp. 342–7.

Tayeb, M.H. (1990b) 'Japanese Management Style', in R. Daily (with contributions from T. Keenan and M. Tayeb), *Organisational Behaviour*. London: Pitman. pp. 257–82.

Tayeb, M.H. (1991a) 'The Effects of Culture on the Management of Organizations', in S.P. Male and P.K. Stocks (eds), *Competitive Advantage in Construction*. London: Butterworths. pp. 236–47.

Tayeb, M.H. (1991b) 'Capitalism, Socialism and Business Organization', in G. Szell (ed.), *Labour Relations in Transition in Eastern Europe*. Berlin: de Gruyter.

Tayeb, M.H. and Smith, P.B. (1988) 'A Survey of Management Styles in Four Capitalist Countries', paper presented to the Fifth Workshop on Capitalist–Socialist Organizations, Brdo Pri Kranju, Yugoslavia, August.

Taylor, J. (1983) *Shadows of the Rising Sun: A Critical View of the Japanese Miracle*. Tokyo: Charles E. Tuttle.

Trevor, M. (1983) *Japan's Reluctant Multinationals*. London: Frances Pinter.

Triandis, H.C. (1981) 'Dimensions of Cultural Variations as Parameters of Organizational Theories', paper presented at the International Symposium on Cross-cultural Management, Montreal, Canada, October.

Turnbull, P. (1986) 'The "Japanisation" of Production and Industrial Relations at Lucas Electrical', *Industrial Relations Journal*, 17, pp. 193–206.

Vernon, R. (1970) 'Future of the Multinational Enterprise', in C.P. Kindleberger (ed.), *The International Corporation: A Symposium*. Cambridge, Mass.: MIT Press.

Vineall, T. (1988) 'Creating a Multinational Management Team', *Personnel Management*, October, pp. 44–7.

Wallace, C.D. (1982) *Legal Control of the Multinational Enterprise*. The Hague: Martinus Nijhoff.

Wallace, W.V. (1990) 'The Soviet Union and Eastern Europe ', *Future*, June, pp. 451–61.

Wallerstein, I. (1979) *The Capitalist World Economy*. Cambridge: Cambridge University Press.

Weber, M. (1930) *The Protestant Ethic and the Spirit of Capitalism*. London: Allen and Unwin.

Weekly, J.K. and Aggarwal, R. (1987) *International Business: Operating in the Global Economy*. New York: Dryden.

West, P. (1989) 'Cross-Cultural Literacy and the Pacific Rim', *Business Horizon*, March–April, pp. 3–17.

White, M. and Trevor, M. (1983) *Under Japanese Management*. London: Heinemann.

Wickens, P. (1985) 'Nissan: The Thinking Behind the Union Agreement', *Personnel Management*, August.

World Bank (1981) *Accelerated Development in Sub-Saharan Africa: An Agenda for Action*. Quoted in Arnold (1989).

World Bank (1991) *World Development Report*. New York: Oxford University Press.

Yoshino, M.Y. (1975) 'Emerging Japanese Multinational Enterprises', in E. Vogel (ed.), *Modern Japanese Organization and Decision-Making*. Berkeley, Calif.: University of California Press.

Index

220 The global business environment